ASPECTS OF SEVENTEENTH-CENTURY FRENCH DRAMA AND THOUGHT

ASPECTS OF SEVENTEENTH-CENTURY FRENCH DRAMA AND THOUGHT

Robert McBride

Senior Lecturer in French
The Queen's University of Belfast

ROWMAN AND LITTLEFIELD
TOTOWA, NEW JERSEY

© Robert McBride

All rights reserved. No part of this publication may be reproduced or transmitted, in any form or by any means, without permission

First published in the United States 1979 by Rowman and Littlefield, Totowa, N.J.

Library of Congress Cataloging in Publication Data

McBride, Robert.
    Aspects of seventeenth-century French drama and thought.

    Includes index.
    1. French literature — 17th century — History and criticism. 2. French drama — 17th century — History and criticism. 3. Philosophy, French — 17th century. I. Title.
PQ245.M3   1979   842′.4′09   78-21249

ISBN 0-8476-6137-7

Printed in Great Britain

To Valerie

Contents

Acknowledgements	viii
Introduction	1
1 Doubt and the Cornelian Hero	7
2 Absence and Presence in *Andromaque, Britannicus*, and *Bérénice*	37
3 Person and Persona in the *raisonneurs* of Molière's *Ecoles*	74
4 The Triumph of Art over Nature in the *Maximes*	90
5 The Paradox of Pascal's *Pensées*	112
6 Doubt and Certainty in Cartesianism	147
7 The Paradoxes of Orasius Tubero	165
Notes	177
Index	189

Acknowledgements

I would like to express my warm thanks to The Queen's University of Belfast for granting me study leave during the academic year 1976-7; to the editorial committee of *Studi Francesi* and M. J. Morel, secretary of *XVIIe Siècle*, for kind permission to make use here of the following articles in somewhat different form: 'Le rôle de Rome dans *Bérénice*', *Studi Francesi*, 52 (January-April 1974), pp. 86-91; 'Quelques réflexions sur le héros cornélien', *XVIIe Siècle*, 104 (1974), pp. 45-60; 'La question du *raisonneur* dans les *Ecoles* de Molière', *XVIIe Siècle*, 113 (1976), pp. 59-73; and to Miss G. Greig, Mrs. G. Carse and Miss W. Johnston for typing the manuscript with such cheerful efficiency.

Introduction

This study does not presume to examine or define the characteristics of what has come to be known as seventeenth-century French classical literature. This would call for a far wider and more systematic investigation into the structure, form and content of that literature than has been attempted here. It seeks rather to discern several of the recurrent features in the works of some of the major dramatists and thinkers of the century, and suggests that there may be a common complex principle underlying their diverse dramatic and philosophic visions, a principle most comprehensively covered by the term paradox. By the term I mean the holding in balanced tension of apparently incompatible elements and it seems to me to be suggested in and through the very diversity of those visions, in each of which it possesses its own coherence and characteristic expression. The works studied have been chosen because they appear to me to exemplify that common principle in their vastly different forms as well as being characteristic of the minds which created them.

Some readers may be surprised by the inclusion of a chapter on La Mothe Le Vayer. It is true that today he is largely a background figure in seventeenth-century studies. In his time however, he was a leading and widely read exponent of scepticism, who, far from being a servile imitator of Montaigne, developed a more radical scepticism than that of the author of the *Essais*. He represents a strong current of scepticism of which Descartes and Pascal were fully aware and which they sought to counteract, as well as providing a source and influence for many of Molière's comedies.

The long-established view of the seventeenth century as formulated by G. Lanson, F. Brunetière, E. Faguet and many other scholars perceived a unity of spirit above all in the sense of order and reason which classical literature was thought to embody. The view that the century represented the age of reason *par excellence* was firmly grounded in the belief that Cartesian reason incarnated its essential spirit. This spirit was seen to be illustrated in drama by the glorification of reason and will in Corneille's plays, by the justification of the golden mean in all things by the so-called *raisonneurs* of Molière's comedies and finally confirmed by Boileau's injunction in his *Art Poétique* to his fellow classical writers: 'Aimez donc la raison: que toujours vos écrits/Empruntent d'elle seule et leur lustre et leur prix.' However simplistic and inadequate this view appears today, it illustrates the way in which the formal perfection and beauty of so much classical literature may mislead us about the significance of its underlying content. Aesthetically the work of art transmutes the tensions and contrasts of its material into harmony and balance. In this sense it is true to say with Gide that 'à vrai dire, en art, il n'y a pas de problèmes — dont l'oeuvre d'art ne soit la suffisante solution'.[1] But it is also true to say that this aesthetic harmony is frequently achieved in spite of, and not because of, the underlying vision and content. This paradox of artistic creation is not, of course, confined to seventeenth-century classical literature and is universal in its scope. But it is all the deeper and more surprising on account of the sustained aesthetic perfection of that literature. H. Lefebvre has neatly crystallized this paradox in a sentence which discerns manifold tensions and conflicting forces under apparently static perfection: 'Les apologistes du classicisme n'ont vu qu'ordre, clarté, perfection, là où il n'y eut en fait que malaise, paradoxe, confusion, crise larvée . . . où par conséquent la perfection de la forme fut, par rapport au contenu, confus et fuyant, à la fois une conquête durement gagnée et en échappatoire.'[2]

If this is at all true, the implicit tension between form and content reflects a dynamic and complex vision rather than a static formal one.

Drama implies conflict and it is here that the tensions in situation and in character are most evidently and paradoxically transmuted into aesthetic balance by the dramatist's sense of unity between word, gesture and rhythm. The fierce clash of the intransigent wills of Don Diègue and Le Comte in *Le Cid* (Act I, Sc. 3) or of Polyeucte and Pauline (*Polyeucte*, Act IV, Sc. 3) are expressed in a series of structured and balanced stichomythias conveying an overall sense of poetic and dramatic symmetry which serve both to mitigate and heighten the underlying discordances. Racine's tragedies involving characters who lose their reason are written from the standpoint of reason and make of such disintegration a rational poetic structure. It is in Phèdre's last words that we witness the final restoration of the order of things which her life has disrupted: 'Et la mort, à mes yeux dérobant la clarté,/ Rend au jour, qu'ils souillaient, toute sa pureté' (Act V, Sc. 7. lines 1643-4).

The mutual acceptance by Bérénice and Titus of definitive separation and destruction of present and future happiness is expressed in a line which achieves double poetic balance in its twofold antithesis as the former declares 'Je l'aime, je le fuis; Titus m'aime, il me quitte' (Act V, Sc. 7. line 1500). Molière's comedies are rationally structured to point up the absurdity of a particular monomania. He uses his unerring sense of comic form to show irrationality lurking at each moment under the guise of studied calm and reason. In the famous scene of the sonnet in *Le Misanthrope* (Act I, Sc. 2) Alceste and Oronte are progressively divested of rational appearances in a symmetrical ballet-like sequence of retorts to reveal their naked combative egos jostling for social supremacy. M. Jourdain's various 'maîtres' likewise forfeit their self-possession as they defend the merits of their respective arts; it is however only with the arrival of the 'maître de philosophie' that unreason is brought to its climax and we witness the familiar spectacle in Molière's theatre of reason attempting to order human nature *(Le Bourgeois Gentilhomme*, Act II, Sc. 2 and 3). Under the poetic and dramatic symmetry lie disorder, contradiction, and paradox, rationally structured to a comic end.

Nor is this artistic paradox peculiar to the dramatists mentioned. It may also be seen clearly in the work of two of the most stringently logical minds of the century, Descartes and Pascal. The structure and architecture of *Le Discours de la Méthode* and the *Pensées* at each stage bear the imprint of geometrical logic as the part leads and subordinates itself to the overall design which is unfailingly kept in view. Their logic is ever conscious of the full range of arguments invalidating a rational interpretation of man and the world and proceeds accordingly. The rationalism of Descartes is at each level of its development an answer to reason's ability to raise the most far-reaching doubts about its premises and conclusions. The apex of his thought in the *Discours*, the *cogito*, is the direct result of rationally conducted doubt, doubt which is, even at the point of Cartesian reason's supreme triumph, directly relevant to his thought. Pascal's logic perceives the innumerable contradictions in man's nature and life and climaxes its operation by merging into faith, which represents both the defeat and triumph of reason in the *Pensées*. The closed and polished form of La Rochefoucauld's *Maximes* covers a highly complex undogmatic view of man, which may not be summarized in neat formulae.

In the area of seventeenth-century drama W.G. Moore has taught us to begin at the beginning.[3] That is, not with convenient generalisations about the authors' intentions and their place in the literary scheme of things in the century, but with the evidence at our disposal. This means above all due respect for the dramatic context of the plays rather than preoccupation in the first instance with the psychology of the characters and the social and historical background to the plays. The importance of treating the plays as plays and not as condensations of philosophy has been recognised increasingly in the cases of Corneille and Molière. The former's characters have often been isolated from the dramatic context to be viewed as abstractions of will and reason, ideal figures whose words and actions necessarily correspond. This tendency has perhaps resulted in the diminution of the dramatic content of the plays which become schools for heroic ethics and stock attitudes of the time. One wonders if this was the experience of the contemporary spectators for whom Corneille wrote. The plays of Corneille, Racine and Molière are still performed because they are dramatically effective, as P. Larthomas has reminded us in his excellent study of the nature and techniques of dramatic language.[4] No-one was more aware of the importance of surprise, shock and suspense in plot than Corneille, or of the importance of maintaining what he termed 'une agréable suspension' in the mind of the spectator.[5] In the cases in which reason and will do triumph, their triumph is more often belated than spontaneous, strenuous than effortless, more the reaction to exceptional dramatic circumstances than a calculated attitude. More often than not the theatrically effective manifestations of mastery and self-mastery contain unresolved tensions pointed up in the course of the multifaceted vision of the play. The famous verses of Pauline to Sévère provide perhaps a case in point: outwardly Pauline does not give way to her feelings for him, but undergoes a severe inner conflict in which reason and passion stand in precarious co-existence:

Ma raison, il est vrai, dompte mes sentiments;
Mais, quelque autorité que sur eux elle ait prise,
Elle n'y règne pas, elle les tyrannise;
Et quoique le dehors soit sans émotion,
Le dedans n'est que trouble et que sédition.
(Act II, Sc. 2, lines 500-4)

Where apparent order and reason reign, the dramatic vision points to instability and antimonies barely held in check.

In spite of the different dramatic expressions and reactions of characters in the theatres of Corneille and Racine, they are all a prey to unforeseen forces, continually aware of the need to affirm their identity in the face of events and other characters. If Corneille's characters react differently to their past and heredity, their reactions are no less ambiguous and complex than those of Racine's. Behind the acceptance of Cornelian *devoir*, that decision is shown to be no more simple in nature or in consequence than Pyrrhus' decision to marry Andromaque, Néron's to murder Britannicus, or Titus' to separate from Bérénice. The complexity of decision and of dramatic reaction to it in Corneille's plays has perhaps been diminished by viewing them too closely within the historical and social framework of the time. In this framework Corneille's characters exemplify the self-confidence of the aristocratic ethic, and Racine's the sense of inner disarray of the dispossessed Frondeurs.[6] A *maxime* of La Rochefoucauld seems to me to express the complex motivation of characters at the point of decision which both dramatists illuminate in their characteristic ways: 'L'homme croit souvent se conduire lorsqu'il est conduit; et pendant que par son esprit il tend à un but, son coeur l'entraîne insensiblement à un autre'.[7] The Cornelian character's response to his *devoir* may be shaped by forces over which he has no direct control, imposing on him attitudes opposed to his actual desires. The Racinian character's lucidity may, in fact, be a form of tragic blindness, his wish to escape the bondage of the past and of others merely the acceptance of a more destructive one. Molière's *imaginaire*, supposing himself to be in full control of the situation, is shown to be dependent on nothing more substantial than his fixation and ultimately his *humeur*. One can never be totally in control of self and events, opine the *raisonneurs*, who turn their backs on their own opinions to become actors in the social comedy.

The sense of complexity discernible in these dramatic visions continually underscores the disparity between the relative nature of the characters and the absolute nature of their aspirations. It is in Corneille's plays that the character seems to come closest to harmonizing his nature and his aspirations. Yet the dramatist's vision of his play — not to be identified with a particular character at a particular moment in his development — shows the human consequences which follow in the wake of absolute patriotism or heroism. The *dénouements* of *Le Cid* and *Horace* point to the fact that the need to be released from the ideal image of self may be just as great as the need to create it. The underlying sense of contingency of these visions derives from their implicit awareness of the divorce between the person and the persona, a sense expressed memorably in Montaigne's *Essais*: 'Le peuple reconvoye celuy-là [le héros miraculeux au monde] d'un acte public, avec estonnement, jusqu'à sa porte; il laisse avec sa robbe ce rolle, il en retombe d'autant plus bas qu'il s'estoit plus haut monté; au dedans, chez luy, tout est tumultuaire et vile.'[8]

Horace is no less aware of the discrepancy between outward gesture and inner reality when he declares during his trial that 'Il [le peuple] veut qu'on soit égal en tout temps, en tous lieux' (Act V, Sc. 2, line 1565) than Auguste in the speech to the conspirators in which he expresses his wish to renounce his imperial charge (*Cinna*, Act II, Sc. 1).

This sense of contingency provides perhaps a point of convergence between the dramatic and philosophic visions. It is the *Essais* which provide much of the inspiration for La Rochefoucauld, Pascal, Descartes and Le Vayer, and each of these writers uses them in a vastly different way: La Rochefoucauld to underline unsystematically the ways in which our actions rarely coincide with our words and intentions and the forces which combine to thwart the latter; Pascal more systematically to reinforce reason's view of man without God as a complex of irreconcilable contradictions. Descartes and Le Vayer both make use of Montaigne's sceptical doubt, the former as a stimulus and test for his philosophic conclusions, the latter to intensify man's inability to understand either himself or the world. Whether Montaigne's description of man is accepted, modified or transcended by these writers, it invariably adds a dimension of complexity and paradox to their visions, a dimension which provides a focal point of so much dramatic and philosophic expression in the seventeenth century.[9] Herein may lie one of the reasons for the continuing vitality and relevance of that century's literature. In an age when the temptation to explicate man's nature and his actions in scientific, historical, economical, sociological, psychological and other frames of reference has perhaps never been greater, the vision of his elusive unanalysable essence is made at once more salient and challenging by the diversity of forms in which it is expressed.

1 Doubt and the Cornelian Hero

1

No greater proof of the vitality of Corneille's theatre could be found than that provided by the variety of different interpretations to which his heroes have given rise in modern criticism. One does not need to list the imposing bibliography which has grown up around him to be convinced of this. Among the innumerable expressions of critical viewpoints, not all are of equal importance, and in the field of Cornelian criticism, as in every other, some establish themselves on account of their lucidity and coherence. The conclusions of such seminal works may be modified and nuanced *ad infinitum* and thus dominate, in one form or another, the critical tendencies of their age. At the beginning of this century, the commonly accepted view of the Cornelian hero was founded on the authority of Gustave Lanson. In an article which is justifiably famous, he established a parallel between the heroes of Corneille's plays and the conception of the *généreux* as formulated in Descartes' *Traité des Passions*.[1] According to Lanson, Cornelian heroism was essentially a heroism of the will and the reason, detached from any movement of the passions and following with equanimity its resolute and unshakeable decision. This view of the hero remained intact for some fifty years, and it was not until the publication of the studies of Cornelian heroism of Paul Bénichou and Octave Nadal that the critical framework which sustained it was seen to be seriously flawed and finally dismantled.[2] These two scholars in particular have provided us with many invaluable insights into the nature of Corneille's heroes. His heroes were viewed no longer as following the dictates of reason alone and as being incapable of yielding to passion, as Lanson had argued; reason and passion, far from being irreconcilable elements, now fused to form the idealized conception of himself which the hero was anxious to project to others. The 'éthique de gloire' became the passion which motivated him, as well as the ideal to which he sought to raise his conduct.[3] Heroic attitudes which in the earlier perspective of Cornelian criticism were seen as emanating from the exercise of reason and the firm control of the will, now stemmed from the passion of pride in aristocratic rank according to Bénichou and from the hero's faith in himself, according to Nadal. In the two more recent views of the hero, the motivations for his actions are apparently far from Lanson's interpretation of him. In spite of this, there is a surprising agreement between the older and the more recent views on the resolution which undergirds and characterizes the heroic act in Corneille's plays. In the opinion of Nadal, 'Pour le héros cornélien, il n'y a aucune espèce de doute dans la décision: un parti pris souverain avant toute délibération a fait le choix de vouloir'[4] and for Bénichou, 'Douter de soi serait, pour n'importe lequel d'entre eux, sortir du caractère héroïque'.[5] One may well ask whether in the final analysis one systematic way of viewing the Cornelian hero has not been succeeded by another one, which, although less doctrinaire in appearance, in reality may be even more so. For the view of the hero who moves in a world of superhuman and aristocratic dimensions is nothing less than a kind of modern sophisticated variation of the famous opinion of La Bruyère on Corneille's characters in comparison with those of Racine: '[Corneille] peint les hommes comme ils devraient être, [Racine] les peint tels qu'ils sont.'[6]

It is possible to become so obsessed with the psychology and social origins of the hero that one forgets the role which he has been given to play within a dramatic context. Corneille does not present us in his theatre with characters who achieve instantaneous and complete heroic development, or who in the first instance exemplify theories of heroic behaviour, but rather with dramatic creations whom he endows with life on the stage and who by no means evolve in a linear or logical fashion. All the defiant and epigrammatic Cornelian retorts are fashioned in a particular dramatic situation and have their origins in contact with other characters. The characters are in frequent rivalry and conflict with each other, continually contradicting and seeking to outstrip each other in language and action. What has come to be known as 'le sublime cornélien' may on close inspection often reveal itself to be nothing more than a rhetorical or dramatic effort on the part of the hero to disguise or suppress his real motivation, which may well be that of hesitation, doubt and even despair.[7] In order to test this view with reference to specific characters, I should like to examine the hero and his development in four plays, *Le Cid*, *Horace*, *Cinna* and *Polyeucte*, which are generally accepted as representing the apogee of heroism in Corneille's theatre.[8]

2

In the famous *Stances* of *Le Cid* (Act 1, Sc. 6) we find Rodrigue faced with the agonizing decision which has been forced upon him by the quarrel between his father and Dom Gomez, the father of his *amante* Chimène. He is so deeply divided by the irreconcilable conflict of loyalties represented by his love for the daughter of the man who has insulted his father on the one hand and by his keen sense of ancestral, filial and personal honour on the other, that he devotes thirty or so lines to the most indecisive self-questioning. It is at this point that the acute nature of his dilemma prompts the suggestion that he allow himself to be killed in the duel with Dom Gomez, and so spare Chimène's suffering for the death of her father and at the same time leave tarnished the *gloire* of his family and name (lines 321-30). This amplification of his doubt about what he ought to do, which he carries to the point of wishing for death in the most supine of ways, is far from being a mere rhetorical device in which the certainty of eventual triumph over difficulty is implied. It is rather a psychological as well as a dramatic mechanism by which Rodrigue will seek to galvanise his will in the circumstances. He must portray to himself the real possibilities of his own death and the ignominious loss of his *gloire* in order to raise himself to the point at which he will eventually take his far-reaching decision, which, in the event of his survival, will radically alter his relationship with Chimène. Without representing to himself in the most vivid fashion the magnitude of his possible disgrace in the eyes of others as well as in his own, he cannot find the strength of will necessary to overcome his conflict of loyalties. The transformation from self-doubt to decision is fully mirrored in the instantaneous and otherwise incomprehensible transition which occurs in his attitude: from the most dejected state of inertia imaginable in his lines about sacrificing himself

> Allons, mon âme; et puisqu'il faut mourir,
> Mourons du moins sans offenser Chimène.
>
> (lines 329—30)

he passes at once to his great decision:

> Mourir sans tirer ma raison!
> Rechercher un trépas si mortel à ma gloire,
> Endurer que l'Espagne impute à ma mémoire
> D'avoir mal soutenu l'honneur de ma maison!
> Respecter un amour dont mon âme égarée
>   Voit la perte assurée!
> N'écoutons plus ce penser suborneur,
>   Qui ne sert qu'à ma peine.
> Allons, mon bras, sauvons du moins l'honneur,
> Puisqu'après tout il faut perdre Chimène.
>
> (lines 331—40)

The importance of Rodrigue's doubt in this scene may now be measured. It is a reflex which subjects the hero's intrinsic worth to a searching examination, and, by virtue of its sheer negative and destructive force, unleashes in him a counter-reflex, which is more positive and creative in nature. This second reflex is nothing less than faith in himself and his family, in other words, in his *gloire*. His *gloire* cannot be conceived of without a degree of self-doubt, which is the necessary stimulus to sustain it.

Having killed Dom Gomez in the duel, Rodrigue must attempt to give his explanation of his deed to Chimène (Act III, Sc. 4). It is true that several of the lines which he speaks in this scene could easily be used as evidence to support the Lansonian idea of the lucid and unflinching hero, but they would first have to be divorced from their dramatic context in order to acquire the full effect of heroic maxims. His lines 'Je le ferais encor, si j'avais à le faire' (line 878) and 'J'ai fait ce que j'ai dû, je fais ce que je dois' (line 900) reflect a mind impervious to the inner conflict which has not however been resolved by the death of his father's enemy but rather exacerbated for Rodrigue beyond measure. His wish to maintain the coherence between his past action and his present attitude in front of Chimène, that is, to remain true to his sense of *gloire*, stems directly from the belief in himself which he rediscovered in the *Stances* and which succeeded his doubts. He must endeavour at all costs to maintain here this coherence, otherwise he will inevitably lapse again into that fatal state of doubt formerly stigmatised as 'ce penser suborneur' (line 337) which is so destructive of the *élan* necessary for the achievement of *gloire*. Hence the fresh dilemma for Rodrigue in this scene, which is a direct result of the maintenance of his *gloire* and indicates the manner in which self-doubt and faith in himself alternately seek to possess the hero's will. The *gloire* which his action in killing Chimène's father has acquired for him does not allow him to disavow his action in public. But his love for Chimène seeks now to compensate itself for its suppression by pretexting that it provided the real motivation for his deed: '. . . un homme sans honneur ne te méritait pas' (line 888). The sharp conflict focused here between *gloire* which must maintain itself in front of others and love which threatens to undermine it by stealth forces Rodrigue to rationalise his act. By so doing, he is able to enjoy the reputation which *gloire* brings and at the same time to idealise the origin of it by making Chimène the ultimate inspiration for it.

The same conflict between the abstract demand of ideal appearances (*gloire*) and love can also be discerned in the role which Chimène opposes to Rodrigue. Her argument proceeds in an inverse direction to his. He has claimed that it was she who inspired him to maintain his *gloire* and asks her to pronounce sentence upon his action: in other words, his *gloire* is the ground which unites him to her in marriage, or in death, as he willingly offers himself to her vengeance (lines 901—4). Chimène, on the other hand, pretexts that her *gloire* is the definitive obstacle to their union, and refuses Rodrigue's implication that she participates in his *gloire*:

Ta funeste valeur m'instruit par ta victoire;
Elle a vengé ton père et soutenu ta gloire:

Même soin me regarde, et j'ai, pour m'affliger,
Ma gloire à soutenir, et mon père à venger.

(lines 913—16)

Her apparent firmness and implacable attitude are imposed on her by the role which Rodrigue's defence of his action obliges her to sustain.[9] Just as he uses the argument of his *gloire* to conceal his inner turmoil, so too Chimène uses her unrelenting fidelity to her father's memory to hide her emotional disarray. She is increasingly forced to pursue the murderer of her father by the exigency of her *gloire* as well as by Rodrigue's blunt emotional pressure on her to do so, whilst expressing the wish not to be able to punish him:

Malgré des feux si beaux qui troublent ma colère,
Je ferai mon possible à bien venger mon père;
Mais, malgré la rigueur d'un si cruel devoir,
Mon unique souhait est de ne rien pouvoir.

(lines 981—4)

As was the case with Rodrigue in the *Stances*, the conflict between the demands of reality (love) and appearances (*devoir*) leads Chimène into an impasse. But following the example of Rodrigue, she likewise has recourse to her *gloire*, that is, the means by which appearances can be made to triumph over reality. In both cases a sublimated form of reality is consciously put in place of reality and personal feelings, a form of reality which is nothing else than a refuge from despair and doubt. *Gloire* becomes therefore the symbol of the divorce between the persona and the person, the appearances with which the vulnerable ego would wish to invest itself. From this point onwards, both protagonists play out their parts in a fiction in which Chimène agrees to pursue Rodrigue to death whilst passionately hoping that the object of her pursuit, her *gloire*, will not be achieved. This fiction is prolonged throughout the scene in which she engages Dom Sanche to fight on her behalf in her quarrel with Rodrigue (Act IV, Sc. 5) and through another avowal of love for him, an avowal which is all the more authentic because it is made involuntarily when she thinks that Rodrigue intends to satisfy the demands of her *gloire* by sacrificing himself to the sword of Dom Sanche (lines 1549—56). Chimène and Rodrigue can only be liberated from this vicious circle by a *deus ex machina*, that is, by the king himself; by freeing her from the requirement to maintain her *gloire* at the expense of the person she loves, he saves both characters from the personas which *gloire* has obliged them to assume, and thus restores their real identities to them.

3

Horace, like the other plays studied in this chapter, does not offer us a single point of view on the hero, and still less the portrayal of a character who remains unchanged throughout. Its subject is the heroism of the Roman Horace as it is affected, and in turn affects other characters, in a particular dramatic context, and this subject is illuminated from more than one side. The other characters, Curiace, le vieil Horace, Sabine, Camille, as well as Horace himself, bring their own view to bear on it. The complex of views, which at first sight appear incompatible, interpenetrate within the universe of the play to form what may be called a vision of Horace's heroism, which is viewed in the light of his speeches with Curiace and the latter's reaction to them in Act II, Sc. 1 and 3, in the scene where Camille's murder takes place after the combat (Act IV, Sc. 5), and in the forensic elucidation of the final Act, where his heroism is left to face the future with nothing but its own diminished resources.

When Horace appears on stage for the first time (Act II, Sc. 1) we learn two facts about his situation which also affect his friend Curiace. He has been chosen with his brothers by Rome to settle their quarrel with Alba, and the Alban Curiace, already Horace's brother-in-law, is shortly to be married to Horace's sister, Camille. Thus they find themselves in a situation in which friendship stands in direct opposition to duty, and their initial reactions are characterized by contradiction and ambiguity. Curiace appreciates as fully as a foreigner can the honour which Rome bestows on Horace by its signal choice of him, but is apprehensive of the consequences of such a choice for Alba. This dual movement of admiration and then of detachment is repeated, but in an inverse direction, in the speeches of Horace. He deprecates the choice which Rome has made to maintain its honour, averring that others could well perform the task more effectively than he. On the one hand, he fears that the combat may hold out for him no greater promise than a 'cercueil' (line 377), but on the other he feels uplifted by 'une mâle assurance' (line 379). Of course this might only be the expression of false modesty on his part, as he intimates that Rome is placing too much confidence in him. Is he not in reality only too proud to accept its decision with joy, whilst conveying the impression that it has been foisted on him *malgré lui*? It must be agreed that this is a possible interpretation of his attitude in this scene, but it does not seem legitimate to ascribe motives to Horace which he may very well not have at this point of the play. If, however, we approach this scene without the preconceived notion of the Cornelian hero whose mind is never troubled by self-doubt, we discover that Horace does in fact experience a momentary hesitation and doubt expressed in the opening lines of his speech to Curiace:

Loin de trembler pour Albe, il vous faut plaindre Rome,
Voyant ceux qu'elle oublie, et les trois qu'elle nomme.
C'est un aveuglement pour elle bien fatal
D'avoir tant à choisir, et de choisir si mal.

Mille de ses enfants beaucoup plus dignes d'elle
Pouvaient bien mieux que nous soutenir sa querelle.

(lines 371—6)

If Horace doubts his own ability to perform his allotted task for Rome, his doubt acts as a kind of spring-board from which he can take his heroic decision and thus conquer doubt. Doubt, far from being alien to the Cornelian hero, is on the contrary a permanent attribute. It is the reflex which stimulates him continually to question his worth and his capacity to perform his heroic deed. Once deprived of this interrogative and creative doubt, he is helpless, for only in the action to which it goads him does he perceive the possibility of emerging from its miasma into the serenity of heroic self-fulfilment. We see here the effect of Horace's doubt on himself as well as on Curiace and it provides the basis for the dramatic clash of this scene. The initial doubt of Horace's opening speech has the immediate effect of stimulating in him the 'juste orgueil' (line 378) with which Rome's honour fills him, together with his determination to comport himself valorously, come what may. This lyrical outburst drives Curiace even further into his doubts about the fate of his country and of his friend (lines 389—97) to which he has already given expression, but in less plaintive tones than those which now convey his dilemma:

Quels voeux puis-je former, et quel bonheur attendre?
De tous les deux côtés, j'ai des pleurs à répandre;
De tous les deux côtés mes désirs sont trahis.

(lines 395—7)

This difference in attitude towards their situation, if not in their evaluation of it, ought not to blind us to one fundamental point on which their views coincide, which Corneille will point up presently with great dramatic skill. Curiace and Horace both agree about the supreme honour which Rome has conferred on Horace in choosing him as their representative in the imminent combat. But the tentative tone adopted by Curiace in this scene would lead us to suppose that if he were to be nominated for a similar task by Alba, he would experience the gravest doubt about accepting it. At least he has gone on record as saying to Horace that he cares as much for his personal happiness as for *gloire*: 'La gloire en est pour vous, et la perte pour eux' (line 405) is how he and Horace's friends envisage the possible death of the Roman. The paradox latent in the attitude of the Cornelian hero towards his duty manifests itself in dramatic fashion as Curiace hears immediately from the Alban army that he has in fact been chosen to represent his country in the combat (Act II, Sc. 2). He receives the news in terms similar to those which Horace has just employed to explain his acceptance of his choice by Rome to Curiace: an expression of modesty is succeeded by an acknowledgement of the honour which has been conferred upon him: 'Je m'estimais trop peu pour un honneur si grand' (line 414). That both the form and content of Horace's speech to Curiace in the previous scene should now be reflected in the latter's reaction to Alba's choice of him underlines the good faith with which Horace has just expressed his similar feelings. In addition it is significant that both characters have experienced the same private doubts, which they will suppress in front of other people.

The second part of the debate between Curiace and Horace takes place against the background of the doubly dramatic situation into which both have now been placed by circumstances, and the different attitudes towards their common situation are given correspondingly sharper emphasis. Curiace laments his fate anew, but in terms which are more emotional and bitter, and Horace for his part takes up his heroic stance even more firmly than before. In the first scene of this Act he had merely spoken of *gloire* in abstract and general terms. Here, on the other hand, he considers the common situation in more measured terms, which may at first sight seem coldly inhuman. He evokes without flinching the awful reality of the friend-to-friend combat with all its implications:

> S'attacher au combat contre un autre soi-même,
> Attaquer un parti qui prend pour défenseur
> Le frère d'une femme et l'amant d'une soeur,
> Et, rompant tous ces noeuds, s'armer pour la patrie
> Contre un sang qu'on voudrait racheter de sa vie;
> Une telle vertu n'appartenait qu'à nous.
>
> (lines 444—9)

The attitude of Horace seems all the more unnatural and inhuman as he urges his friend to think of the renown which their unique combat will earn for them (lines 450—2). It must be said that it is difficult to glimpse behind such words the anguished hero in whom L. Herland invites us to believe.[10] This is of course a salutary attempt to counter much adverse criticism of the character, but it ends up by making Horace unrecognizable for us. A more exact picture of him may emerge if we take into consideration his dramatic situation. In order to face the imminent combat without giving way to his human emotions, Horace forces himself to use the despairing outburst of Curiace as a stimulus for his speech on their future *gloire* and thus attempts to see further than the reality of their present dilemma. He must transcend the doubt of Curiace because he himself has voiced it already in his first reaction to the news that Rome has chosen him for the combat and doubtless still shares it in his innermost thoughts. In other words, the feelings here of Curiace and Horace are fundamentally the same, with one difference: this is that the former gives vent verbally to his feelings, and the latter knows that words of revolt and despair will not materially affect their present situation. If Curiace taunts Horace with displaying his 'fermeté [qui] tient un peu du barbare' (line 456) it is not, as Curiace imagines it to be, the unquestioning acceptance of an inhuman *devoir* on the part of Horace: he himself has just accepted the same task as Horace, and he tells us here that

> Je n'ai point consulté, pour suivre mon devoir;
> Notre longue amitié, l'amour ni l'alliance,
> N'ont pu mettre un moment mon esprit en balance.
>
> (lines 462—4)

The 'fermeté' which Curiace finds so reprehensible in Horace's attitude is rather the latter's determination not to give way to self-pity and grief by his realistic and unemotional evaluation of their common situation. The fact that they have both accepted the proposal of the combat implies the same 'fermeté' on the part of both characters but they explain it in different words and attitudes to each other and to themselves. The tragedy of their situation is immeasurably heightened in the perspective of the spectator by the co-existence of the basic similarity of their position and the sharp difference in their attitudes: for their tragic situation does not merely reside in a state of things which they are powerless to change, but also in the fact that they disagree about the way in which they should describe and react to a situation which they have mutually accepted.

The reproach which Curiace has just made about Horace's inhuman attitude to their position is not borne out by the speech in which the latter defends himself against the criticism of his friend. After rebutting Curiace's charge that to be Roman is to be inhuman, he admits at once that 'Notre malheur est grand, il est au plus haut point' (line 489). When he says that the *gloire* of defending one's country 'Doit étouffer en nous tous autres sentiments' (line 494) he gives the clearest proof that Curiace has seriously misjudged his attitude towards their combat. For in speaking of the need to suppress one's natural feelings at such a time, he lets us glimpse the immense effort he is making to control them consciously. Curiace may give expression as he pleases to his feelings in their critical position; Horace's realistic view of that position forces him not only to accomplish his supreme but terrible *devoir* (as Curiace does also in spite of his emotional outbursts in this scene), but also to resist the temptation to express his doubt about the sacrifice of life and friendship which it will necessarily entail in the only way open to him, that is, verbally. Thus his flat statement 'Rome a choisi mon bras, je n'examine rien' (line 498) is not at all to be seen as the brutal utterance of a warrior about to rid himself of the last vestige of his humanity. It is rather a supremely pragmatic attitude adopted in a situation of crisis and which by its very intensity serves as a bulwark against inner doubt and despair.[11]

In interpreting Horace's role in such a way, it is not at all my intention to discredit the character of Curiace who remains as moving and as pathetic in his dilemma as does Horace. For L. Herland, on the contrary, Curiace is a character who boasts in a tiresome and complacent manner about his own capability to entertain human feelings.[12] It is not hard for us, however, to sympathize with his verbal revolt against what seems to him to be Horace's irritatingly calm and unfeeling acceptance of their position when we remember that he has a reason of compelling force which makes such acceptance on his part a sheer impossibility: he is due to marry Horace's sister, Camille, tomorrow, that is, the day after the combat. He is on the verge of self-fulfilment which events will at best diminish and at worst destroy, and it is not at all surprising that he should agonize over the unjust and arbitrary blow which fate has just dealt to his happiness. Each responds therefore to the situation in terms shaped by individual nature, temperament, and, particularly in the case of Curiace, by circumstances: Curiace must continue to submit to his private doubt his definitive decision which he has made in public, and Horace must remain convinced of the futility of any outward display of anguish or remorse. A barrier of language separates one from the other, but in both human feelings are as helpless and as crushed. Curiace stubbornly and pathetically attempts to understand in terms of human feelings and language the full horror of their inhuman *devoir*. Horace's lucidity encases him in the bitter awareness that language can never approximate to, still less give an account of, his inhuman *devoir*.

In the following scene with Camille, however, Horace does attempt to bridge the gap between his realistic attitude adopted in the scenes with Curiace and a more evidently humane attitude which brings him closer to that of the Alban and also reveals something of the effort, and its cost to his own feelings, which he makes to keep them under stern control. In so doing, he involves himself in a painful dialectic, which is made all the more so for him because he still retains his lucid awareness of their present, and their possible, situation. He considers each of the two choices with which Camille will be faced as a result of the outcome of the combat and endeavours painfully but firmly to suggest to her how she should react to each of them. If Curiace should emerge as the victor, he advises her not to treat him as a warrior who has just murdered her brother, but rather to welcome him as an honourable man who has just fulfilled the requirements of his *devoir*. And in the event of Horace returning as the victorious hero of the combat, he will expect the same reaction from her. His method of envisaging the possible situation in which Camille may find herself may appear at first sight altogether too cruel and coldly intellectual. But his speech of farewell to his sister is worthy of closer scrutiny than this, for it reveals great awareness of the frailty of human nature and at the same time a strong conviction that life will have to continue after the event. He knows that depending on the outcome of the combat it will be all too tempting and all too human to view Curiace as the murderer of her brother or Horace himself as the assassin of her fiancé. But once the combat is over, it will not be possible to live on simply as though nothing at all had happened. And thus the essence of his advice to Camille seems to be as follows: 'Do your best, by a supreme effort of will and understanding, not to foist upon the victor, whoever he may be, your understandable feeling of resentment.'

It was said above that the difference in attitude in Curiace and Horace to their situation was one of form and not of content. It consists essentially in the different manner in which each of the characters comes to terms with the feeling of doubt which can undermine his will and jeopardize his *gloire*. It is manifestly the *raison d'être* of the two scenes in which their attitudes are defined towards their duty and each other. But when other characters attempt to question the demands which *gloire* makes on them, they at once react in the same way to the common enemy. The mechanism of heroism, which has already been seen at work in Rodrigue's attitude to Chimène, comes into play in Curiace's reaction to Camille (Act II, Sc. 5). In reply to her passionate reproaches that he is betraying her for the sake of his *gloire* he says 'Avant que d'être à vous je suis à mon pays' (line 562). His words here echo in mitigated form one of Horace's lines spoken to him at the end of their earlier encounter: 'Albe vous a nommé, je ne vous connais plus' (line 502), which provoked from Curiace the offended reply 'Je vous connais encore, et c'est ce qui me tue' (line 503); ironically, Curiace in the scene with Camille assumes the attitude which he has earlier criticised in Horace, as he now attempts to minimize their suffering by rationalizing the situation in the anonymous language of *devoir*. As he does so, we see that the assumed attitude of rigid patriotism is more than a means of suppressing his doubts about the human consequences of the imminent combat: it also gives to us the spectators the means of measuring the full extent of suffering which the truly tragic dilemma of Horace and Curiace involves for all the protagonists.

The future combatants join forces more and more as their combat draws closer. With consummate dramatic skill, Corneille thus orchestrates his play towards its climax, and in so doing endows his characters with a profound sense of tragic urgency and vitality which produces one of the most moving scenes of the play at the end of the second Act. Camille and Sabine act jointly to reverse the decision of Curiace and Horace to fight (Act II, Sc. 6). The combatants are in fact reduced to the point of extreme vacillation between the demands of love and their *devoir*, as their heroic resolve weakens visibly:

    CAMILLE: Courage! ils s'amollissent!

    SABINE: Vous poussez des soupirs! vos visages pâlissent!
                                                                          (lines 663—4)

The last view that Corneille gives us of Curiace and Horace before the combat is that of the two combatants who waver in the face of the emotional assault of Camille and Sabine on their *gloire*, and are rescued from this threat by the brusque intervention of le vieil Horace. Horace does not reappear until after his victory in the combat in which he has killed the Curiace brothers single-handed. There is a remarkable difference between his attitude displayed before the event and that after it. Before the combat, he had let us glimpse his pity for Camille and his understanding of her position, and the feelings shared with Curiace about their common undertaking. Confronted with his supreme test, he has, true to his nature, regained that total control over his doubt and feelings which was seriously threatened by the other characters prior to the combat. Fresh from his epic victory, he now presents himself to Camille as the hero who, through his perfect self-control, has changed the course of Roman history, and he expects the same self-control from her:

> Ma soeur, voici le bras qui venge nos deux frères,
> Le bras qui rompt le cours de nos destins contraires,
> Qui nous rend maîtres d'Albe; enfin voici le bras
> Qui seul fait aujourd'hui le sort de deux Etats;
> Vois ces marques d'honneur, ces témoins de ma gloire,
> Et rends ce que tu dois à l'heur de ma victoire.
>
> (lines 1251—6)

But Camille cannot dissociate the person she loves from the abstraction of public *devoir* to which Horace exhorts her to give formal acknowledgement. What Horace brands as the public enemy of Rome is nothing less than 'mon cher Curiace!' to Camille (line 1267). This plaintive cry at once brings into question Horace's epic deed and renders superfluous his rigid self-control displayed in the previous scenes with Camille and Curiace. There is no point in his role at which it is more necessary for the spectator and reader to place themselves imaginatively within the perspective which Horace has on Camille's furious reaction to his victorious attitude in this scene. What he must find most offensive and provocative in her words here is the fact that she reminds him, but *après coup* and in a much more truculent fashion, of the argument which Curiace had advanced to him at the beginning of the play and which he had steeled himself to resist. Like her fiancé, Camille asks him here to question his whole attitude and his deed; but having accomplished what is now irreversible, there is no room for doubt or self-pity in his mind. This was precisely what he had tried, unsuccessfully, to make her understand too prior to the combat (Act II, Sc. 4, lines 517—30). It is only by immersing himself in action that Horace can rid himself of the spectre of insidious doubt which Camille's outburst conjures up to his mind — hence her murder. It is therefore not simply out of love for Rome or his *gloire* that he takes his vengeance on his sister. Of course he does invoke Rome in this scene (lines 1257—61), but the word acts upon him as an abstraction which anaesthetizes his sensitivity to the feelings of others and to his own.[13] It is rather out of inner necessity that he commits the murder: as long as Camille remains alive, he will be a prey to thoughts of self-recrimination and doubt evoked by her in his mind. Either he chooses to live on the public and heroic level where heroism and *gloire* banish doubt by action, or else he falls victim, like Curiace, to questioning the demands which they impose on the individual.

In his *Examen* of the play (1660) Corneille was of the opinion that the murder of Camille had been insufficiently prepared even by the description of Horace's 'vertu farouche' and his firm counsel to her before the combat. He goes on to deny that there is any dramaturgical necessity for her death:

> ... cette mort fait une action double, par le second péril où tombe Horace après être sorti du premier. L'unité de péril d'un héros dans la tragédie fait l'unité d'action, et quand il en est garanti, la pièce est finie, si ce n'est que la sortie même de ce péril l'engage si nécessairement dans un autre, que la liaison et la continuité des deux n'en fasse qu'une action: ce qui n'arrive point ici, où Horace revient triomphant sans aucun besoin de tuer sa soeur, ni même de parler à elle.[14]

In spite of Corneille's dramaturgical misgivings about the murder, it is undeniably a logical psychological consequence of Horace's perfervid patriotism which steels him to place his country's interests in front of those of kith and kin. If one compares the exacerbated attitude of Horace in the scene of the murder with the words which he speaks to Camille prior to the combat, it is evident that the absolute line of conduct which he prescribes to her in the event of the death of Curiace or of himself does in fact leave him little or no scope for accommodation to her fierce attack on him after the combat. In the *Examen* Corneille also thought that the action might well have ended with the victory of Horace over the Albans.[15] This might well have been acceptable within a strictly Cornelian definition of tragedy in which the hero is subjected to what Corneille in his first *Discours* on dramatic poetry calls 'péril de vie, des pertes d'Etats, ou de bannissement' but not necessarily to suffering or death.[16] If the question is considered in a wider framework than this the ending of the play with the victory of Horace over the Curiace brothers would undoubtedly make him into a less tragic figure than he is at the end of the fifth Act. For the ending of the action with his victory would mean that he would not experience the fall of the tragic hero which gives rise to tragic emotions or the inner conflict which he undergoes in the final Act, where he comes back to reality within the universe of the play.

His return to this reality does not begin immediately after the murder of Camille. The full recognition of his situation is all the more overwhelming for him on account of this delay. Even after the murder, he can still speak of himself as being the perpetrator of 'un acte de justice' (line 1323), and enjoin his wife who mourns her three brothers to share in his *gloire* and *vertu* (lines 1348—62) — in other words, not to give way to self-pity and futile recrimination. Not until Sabine implores him to kill her does he reveal himself as incapable of sustaining his inhuman attitude any longer:

> Quelle injustice aux dieux d'abandonner aux femmes
> Un empire si grand sur les plus belles âmes,
> Et de se plaire à voir de si faibles vainqueurs
> Régner si puissamment sur les plus nobles coeurs!
> A quel point ma vertu devient-elle réduite!
> Rien ne la saurait plus garantir que la fuite.
>
> (lines 1391—6)

This remarkable avowal of his weakness reveals his dependence on the opinion which Sabine has of him; it marks the point at which the heroic concentration is broken and the exaltation of the hero falls, and is the end of his attempt to control himself and events in the play.

The death of Camille has in fact broken the heroic resolve which undergirds Horace's actions, that is, the certainty that in acting he achieves that mastery over himself and others which results in his personal and public *gloire*. This mastery and *gloire* which serve to stimulate each other in the acts of the Cornelian hero have now been seriously diminished. In killing Camille Horace has forfeited that heroic sense which galvanizes abstract ideals so that noble and sublime actions result and which are recognised by others as such. The hero has fallen and shows his awareness of his fall by asking his father to dispose of his life:

> Reprenez tout ce sang de qui ma lâcheté
> A si brutalement souillé la pureté.
> Ma main n'a pu souffrir de crime en votre race;
> Ne souffrez point de tache en la maison d'Horace.
>
> (lines 1425—8)

It is the same fallen hero whom we find in the scenes of judgement in front of the king in the final Act, which provides a structural and thematic counter-balance to Act II.[17] There the heroism of Horace had striven to rise above all others, even above Curiace who had been entrusted with an honour similar to his own, and had expressed itself in terms of lyrical exultation. Now, however, the fallen hero only aspires to the common fate of mortals, death, since he cannot live on the same terms as the most unimportant creature: 'D'autres aiment la vie, et je la dois haïr' (line 1546). He is impelled to wish for death not by an ill-defined *Todeswunsch*, but because the spring of his heroism, the desire to achieve self-mastery and his *gloire*, is as it were flawed in its essence since the murder of his sister. The hero can only act to good effect if he rediscovers in his action the certainty of his superiority which is both the objective and the motive of his quest, dispelling all his doubts. In its initial stages heroism emanates from doubt, but of course transcends it as it is spurred on by self and others to commit action of a unique kind, capable of securing *gloire*. But the deep paradox of *gloire* is that it implies in itself the death of heroism. Once *gloire* has been achieved by the hero, he is obliged by his own and by its nature not to fall below its supreme standard. Horace recognizes that other people will scarcely forgive him if he fails to maintain his remarkable standard of *vertu* in future actions:

> Le peuple, qui voit tout seulement par l'écorce,
> S'attache à son effet pour juger de sa force;
> Il veut que ses dehors gardent un même cours,
> Qu'ayant fait un miracle, elle en fasse toujours:
> Après une action pleine, haute, éclatante,
> Tout ce qui brille moins remplit mal son attente:
> Il veut qu'on soit égal en tout temps, en tous lieux;
> Il n'examine point si lors on pouvait mieux,
> Ni que, s'il ne voit pas sans cesse une merveille,
> L'occasion est moindre, et la vertu pareille:
> Son injustice accable et détruit les grands noms;
> L'honneur des premiers faits se perd par les seconds;
> Et quand la renommée a passé l'ordinaire,
> Si l'on n'en veut déchoir, il ne faut plus rien faire.
>   (lines 1559—72)

Here lies the essence of his tragic position of which he is fully aware: it is the only reason which can make him seek death, and it makes him the most profoundly tragic character in Corneille's theatre.[18] His tragedy does not merely consist in the fact that he expresses the ardent wish to die and that the royal decree condemns him to live on. Corneille's heroes are after all eminently equipped to triumph eventually over difficulty and misunderstanding. The roots of his tragedy go deeper and are more ineradicable than this. For the first time, doubt has taken full possession of the hero's mind. The sacrifice of Camille to his patriotic zeal, which is an act devoid of danger and therefore unworthy of the heroic mind, has compromised his *gloire* and makes him doubt it. And he also doubts his own capacity to emulate the extraordinary action which he has just accomplished.

4

It is generally agreed that the real hero of *Cinna* is Auguste and this appears to be borne out by the original title of the play which read as *Cinna ou la clémence d'Auguste*. The grandeur of his role and his extraordinary act of clemency at the end of the play are reasons which are held to account for his superiority over the unsuccessful conspirator against him, Cinna, who is overshadowed by and in his presence.[19] If the latter is viewed as generally vacillating, weak and strangely unheroic in his actions, Auguste is thought to exemplify the very idea of coherence and self-possession, and has even been described as 'le Grand Prêtre de la Maîtrise'.[20] The fixed gulf seen between the status of the two characters in the play would seem to have been created by a particular and definite idea as to what constitutes Cornelian heroism and what does not. The view which will be argued here is that the heroism of Auguste is acquired painfully through the various peripeties of the play and is in essence no different to that of Cinna at the end, sharing with it the same fragile basis, *gloire*. If Cinna's words and actions are characterized by vacillation in the earlier Acts, it must be remembered that he raises himself to the level of Auguste and Emilie as they seek to outdo each other in *générosité* in the final Act (lines 1616—44). If Cornelian heroism is viewed solely at the apogee of its *gloire*, that is as it exults lyrically in its victory over self and others, we run the danger of totally misjudging its nature and its effect. It is true that it is easy to be so dazzled by the apparently effortless mastery and will-power which heroism delights to celebrate that one overlooks the different stages through which it develops and which reflect more faithfully its essential character. Once considered in this light, the heroism of Auguste may well appear to be much less far removed from that of Cinna; both indeed may be similar in that they emerge gradually as laborious attempts to dominate nature and will and that they represent the very antithesis of the effortless and spontaneous self-mastery of the superhero. The heroism of Auguste seems to provide a salient case in point.

Our first view of Auguste is of the omnipotent Emperor who has achieved his power at the expense of his peace of mind. The Emperor who intimates his wish to relinquish his imperial power in the presence of the conspirators Cinna and Maxime is a man wearied by the continuing plots against his life, seeking only escape from the fruits of his ambition:

L'ambition déplaît quand elle est assouvie,
D'une contraire ardeur son ardeur est suivie;
Et comme notre esprit, jusqu'au dernier soupir,
Toujours vers quelque objet pousse quelque désir,
Il se ramène en soi, n'ayant plus où se prendre,
Et, monté sur le faîte, il aspire à descendre.

J'ai souhaité l'empire, et j'y suis parvenu;
Mais, en le souhaitant, je ne l'ai pas connu:
Dans sa possession, j'ai trouvé pour tous charmes
D'effroyables soucis, d'éternelles alarmes,
Mille ennemis secrets, la mort à tous propos,
Point de plaisir sans trouble, et jamais de repos.
(Act II, Sc. 1, lines 365—76)

Several Acts later he is told of Cinna's plot against him and in his lengthy speech in which he attempts to fathom for himself the reasons which have driven his confidant to betray his Emperor he has obviously lost both his self-control and all control of the situation (Act IV, Sc. 2). Initially the shock of hearing of the plot induces in him a deep feeling of self-pity (lines 1121—9), then a mood of black introspection as he blames himself for having provided inspiration for the conspiracy by his own bloody deeds (lines 1131—48). He is overwhelmed by the knowledge that his trusted counsellor is the instigator of it, but pulls himself together and decides to punish the traitor (lines 1150—61); but he rejects the idea of reprisals, since they will inevitably bring in their wake counter-violence and counter-repression, so prolonging the vicious circle from which he has been seeking to escape; he next resolves to kill both himself and the leader of the intrigue thus satisfying his vengeance and resolving his personal dilemma (lines 1170—86); and at the end of this long period of reflection and self-absorption he has come to no clearer view of his future actions than that which he had at the beginning of the scene, and his last line is an adequate summary of his inner turmoil and despair: 'Ou laissez-moi périr, ou laissez-moi régner' (line 1192).

The inspiration to pardon the conspirator-in-chief does not come of its own accord to Auguste's mind. It is rather his wife, Livie, who makes the suggestion to him: 'Essayez sur Cinna ce que peut la clémence; / Faites son châtiment de sa confusion' (lines 1210—11). She envisages the idea of the pardon as offering Auguste a last chance to end the repeated intrigues against his life and to succeed where past punishment has failed. But the very idea of pardoning the conspirators runs completely counter to everything that Auguste has done in the past and to his intentions for the future, confused though they may be. His wife endeavours to win him over to her idea by appealing to his sense of *générosité*: 'C'est régner sur vous-même, et, par un noble choix, / Pratiquer la vertu la plus digne des rois' (lines 1243—4).

The tormented Emperor rejects her suggestion scornfully as mere 'conseils d'une femme' (line 1245). He leaves this scene in deep disagreement with his wife and in the most complete disarray; but, with a truly theatrical *tour de force*, Corneille presents him as the apparently self-possessed judge and the poised Emperor of Cinna in the opening scene of the final Act.

But in spite of appearances, Auguste has not yet accepted the advice of Livie, and his self-mastery and serenity have not been acquired. He may well seem to be in perfect self-control as he enumerates the many ways in which he has been Cinna's benefactor, emphasizing the conspirator's dependence on him and savouring fully the total confusion of his confidant who imagined that his position placed him beyond all suspicion. Cinna may well be shaken in this scene of confrontation with the Emperor, but manages to resist the pressure which is exerted on him by displaying an insolent and impenitent attitude. He even challenges the omnipotent Emperor, provoking him to the point at which he loses all appearances of his calm self-assurance. In fact Auguste is reduced to proffer threats which merely serve to underline both his growing loss of control over the situation and himself and the superiority of Cinna, which is all the more exasperating to Auguste because he has manifestly failed in his design to reduce his opponent to a position of abject dependence upon him:

> Tu me braves, Cinna, tu fais le magnanime,
> Et, loin de t'excuser, tu couronnes ton crime.
> Voyons si ta constance ira jusques au bout.
> Tu sais ce qui t'est dû, tu vois que je sais tout,
> Fais ton arrêt toi-même, et choisis tes supplices.
>
> (lines 1557—61)

His helpless exasperation gives way to shock on learning of Emilie's defection to the cause of the conspirator in the following scene. Like Cinna, she too confronts the Emperor with impenitent defiance, admitting proudly that it was she who instigated the plot against his life in order to avenge her father whom Auguste murdered, and that she has used Cinna's love for her to further it. By flaunting the love which unites them in hatred of Auguste, she provokes him to his most vehement threats of physical force against both of them, threats which only heighten our impression of the tyrant's weakness and despair which they are intended to conceal:

> Oui, je vous unirai, couple ingrat et perfide,
> Et plus mon ennemi qu'Antoine ni Lépide:
> Oui, je vous unirai, puisque vous le voulez;
> Il faut bien satisfaire aux feux dont vous brûlez;
> Et que tout l'univers, sachant ce qui m'anime,
> S'étonne du supplice aussi bien que du crime.
>
> (lines 1657—62)

A still greater shock is reserved for Auguste in the following scene, as the character who has revealed the existence of the plot to him and whom Auguste imagines to be his staunchest ally, Maxime, confesses that he is the most mendacious of all the Emperor's enemies, since he has only betrayed the plotters in order to ruin Cinna in the eyes of Auguste and to win Emilie for himself. Faced with the magnitude of this triple defection of his trusted friends, the hero is in the familiar position of being deprived of all apparent inner and outer resources: the moment is thus ripe for the mechanism of Cornelian *gloire* to come into play in the hero's psychology. The more he feels himself to be crushed and immobilized by the blows of fate, the greater his effort to assert himself against it. But what is really the underlying significance of the munificent pardon issued so unexpectedly by Auguste to the conspirators through which he asserts his presence against fate and his enemies? It has been suggested that nothing less than Auguste's religious conversion can account for his dramatic gesture.[21] Without excluding the sudden manifestation of divine grace in Auguste as in Polyeucte, it seems difficult to maintain this view with the dramatic evidence at our disposal. The verses which convey the transition of Auguste from despair to the magnanimity of his pardon contain no trace of religious feeling on his part, unless we take his exclamation 'ô ciel!' as evidence to this effect as he says: 'En est-ce assez, ô ciel! et le sort, pour me nuire, / A-t-il quelqu'un des miens qu'il veuille encor séduire?' (lines 1693—4).

But as the context implies, this exclamation is the measure of his stupefaction at having been betrayed by his intimate friends, and a flimsy basis on which to erect the hypothesis of his conversion. Divine grace may erupt spontaneously as in Polyeucte, but in that case Corneille at least prepares us dramatically for it as he makes its manifestation in the hero coincide with his baptism. Besides, the combat of *gloire* which the Emperor proposes to Cinna, in which the opponents will strive to outbid each other in *générosité*, fits uneasily into the spirit of self-denial and humility of religion. In the context of Auguste's proposal to Cinna, one of the maxims of La Rochefoucauld on humility is extremely pertinent: 'L'humilité est la véritable preuve des vertus chrétiennes: sans elle nous conservons tous nos défauts, et ils sont seulement couverts par l'orgueil qui les cache aux autres, et souvent à nous-mêmes' (No. 358).

Of course the pardon of Auguste has the character of pure inspiration to the extent that it is not solely explicable in terms of calculated political self-interest on his part.[22] It is true that Auguste does indeed follow the earlier suggestion by his wife that he show nobility of mind in pardoning the conspirators; but he adopts her idea belatedly and spontaneously, just at the moment when his decision to put them to death has been overtaken by the shattering news that Maxime is also one of the traitors. On the one hand then the pardon is the sudden germination of an idea which Livie has sown much earlier in his mind; and on the other, it inevitably contains some degree of self-interest, since in attempting to make the pact of friendship with his enemies

Auguste hopes to eliminate future intrigues against him.[23] But in the unexpected change in the Emperor's attitude there is also a hidden dimension which emerges in the dramatic movement of the *dénouement*. Confronted with the spectacle of his own despair caused by the betrayals of which he is both cause and victim, Auguste is enabled to rise above unpalatable reality by his inherent reflex of *gloire*:

> En est-ce assez, ô ciel! et le sort, pour me nuire,
> A-t-il quelqu'un des miens qu'il veuille encor séduire?
> Qu'il joigne à ses efforts le secours des enfers;
> Je suis maître de moi comme de l'univers;
> Je le suis, je veux l'être. O siècles, ô mémoire!
> Conservez à jamais ma dernière victoire!
>
> (lines 1693—8)

Auguste may well celebrate his pardon and self-mastery in these lyrical tones, but they represent a despairing gesture on his part and his ultimate attempt to assert himself in the face of a situation which threatens to engulf him. In this respect his *gloire* resembles that of Cinna: in both characters *gloire* derives from the most acute perception on their part of their utter helplessness in the situation and from the supreme attempt to transcend it, which is the consequence of this perception; they seek to transcend it however not by pitting themselves directly against the reality of their situation, but by pretending that it can be idealized in a way consonant with their highest idea of themselves. Realism precedes idealism in the achievement of the hero's *gloire*, and the latter is born from the former. The 'dernière victoire' which Auguste anticipates lyrically can only come about if the other characters agree to forsake the impasse of their real situation for the idealized reality of *gloire*. Thus *gloire* may well be less the sublime habitat of the superhuman hero than the sign of a final supremely dramatic attempt on the character's part to come to terms with despair and defeat. I do not at all conclude that Corneille set out consciously to question the notion of *gloire* in his plays; rather that his vision of heroism is formed not just of one monolithic view of the hero at a particular moment of triumphant self-assertion, but of many frequently contrasting views illuminated in the course of the drama. This vision is both complex and dynamic, holding in precarious balance more unresolved tensions than the traditional interpretation of *gloire* as the stable and enduring value of heroism would suggest. Under the rhetoric of heroism the characters are constant prey to contradiction, doubt and conflict. We may well see less distance than has been imagined between the world of Corneille's heroes and La Rochefoucauld's view that '. . . à une grande vanité près les héros sont faits comme les autres hommes', if we substitute the word *gloire* for *vanité* in his maxim.[24]

5

In his *Examen* of *Polyeucte* Corneille writes that 'Ceux qui veulent arrêter nos héros dans une médiocre bonté, où quelques interprètes d'Aristote bornent leur vertu, ne trouveront pas ici leur compte, puisque celle de Polyeucte va jusqu'à la sainteté, et n'a aucun mélange de faiblesse'. Corneille thus implicitly rejects the Aristotelian prescription that a tragic plot should show an intermediate kind of personage, who is neither too good nor too bad, who suffers misfortune through some error of judgement, arousing thus in the spectator's mind the tragic emotions of pity and fear through which a catharsis is effected. Elsewhere, Corneille denies that the tragic hero need excite both pity and fear in order to achieve this tragic effect: in his second *Discours* on dramatic poetry he cites Polyeucte as one of the completely virtuous characters whose misfortune arouses only pity on the part of the spectator.[25] For his author, Polyeucte seems to have been a fitting character for a tragedy because he excites our pity and admiration by his unwavering determination to die for his faith in the midst of great danger. (In the *Examen* of *Nicomède* Corneille indicates that the hero's steadfastness in peril arouses our admiration which can lead to a purgation of the passions just as effectively as Aristotle's pity and fear.) We may agree that this is an apt description of the Polyeucte who in his last scene declares defiantly to Félix that he will not disavow his sacrilegious act in the temple: 'Je le ferais encor, si j'avais à le faire' (line 1671). But how adequate is this view of Polyeucte the unbending and defiant hero as a summary of the character who evolves dramatically throughout the preceding four Acts?

Polyeucte, as we see him in the first scene of the play, is a new convert to Christianity who has not yet professed his faith publicly by his baptism, which is however imminent. Within the dramatic situation of the play, he is in a transitional state: having espoused a faith diametrically opposed to his former pagan way of life, he has not yet committed the sacrilegious act of breaking the idols in the temple which marks in a spectacular manner the separation from paganism which his baptism will signify inwardly. He finds himself simultaneously pulled between two poles of attraction: between the 'ardeur' with which the new faith makes him burn (lines 41, 94), and his equally ardent love for Pauline whom he has just married, and who in a dream has seen him in great danger from her former *amant* Sévère, as well as from seditious Christians. His uncertain state of mind is crystallized in his questions to his Christian mentor Néarque about the necessity of obeying at once God's call to baptism: 'L'occasion, Néarque, est-elle si pressante/Qu'il faille être insensible aux soupirs d'une amante?' and 'Pour se donner à lui faut-il n'aimer personne?' (lines 21-2, 69). When Pauline arrives to prevent him from leaving the palace, he is so moved by her pleas to stay that he knows that the only way he can resist them is by leaving her presence altogether, as do Horace and Curiace when faced with the combined opposition of Camille and Sabine to their combat: 'Je sens déjà mon coeur prêt à se révolter,/Et ce n'est qu'en fuyant que j'y puis résister' (lines 123—4).

In the opening scenes of the play, therefore, Corneille shows us a Polyeucte who is far from unified in his purpose and in deep conflict within himself, with his friend Néarque, and with his pagan wife. In Scene 3 Pauline laments to her *confidente* the lack of power which she has over her husband at the very moment when she has so much power over him that he cannot afford to reveal to her the reason for his sudden departure. So to the person whom he loves he is obliged to use a degree of casuistry in his answers in order to maintain his own coherence in the face of her emotional sway over him: 'Quel est donc ce secret?' she asks him and he replies in temporizing fashion, 'Vous le saurez un jour: je vous quitte à regret;/Mais enfin il le faut' and 'Ne craignez rien de mal pour une heure d'absence' (lines 111—13, 121).

It is Polyeucte's sensitivity to his wife's anxiety about him and his extreme reluctance to do anything which will offend her which shed some light on the reasons for his ambiguous attitude to her prior to his decision to destroy the idols in the temple (Act II, Sc. 6). When he comes back from his baptism (Act II, Sc. 4) he attempts to calm his distraught wife, whose presentiment of his death has been intensified by the unexpected arrival of Sévère in Mélitène. Pauline declines to go to the sacrifice in the temple to mark the victory of the Roman Emperor Decius because of the presence of Sévère: it is at this point that Polyeucte announces that he does not fear the possible reprisals of her influential former *amant* against him: 'Et comme je connais sa générosité,/Nous ne nous combattrons que de civilité' (lines 635—6).

But several lines after this statement of intent, he declares to Néarque that he is going to the temple in order to destroy the pagan idols (lines 643—4). In the light of his professed intention, do not his earlier words to Pauline seem blandly deceptive? The point has been put pertinently by R. Lebègue: 'ce vers si courtois, si serein, sonne faux et témoigne d'une dissimulation que Pauline n'a pas méritée et qui est indigne de Polyeucte.'[26] It cannot be doubted that there is a considerable discrepancy between the conciliatory remarks of Polyeucte about Sévère to Pauline and the intransigent tone of the potential iconoclast several lines afterwards. But to infer that he is cynically deceiving Pauline in lying to her about his intentions in the temple is to forget that in the opening scenes of the play he had been at great pains to calm her fears for his life, and had shown himself loath to disregard them in front of Néarque. In view of what we already know about Polyeucte's feelings for his wife, his attitude to her in Act II, Sc. 5 can only be interpreted as a fresh attempt on his part to allay the forebodings of her dream which have been immeasurably increased by the arrival of Sévère. Polyeucte then is certainly guilty of deceiving his wife, but he intends as far as possible to spare her unnecessary suffering, since he knows that her feelings for him are bound sooner or later to conflict with his Christian zeal.

It is important to emphasize the basic humanity of Polyeucte at this point of the action on account of the danger of viewing the Polyeucte of Act II, Sc. 6 who has just undergone the sacrament of baptism as completely different to Polyeucte in his unbaptized state. His baptism has admittedly fired his Christian zeal, present but dormant in the opening scene, with determination to witness for his faith by destroying the pagan gods. In a play about the effects of divine grace in the life of the neophyte its manifestation is obviously central to the dramatic development of the character. One critic in particular has argued trenchantly that there are two entirely different Polyeuctes, 'celui d'avant le baptême, tout possédé de sa femme, celui d'après, tout possédé de Dieu, très éloigné de l'autre, autant dire contraire'.[27] Such a view overlooks entirely the various dramatic situations into which Corneille places his character. In the first scene of the play, before the baptism, Polyeucte experiences the inner conflict of the new convert between loyalty to his faith and loyalty to his love for his wife, a conflict amply indicated in the temporal opposition between Néarque's insistence on 'aujourd'hui' as the time in which to answer God's call (lines 58, 80) and his own procrastinating replies in favour of 'un peu de remise' (lines 23, 52). After his baptism, however, this conflict is reversed: the opposition between the temporizing of Néarque and the urgency of Polyeucte could not receive sharper focus than in the question of the former and the answering question of the latter: 'Vous voulez donc mourir? Vous aimez donc à vivre?' (line 673). In the reversal of the situation of the opening scene Corneille lets us see the overpowering effect of divine grace manifested in Polyeucte's desire for instantaneous action, a desire previously stressed by Néarque, as well as its dramatic potential as it leads first to conflict between them and then to union of mind and heart as they go to prepare the assault on the forces of paganism. But the conflict within Polyeucte between his love for Pauline and his love for God has not disappeared. Relegated to the background by the force of the dramatic movement which Corneille gives to his characters, it will only re-emerge in more acute form in Act IV, Sc. 1.[28]

After the destruction of the idols, the imprisoned Polyeucte hears that Pauline has requested to see him, and his inner conflict is expressed in terms which are at once similar to and more poignant than those used by him to Néarque in the first scene of the play before the baptism and the act of sacrilege:

> O présence, ô combat que surtout j'appréhende!
> Félix, dans la prison j'ai triomphé de toi,
> J'ai ri de ta menace, et t'ai vu sans effroi:
> Tu prends pour t'en venger de plus puissantes armes;
> Je craignais beaucoup moins tes bourreaux que ses larmes.
>
> (lines 1082—6)

It is true that several lines farther on he prays that the already martyred Néarque may help him 'vaincre un si fort ennemi' (line 1091). Is it true then to say that Polyeucte, in his attempt to achieve mastery over himself, his nature and death for the sake of his faith, does not in reality love Pauline?[29] In a very real sense he must, like Horace, suppress his natural feelings if he is at all to be faithful to his purpose in dying as an act of witness to his Christian faith. The fact, however, that he admits here his need of help to achieve this is surely proof that he recognizes his own inability to eradicate his attachment for Pauline as well as of the agonizing nature of his conflict. There is certainly here not the slightest trace of that spontaneous and effortless self-mastery on the part of Corneille's heroes of which Lytton Strachey wrote when he anticipated much later Cornelian criticism by saying that 'they never blench, they never waver, but move adamantine to their doom'.[30] It is precisely at this moment when he doubts his ability to resist Pauline's entreaties to desist from the course of action to which he has committed himself that he requests that Sévère be allowed to visit him in order to hear what he describes as 'un secret important' (line 1099). This secret is none other than the extraordinary offer of Pauline which he will make to his rival in Act IV, Sc. 4. It is highly significant that he should ask to see Sévère just as he feels that his intention to die is threatened most by Pauline's visit. Is the juxtaposition in his mind of his apprehension of her visit and of his projected offer to Sévère not proof both of the depth of his attachment to her and of his desire to strengthen his will by the knowledge that she will not be deprived of the possibility of attaining earthly happiness after his death?

The famous *Stances* of Polyeucte are in this respect a conscious effort to stiffen his resistance to the appeals of Pauline. Like those of Rodrigue in *Le Cid*, they are far from being mere rhetoric, but fulfil the dramatic function of galvanising a will to action which feels itself threatened by emotional persuasion from within and without. Hence the *Stances* represent a counter-persuasion couched in absolute terms, and the fragile honours and pleasures of the world are opposed to the constancy of eternal felicity (lines 1105—14). Rodrigue and Horace both had varying degrees of insight into the brittle nature of earthly *gloire*. The former however transcended the ephemeral doubt which threatened to paralyse his will and engulf his *gloire* and the latter achieved an apparently stable *gloire* at the expense of his natural feelings, but, pursuing it to its logical conclusion by killing Camille, ended up by falling victim himself to its caprice. Polyeucte allows us to have a still more penetrating insight into the fragile basis of *gloire* as he says to Pauline in the following scene

> J'ai de l'ambition, mais plus noble et plus belle:
> Cette grandeur périt, j'en veux une immortelle,
> Un bonheur assuré, sans mesure et sans fin.
> Au-dessus de l'envie, au-dessus du destin.
>
> (lines 1191—4)

Polyeucte's aspiration to the greater and more enduring *gloire* of martyrdom may be viewed in this respect as the culmination of secular heroism whose *gloire* is continually threatened by circumstance and man's finitude and whose stability is strictly provisional. Polyeucte on the other hand is saved from incipient self-doubt by the reflections of the *Stances* on the instability of human achievement. The transformation wrought in him is seen in the contrast between his anxiety at the idea of Pauline's visit (Act IV, Sc. 1) and the last lines of the *Stances* where he envisages her coming in person with self-confidence: 'Je la vois; mais mon coeur, d'un saint zèle enflammé,/N'en goûte plus l'appas dont il était charmé' (lines 1157—8).

Under the impetus of this intensified zeal, Polyeucte grasps the initiative firmly in their meeting (Act IV, Sc. 3). His aggressive questioning with which he greets his wife is couched in such a way that the absolute opposition of the *Stances* between time and eternity is focused in terms of intense personal struggle and rivalry underlined by the strong antitheses within the alexandrines:

> Madame, quel dessein vous fait me demander?
> Est-ce pour *me combattre*, ou pour *me seconder*?
> Cet effort généreux de votre amour parfaite
> Vient-il à *mon secours*, vient-il à *ma défaite*?
> Apportez-vous ici *la haine* ou *l'amitié*,
> Comme *mon ennemie*, ou *ma chère moitié*?
>
> (lines 1161—6) (my italics)

Pauline's argument against her husband's intransigence proceeds in four stages, dealing with his personal attributes, his duty to the state, the manner in which his Christian faith may be professed, and finally with his relationship with her. In the first stage (lines 1167—82) she argues that he is his own enemy and can save himself from death, and so implicitly denies the tension between the world and God on which his resolve is built. She further compounds this error of judgement by going on to speak of Polyeucte's outstanding attributes — 'le sang dont vous sortez', 'Vos grandes actions, vos rares qualités', 'vos exploits', 'votre naissance', 'votre pouvoir', the promising future prospects ('notre espérance') which would be cut short by his untimely death (lines 1173—80) — in short, all the elements which Polyeucte in the *Stances* has placed in the category of the world in opposition to God. To the extent that her argument is based upon his personal worth and rank, Polyeucte finds it easy to oppose it with his idea of a *gloire* which is not subject to the fluctuations of time and circumstance (lines 1191—4). He can likewise cope with the second stage of her argument, namely that Polyeucte owes his life to his Prince, the public, and the state (lines 1199—205) by simply invoking the higher loyalty of God: 'Mais je la dois bien plus au Dieu qui me la donne' (line 1212). She next appeals to him to content himself with his private worship of his God, and to refrain from public profession of his faith. She attenuates this adroitly by adding that he will only need to conceal his new faith until Sévère departs (lines 1221—4). Once more, Polyeucte dismisses the idea of expediency as readily as he has withstood her two previous attempts to weaken the bases of his resolve. The final phase of the argument to undermine his resistance comes only after the failure of her three appeals to his reason. It marks therefore the collapse of her rational argument and her regression to a purely emotional one, as she accuses him of having ceased to love her, and it culminates in the bitter reproach 'Je te suis odieuse après m'être donnée!' (line 1252). It is by far the more effective in its effect upon him: up to this point, he has been able to withstand her argument with apparent effortlessness, couched as it was in terms of loyalty and expediency. His reaction to her emotional onslaught however is very different, and provokes the famous exclamation 'Hélas!' from him (line 1253), which marks the first outward sign of feeling for her throughout their meeting. Does this signify regret for Pauline or forgetfulness of her? A recent interpretation of the play has maintained the latter view and does not see Polyeucte's reaction here as betraying an inner conflict in his nature:

> Les soupirs et les larmes de Polyeucte ne sont pas le signe d'une faiblesse ou d'une déception; ils sont le signe d'une rupture. Endormi par les fumées d'un rêve religieux égoïste, le néophyte avait bel et bien oublié l'engagement personnel qui le liait à Pauline; la vision d'un ciel dont le bonheur ne semblait guère fondé sur la communication d'amour lui avait fait perdre de vue les exigences d'un amour conjugal qu'il avait réduit à la jouissance d'un 'bien' terrestre.[31]

It is true that Polyeucte has apparently been preoccupied with his own salvation to the extent that he reduces Pauline at least in his language if not in his thinking to one of the elements of the world which conspires against his purpose: '... je ne regarde Pauline/Que comme un obstacle à mon bien' (lines 1143—4) he had said prior to this meeting with her. The unfortunate harshness of tone in this absolute statement as well as Polyeucte's rigid duality of the world and salvation do not strike a ready chord in the mind of the modern spectator, still less perhaps in the Christian one. But can it seriously be maintained that he has forgotten the ties which bind him to her? On the contrary, it is because he is so aware of them that he dreads so much her appearance, that he arranges his meeting with Sévère, and that he has to spend nearly sixty lines strengthening his conviction in the enmity of the world and God. It was, after all, only after this lengthy process of reflection that he felt able to withstand her arguments. Pauline's reaction to his show of feeling here bears witness to his struggle with his emotions, paralleling the moment in *Horace* when Sabine and Camille join forces against the inhuman act in which Horace and Curiace are about to participate, as she exclaims 'Mais courage, il s'émeut, je vois couler des larmes' (line 1256). Polyeucte at once explains his emotional reaction as sorrow at the state of pagan ignorance and spiritual darkness in which he will leave Pauline, and prays for her enlightenment. He is so anxious to ensure her conversion because he has given her the highest possible place which a human can occupy in his affections, that is, one that is superior to himself, but inferior to God (lines 1279—80). Within this hierarchy of affection, his love for her is given an entirely new meaning: emptied of its physical connotations (and this will be evidenced later in his renunciation of her to Sévère) it acquires a spiritual quality which he hopes will be instrumental in converting her:

Mais si, dans ce séjour de gloire et de lumière,
Ce Dieu tout juste et bon peut souffrir ma prière;
S'il y daigne écouter un conjugal amour,
Sur votre aveuglement il répandra le jour.

(lines 1263—6)

This scene marks a critical stage in the dramatic development of Polyeucte and the culmination of the intense inner struggle of the *Stances*. For Polyeucte at this point love of Pauline and love of God are no longer in opposition, and love for his wife is but a manifestation of his greater love for God, as she will see retrospectively after his death and her conversion. At this moment of course Pauline can only view his love of God as constituting the supreme obstacle to, and not the supreme fulfilment of, her happiness. The highest form of his love for her does not consist as she imagines in not leaving her as she implores him to do ('Au nom de cet amour, ne m'abandonnez pas') but precisely in asking her to follow his example of martyrdom: 'Au nom de cet amour, daignez suivre mes pas' (lines 1281—2). It is perfectly comprehensible that Pauline should retort 'Va, cruel, va, mourir; tu ne m'aimas jamais' (line 1289), but within the context of the final Acts nothing could be further from the truth. For it is because of the death of

Polyeucte that the pagan Pauline will be converted to the Christian faith and will echo the invitation which he issues to her here to follow his example when she says to Félix in the final Act: 'Polyeucte m'appelle à cet heureux trépas;/Je vois Néarque et lui qui me tendent les bras' (lines 1733—4).

From a strictly human viewpoint, it would naturally be preferable if Polyeucte were to follow the advice proffered at various stages throughout the play by Néarque, Pauline, and Félix that he should bear witness in favour of Christianity by his life. But the only perspective in which Pauline and Félix will be converted in the play is the one involving the death of Polyeucte. In the dramatic context of the play, the prior condition of their conversions is his martyrdom, which thus automatically assumes the character of a sacrifice. Without an understanding of the Christian idea of sacrifice, the divinely appointed way by which God makes man's redemption possible through the death of Christ, the death of Polyeucte becomes an arbitrary and gratuitous act and a vain egotistical attempt at the conquest of absolute self-mastery.[32] As R. Tobin has perceptively pointed out, Pauline, once converted, describes herself as 'cette seconde hostie' (line 1720), the first sacrificial victim of course having been Polyeucte, and an explicit analogy of Christ dying to atone for the sin of the world is thus established.[33] Once seen in the context of Christian sacrifice, the death of Polyeucte, far from being proof of his gross insensitivity to or neglect of his wife becomes the highest manifestation of his love for her: 'Nul n'a plus grand amour que celui-ci: donner sa vie pour ses amis.'[34]

The second aspect of Polyeucte's sacrifice, his renunciation of Pauline to Sévère, is made more comprehensible if not more acceptable for the modern spectator or reader in the light of the first.[35] Unacceptable it still may be, but Corneille has taken care to integrate it into Polyeucte's purpose in dying. In one of his last speeches to Pauline before going to destroy the idols in the temple, he says that he understands how much she has sacrificed for him in giving up her hope of marrying Sévère and how great this sacrifice has been for her *amant*:

O vertu trop parfaite, et devoir trop sincère,
Que vous devez coûter de regrets à Sévère!
Qu'aux dépens d'un beau feu vous me rendez heureux!
Et que vous êtes doux à mon coeur amoureux!
Plus je vois mes défauts et plus je vous contemple,
Plus j'admire ...

(lines 621—6)

One may assume that he has already resolved to sacrifice Pauline to Sévère when he sends for the latter from his prison (Act IV, Sc. 1). There is nothing arbitrary in this sacrifice, which will have the effect in his eyes of bringing together by his death those whom his life has separated from each other, and he makes this explicit to Sévère:

> Ne la refusez pas de la main d'un époux:
> S'il vous a désunis, sa mort vous va rejoindre.
> Qu'un feu jadis si beau n'en devienne pas moindre;
> Rendez-lui votre coeur et recevez sa foi;
> Vivez heureux ensemble et mourez comme moi;
> C'est le bien qu'à tous deux Polyeucte désire.
> (lines 1306—11)

In Act V, Sc. 3 he gives his reasons to Pauline for his decision to give her to her former *amant*; like Horace, who prior to the combat sought in vain to persuade his sister to accept the victor, whoever he might be, without recrimination in order to make life at least bearable afterwards, Polyeucte displays similar comprehension of the situation facing Pauline. Neither Horace nor Polyeucte ask Camille or Pauline to make a greater sacrifice than that which they are prepared to make themselves. Polyeucte communicates his understanding of his wife's position by speaking to her in terms which evince at once compassion and objectivity:

> Mon amour, par pitié, cherche à vous soulager;
> Il voit quelle douleur dans l'âme vous possède,
> Et sait qu'un autre amour en est le seul remède.
> Puisqu'un si grand mérite a pu vous enflammer,
> Sa présence toujours a droit de vous charmer:
> Vous l'aimez, il vous aime, et sa gloire augmentée ...
> (lines 1586—91)

His words may sound as dispassionately cruel as those spoken to Camille by Horace before his combat in her similarly anguished state; they merely produce the unintended effect of exasperating the hearers beyond endurance by virtue of the apparently calm acceptance on the part of the speakers of an intolerable situation. Alike in their reaction to the words of Horace and Polyeucte before the decisive event of the plays, Camille and Pauline are however dissimilar in their reactions after the event. Camille can understand her brother's attitude still less after Curiace's death at his hands than before; she manifests her total rejection of Roman *gloire* by provoking Horace to kill her, thus consummating her revolt by joining the enemy of Rome in death. But only through the death of her husband can Pauline come to an understanding of Christian sacrificial love, and her understanding will impel her to seek to rejoin her martyred husband. Before his death Polyeucte had tried to explain this conception of love to Pauline and

Félix, but in vain, as he described the God whom he worshipped as

> Un Dieu qui, nous aimant d'une amour infinie,
> Voulut mourir pour nous avec ignominie,
> Et qui, par un effort de cet excès d'amour,
> Veut pour nous en victime être offert chaque jour.
>
> (lines 1659—62)

In its supreme manifestation in the death of Christ on the cross Christian love is self-emptying ('kenosis') and self-sacrificial, not self-preserving.[36] In Pauline's wish to follow Polyeucte's example after her conversion in Act V, as he has in turn followed that of the God-made-man, we find human love sanctified by grace attaining to its highest possible expression.

2 Absence and Presence in *Andromaque*, *Britannicus*, and *Bérénice*

1

The character who gives the title to the play does not herself make her first appearance until Act I, Sc. 4, and appears for the last time in Act IV, Sc. 1. (In 1668 and 1673 she re-appeared in Act V, Sc. 3, but this variant was later dropped.) Between her first and last appearances she only appears in five consecutive scenes in Act III, Sc. 4 with Hermione, briefly with Céphise in Scene 5, in Scenes 6 and 7 with Pyrrhus, and again in Scene 8 with Céphise. The somewhat episodic nature of the role has not escaped attention, and has raised serious doubts as to whether or not one can claim that she is the principal character of the tragedy. In his book *The Art of Jean Racine*, Bernard Weinberg for example points to the evident disproportion between the roles of Oreste, Pyrrhus, Hermione and that of Andromaque, and considers this as one of the play's main dramatic weaknesses: 'At both the beginning and the end, then, other persons hold our attention; Andromaque, much as we feel with her while she is present on the stage, is reduced almost to the role of a secondary personage.'[1] Lucien Goldmann has gone even farther than this, stating that 'tout en étant le seul être humain de la pièce, Andromaque n'en est pas le personnage principal. Elle se trouve à la périphérie.'[2] Antoine Adam, on the other hand, comes to a similar conclusion from a consideration of her psychology: he refuses implicitly to give her a different dramatic standing to that of the other characters by describing her as an indecisive character in a play of indecisive characters.[3] Yet the fact remains that Racine gave her name to the title of his play; and whilst one should be careful not to read too much into this, one cannot refrain from thinking that her role and her dilemma in the play must, in some general conclusive sense at least, have epitomised for the playwright the essence of what the tragedy was meant to convey to the spectator and the reader. The paradox of the eponym who is more conspicuous by her absence than by her presence is one which, I suggest, is capable of shedding light on the play's tragic vision.

The structure of *Andromaque*, in which all the characters stand in such close relationship to each other that the action of one must have repercussions on those of all the others, has traditionally been the object of much admiration. Oreste loves Hermione, Hermione loves Pyrrhus, Pyrrhus loves Andromaque, and Andromaque's love is directed towards her dead husband Hector and their son. The decision of Andromaque whether to marry Pyrrhus or to reject his offer in turn affects the rest of the characters and creates the principal focus of the play's dramatic tension. From a dramatic point of view, therefore, the decisions of the other characters depend initially on the decision which Andromaque will make in her first meeting with Pyrrhus in Act 1, Sc. 4. What is perhaps not quite so obvious is the way in which Racine makes Andromaque, directly or indirectly, responsible for the actions of the other characters not only *after* her decision in Act 1, Sc. 4, but from the beginning of the play. In other words, she is not only the pivotal figure in the action, but also the character who, although absent from the action, obliges the other characters to act in a certain way, even when they imagine that they are acting independently.

The action begins with the character who in the hierarchy of decisions to be taken is farthest from Andromaque, that is, Oreste. Oreste tells Pylade that he has come to seek Hermione's love, and in his long narration of events preceding his decision to come to Epirus (lines 37—104) we learn two important facts about him. The first of these is that, spurned in love by Hermione, he had resolved to forget her, and in fact reached the stage where he thought that he had suppressed his feelings for her. The second is that on arriving in Greece, he has learnt that the leaders of the Greek states are greatly perturbed by a dangerous situation: their former ally in the Trojan war, Pyrrhus, is harbouring the infant son of the dead Trojan leader Hector as well as his wife Andromaque. What is of paramount interest to Oreste is the fresh situation into which this event places Pyrrhus and his fiancée Hermione: 'On dit que peu sensible aux charmes d'Hermione, / Mon rival porte ailleurs son coeur et sa couronne' (lines 77—8).[4]

Pyrrhus' neglect of Hermione for Andromaque transforms the dejection of Oreste first into vengeful delight and then into renewed passion for Hermione. It is therefore he who offers himself as the Greek ambassador to Pyrrhus, indifferent to his mission to persuade the latter to give up Hector's son to the Greeks and inspired solely by the hope of gaining Hermione by consent or force. Within the context of the play, it is apparently Oreste who initiates the action on behalf of the Greeks; and later it is apparently Hermione who, before Oreste, is the initiator of the ultimatum of the Greek princes: 'J'ai déjà sur le fils attiré leur colère,' she says to Cléone (Act II, Sc. 1, line 445). But neither of these characters is the ultimate initiator of the tragic action; they are rather unwitting agents of it, imagining themselves to be free, whilst their actions are shaped for them by the character who is Pyrrhus' captive. For in the chain of events preceding the tragedy, it was she who had been the innocent means of arousing the jealousy of Hermione and her determination to avenge herself on the Trojan captive as well as on her unfaithful fiancé, Pyrrhus. The action of Hermione in informing the Greeks of Pyrrhus' infidelity is only the second link in the chain of events external to the play, but it suffices to rekindle Oreste's passion for her and to delude him with the hope that he can win her.

Andromaque is the unwitting cause of the intrusion of the Greeks into the drama from outside, and ultimately of the potentially unstable attitude with which Oreste envisages his new position with regard to Hermione: '...je viens chercher Hermione en ces lieux, / La fléchir, l'enlever, ou mourir à ses yeux' (lines 99—100). Andromaque is also directly but not deliberately responsible for the dangerously unstable attitudes of Pyrrhus and Hermione at the outset of the play, as described for us by Pylade in the opening scene. It is not just the fact that Pyrrhus has fallen in love with Andromaque and has left Hermione which creates the dramatic starting-point of the play, but rather that his captive is the cause of his fluctuations from love to hatred of her, and of Hermione's movements from coldest indifference to Pyrrhus to possessive passion. For Pyrrhus' daily attempt to coerce Andromaque's love for him by the threat to kill her son not only provokes him alternately to reduce her to tears and then to console her (lines 111—14); it also sends him back to Hermione as a means of avenging his unrequited passion. Thus he is, at the start of the play, brought to the extreme point of vacillation between Andromaque and Hermione. It is not merely the fact that he may marry one and refuse the other which gives the dramatic concentration to the opening scene, but rather that in his case sentimental choice is inseparable from emotional and physical violence: he is, Pylade tells us, liable to 'Epouser ce qu'il hait, et punir ce qu'il aime' (line 122). Hermione similarly has been reduced by Pyrrhus' inconstancy and ultimately by Andromaque's constancy to Hector to the point of extreme vacillation in her attitude towards Pyrrhus. On the one hand, she affects coquettishly to spurn his periodic returns to her from Andromaque; in secret however she laments his abandonment of her, and in practice she is 'Toujours prête à partir, et demeurant toujours' (line 131). Like Oreste, who can view with some detachment the events in which he has been caught up ('Je me livre en aveugle au destin qui m'entraîne' (line 98)), she is at the outset of the play at the point where lucidity and illusion about her situation converge in her mind with such frightening intensity that the most insignificant event is liable to unleash a reaction either of extreme love, or of extreme hatred, both of which will be equally as intense if not as destructive in their effects on others. The first scene not only gives the spectator the background information with which to interpret the relationships of Oreste, Hermione, Pyrrhus, Andromaque: it presents all four characters at the point of supreme crisis in their relationships with each other, and leaves us to marvel at the dramatic paradox which Racine has placed at the heart of his play, namely, that the unseen and absent captive Andromaque should be the presence which has not only brought them together at this particular moment at the court of Pyrrhus, but which also, seen or unseen, continues to dominate their reactions to each other.

The second example of this unseen domination by Andromaque of the action is given in Act I, Sc. 2, where Oreste meets Pyrrhus to deliver the message of the Greeks. He begins by saluting in Pyrrhus 'le fils d'Achille et le vainqueur de Troie' (line 146), thus reminding him of his ancestral status and heroic image, an image which the Trojan war has earned for him in the eyes of the Greeks. He evokes this to contrast it with the protection now accorded to the potential reincarnation of the danger to Greece in 'Le fils d'Hector' whose life the Greeks demand. What to the Greeks is a matter of national urgency is to Pyrrhus nothing more than disproportionate alarm about 'la mort d'un enfant' (line 180). Oreste evokes a graphic picture of Hector's son one day wrecking havoc on the Greek fleet, as did his father (lines 161—4) which draws from Pyrrhus the flat and undramatic 'Je ne sais point prévoir les malheurs de si loin' (line 196). In contrast to Oreste's flight of fancy, he states that the once powerful nation of Troy is now a desolate heap of rubble (lines 197—204). Unlike the Greeks, Pyrrhus makes a distinction between what was right then, and what is right now: 'Tout était juste alors' (line 209). Circumstances at that time conspired to drive him to commit deeds which are now to be regretted:

> La victoire et la nuit, plus cruelles que nous,
> Nous excitaient au meurtre, et confondaient nos coups.
> Mon courroux aux vaincus ne fut que trop sévère.
>
> (lines 211—13)

The remorse of Pyrrhus for his actions will be more fully expressed in his first meeting with Andromaque in Act I, Sc. 4. There we see the cause of his dramatic reversal from his former self to his present readiness to defend Andromaque against his former allies; here we see the effect of this reversal in his rejection of his past deeds, a rejection most sharply expressed in his challenge to the Greeks to come to Epirus and fight against the Trojan victor and the Trojan vanquished (lines 230—2). The extent to which Pyrrhus is prepared to renounce his past and his allies is symbolic of the power which the unseen Andromaque exerts over him. Nowhere, however, does he allude to his love for Andromaque; he rather rationalizes his refusal to hand over her son to Oreste by claiming, with unconscious irony, that he has sole authority to dispose of his own captives from Troy, at the very moment when his actions reveal his full dependence on his Trojan prisoner! The refusal to comply with the demand of the Greeks is quickly followed by a second result of Andromaque's mastery over Pyrrhus, which will have more far-reaching consequences for all the protagonists than the first. Thinking that he is in complete control of the situation, Pyrrhus himself suggests to Oreste that he see Hermione, in spite of the warnings of the prudent Phoenix in the following scene about the danger in Oreste's passion for her. The first consequence of Pyrrhus' error here may be seen in Act II, Sc. 2, where Hermione, although despising Oreste, is so humiliated by her position at Pyrrhus' court that she asks Oreste to seek out Pyrrhus' intentions concerning herself and Andromaque; if Pyrrhus intends to marry Andromaque, she says, she will accompany Oreste to Greece. Oreste promptly interprets this conditional offer in the light of his passion for her (Act II, Sc. 3), only to see his hopes dashed by Pyrrhus' change of mind in the following scene, where he reveals his intention to marry Hermione instead. By Act III, Sc. 1 Oreste has now been pushed by circumstances and his temperament towards that unstable frame of mind which will reluctantly yield to Hermione's command to kill Pyrrhus whom he nevertheless respects (Act IV, Sc. 3). But in Act I, Sc. 3 Pyrrhus is totally oblivious to the potential danger in his slighting of Hermione and in the freedom he allows Oreste to have. So filled is he with the vision of Andromaque that he is unconcerned with the Greek's ultimatum, the jealousy of Hermione and the rivalry of Oreste, his personal security and the sober realism of Phoenix, whom he dismisses by saying 'Une autre fois je t'ouvrirai mon âme:/Andromaque paraît' (lines 257—8).

The last verse of Act I, Sc. 3 marks the moment at which Andromaque's presence becomes visible on the stage. It is a moment of climax up to which the play has been leading. The invisible presence of Andromaque has been everywhere increasingly discernible, all the while focusing more sharply in the actions of the characters. For her presence provides the pretext for Oreste's coming, it is the cause of Pyrrhus' rejection of Hermione, of the Greek ultimatum, of Pyrrhus' cecity regarding Oreste's intentions, and finally of the trance-like state which her actual appearance induces in Pyrrhus. Andromaque's presence is the only one which matters for Pyrrhus; but since he is the character who hangs on her decision to marry him or not and who in the structural hierarchy of the play is in the position of influencing the actions of Hermione and Oreste, Andromaque's presence is, ultimately, the only one which matters for them also. But it is not Pyrrhus but the past which commands her loyalty, casting its shadow over her even before her first appearance and shaping the outcome of the tragedy. It is Andromaque's past which is the determinant of her actions in the present, and consequently of the reactions of all the other protagonists, initially and most directly of Pyrrhus.

2

Pyrrhus, having momentarily recovered his lucidity before his next passionate return to Andromaque, shows an awareness of the great gulf which past events in Troy place between them when he says to Phoenix in Act II, Sc. 5, 'Elle est veuve d'Hector, et je suis fils d'Achille:/Trop de haine sépare Andromaque et Pyrrhus' (lines 662—3). It is the fate of Hector and the outcome of the Trojan war which shape the two crucial decisions which Andromaque takes in the play, decisions which in their turn affect all the other characters. The second decision is a reversal of the first one, but both are shaped by the same past inspiration. Andromaque takes the first of her decisions in Act I, Sc. 4, when, in answer to Pyrrhus' 'offer' to save the life of her son from the Greeks if she marries him, she says 'Hélas! il mourra donc' (line 373). The second one is taken in Act IV, Sc. 1, as she says to Céphise, 'Je vais, en recevant sa foi [i.e. of Pyrrhus] sur les autels, / L'engager à mon fils par des noeuds immortels' (lines 1091—2). She takes both decisions with the full knowledge of the impossible distance which separates the victor of Troy from the widow of Hector, a distance which Pyrrhus measured accurately above and which is expressed for Andromaque in her intention to commit suicide immediately after their marriage. What is for Pyrrhus a temporary insight into his dilemma is her permanent and personal truth. For in reality Pyrrhus aspires to forget the *haine* which separates them.There is nothing which he would like to erase from his memory so much as his part in the Trojan war; this is signified by his rejection of the Greeks' demand to give up Hector's son, by regret for his past cruelties expressed to their emissary as well as to Andromaque in Act I, Sc. 4. Reminded forcefully by Hermione of his atrocities in Troy (Act IV, Sc. 5) he says 'Mais enfin je consens d'oublier le passé' (line 1344). The deeds about which she waxes so rhapsodic are now to Pyrrhus excesses due to time and circumstance.[5] His vacillations between Hermione and Andromaque can be viewed as his movement away from the glory of 'le fils et le rival d'Achille' whom Phoenix recognises as the authentic Pyrrhus (line 630) to the Pyrrhus ready to renounce his former deeds and allies for Andromaque (lines 230—2, 283—8). But the tragic conflict of Pyrrhus goes more deeply than that. He is not merely a man haunted by his past, but rather one who is not allowed to erase his past from his mind by Hermione and more especially by Andromaque. The more he loves Andromaque the closer she brings him to that past, both in her refusal to marry him and in her eventual acceptance of his 'offer'.

It is Andromaque's vision of the past which is responsible in his eyes for the agony of his dilemma: 'Hélas! fus-je jamais si cruel que vous l'êtes?' (line 322) he asks her in their first meeting. But in his passion for her, he forgets voluntarily that it is he himself who is responsible for her traumatic vision of the massacre of Troy which has seared itself indelibly into her mind and emotions. When her *confidente* argues that she should not despise marriage with someone who no longer seems to remember his ancestry and past deeds (lines 985—91) Andromaque evokes vividly the past which will always be present to her. Pyrrhus' presence is inseparably bound up with that tragic past, serving only to actualise and perpetuate in all their horror his acts at Troy:

> Dois-je les oublier, s'il ne s'en souvient plus?
> Dois-je oublier Hector privé de funérailles,
> Et traîné sans honneur autour de nos murailles?
> Dois-je oublier son père à mes pieds renversé,
> Ensanglantant l'autel qu'il tenait embrassé?
> Songe, songe, Céphise, à cette nuit cruelle
> Qui fut pour tout un peuple une nuit éternelle.
> Figure-toi Pyrrhus, les yeux étincelants,
> Entrant à la lueur de nos palais brûlants,
> Sur tous mes frères morts se faisant un passage,
> Et de sang tout couvert échauffant le carnage.
> Songe aux cris des vainqueurs, songe aux cris des mourants,
> Dans la flamme étouffés, sous le fer expirants.
> Peins-toi dans ces horreurs Andromaque éperdue:
> Voilà comme Pyrrhus vint s'offrir à ma vue:
> Voilà par quels exploits il sut se couronner;
> Enfin voilà l'époux que tu me veux donner.
>
> (lines 992—1008)[6]

We have already seen the effects which this irrevocable hold of Andromaque's traumatic vision of Troy, Pyrrhus and Hector has produced, in her rejection of Pyrrhus' conditional offer to free her son (Act I, Sc. 4). Her alienation from Pyrrhus is present fact; by delaying and superimposing this horrendous vision on present fact towards the end of Act III Racine manages to create the impression of continuing horror, which increases rather than diminishes with time in Andromaque's mind. This powerful re-enactment in the present by Andromaque of the fall of Troy gives a new dimension to the apparently elegiac and passive Andromaque of Act I, Sc. 4, who to all appearances has been at the complete mercy of the cruel Pyrrhus. The closer Racine brings her to the point where she will finally take the tragic decision to marry Pyrrhus (Act IV, Sc. 1) the more we see her as a character whose hatred and revulsion of him extend into the future, fed as they are by the actual image of his past atrocities: 'Qu'il nous prenne, s'il veut, pour dernières victimes. / Tous mes ressentiments lui seraient asservis' (lines 1010—11).[7]

It is in communion with the dead Hector that Andromaque receives the inspiration for her decision, the 'innocent stratagème' (line 1097) by which she will save her son's life in marrying Pyrrhus and then commit suicide. The effect of this communion with the past is seen in the fact that she now appears 'calm of mind, all passion spent'. The extreme revulsion which she experienced towards Pyrrhus before her decision has disappeared, since it is no longer union with the conqueror of Hector which is the focus of her attention but rather the survival of her son. With some ingenuousness she argues that Pyrrhus will, even after her death, keep his promise to protect Astyanax: 'Je sais quel est Pyrrhus. Violent, mais sincère' (line 1085).[8] The temporal and spatial dimensions of her decision are bounded by her visit to Hector's grave: 'Allons sur son tombeau consulter mon époux' (line 1048) she had said prior to her critical decision, and she envisages her reunion with him at the altar, where she will be Pyrrhus' bride in appearance, but in reality his sacrifice and Hector's eternal bride in death: 'J'irai seule rejoindre Hector et mes aïeux' (line 1099).[9] By her death and her son's survival she will remain faithful to Hector as well as to 'le fils d'Hector': in other words, to the past and to the future of Troy by her present sacrifice.

3

Racine reinforces the intensity of Andromaque's vision of the last moments of her family and the fall of Troy by skilfully working with certain key-words in her role, which gradually acquire a new meaning and depth far transcending their original connotation.[10] They come, through a combination of circumstance, character and repetition, to symbolize an attitude which can only view the present through the veil of past events. When Pyrrhus informs Andromaque of the decision of the Greeks to demand her son's death, she replies, 'Hélas! on ne craint point qu'il venge un jour son père;/On craint qu'il n'essuyât les larmes de sa mère' (lines 277—8).

Racine chooses the weakest and most insipid exclamation ('hélas') in her response to the threat to the life of her son in whom she finds her sole consolation for the tragedy of Troy. Likewise, her only answer to Pyrrhus' reintensified blackmail at the end of this scene is simply the passive 'Hélas! il mourra donc' (line 373). When she later comes to Hermione to entreat her to intercede with Pyrrhus for the life of her son, she disclaims any jealousy of Hermione's position as Pyrrhus' fiancée, and says that all her love died with Hector: 'Par une main cruelle, hélas! j'ai vu percer / Le seul où mes regards prétendaient s'adresser' (lines 863—4). In the same speech to Hermione, 'hélas!' prefaces a reference to the captivity of Hermione's mother, Helen, in Troy, and to Hector's attempts to ensure more favourable treatment for her at Andromaque's instigation (lines 873—5). When Hermione refuses to intercede on behalf of Astyanax, Céphise encourages her mistress to use her charm to reassert her influence over Pyrrhus. She replies plaintively 'Hélas! tout m'abandonne' (line 893) and 'Hélas! de quel effet tes discours sont suivis!' (line 979). As Andromaque rejects Céphise's counsel of expediency, which sees no obstacle to marriage with Pyrrhus, the *confidente* tries to force Andromaque's hand by saying that they should go instead to see the sacrifice of her son: Andromaque's immediate reaction is a pathetic evocation of Hector's last words to her concerning their son, prefaced by the lament 'Hélas! je m'en souviens' (line 1018). As she is again urged by Céphise to marry Pyrrhus, and to give him her promise without delay, she queries such a pragmatic approach to her dilemma: 'Hélas! pour la promettre [la foi] est-elle encore à moi?' (line 1044). 'Hélas!' expresses then, at least up to the point where Andromaque's decision is finally taken, her recurrent feeling of helplessness as she envisages her personal dilemma or her son's, or as she is painfully reminded of the fate of Hector and the deposit of his trust in her which makes personal compromise with his victor morally unacceptable. The apparent pathos inherent in the word is somewhat misleading in Racine's use of it here, for it comes to stand for the final authority of the past over her present actions, as well as for the finality of her present situation. It symbolizes both strength and weakness: the moral strength to be gained from the continuing inspiration of the past, and her present vulnerability which that past has produced.

A second of the key-words which Racine invests with new depths of meaning to convey Andromaque's dilemma symbolically is the adjective 'importun'. In Act I, Sc. 4, she describes herself as being 'Captive, toujours triste, importune à moi-même' (line 301). Held prisoner in the physical sense by Pyrrhus, her will is not in his power since it derives its moral strength from the past. She belongs to the past even, or specially, in her desire to ensure the survival of her son. This had been the sacred trust which she received from Hector on the day of his death (lines 1018—26), and it is in her fidelity to 'l'image d'Hector' (line 1016) that the hold of the past over her is supremely revealed. In Act III, Sc. 6 she refuses once more Pyrrhus' 'offer' to save her son, adducing as her reason for so doing 'Ce reste de fierté, qui craint d'être importune' (line 914), that is, her pride which is out of place in the present because it has lost its *raison d'être*, Hector. But 'importun', like 'hélas', is ambivalent, because of the paradoxical survival of the past into the present. Attachment to her past on the one hand deprives Andromaque of all will to act in the present (Act I, Sc. 4), and culminates, under the pressure of Pyrrhus, in the logical decision to commit suicide (Act IV, Sc. 1). Yet on the other hand the past provides her with the very moral dynamism for her 'innocent stratagème' which underlies her decision to ensure the future of Hector and Troy by her self-sacrifice.

But it is principally the tear-stained glance of Andromaque which mirrors the tragic Trojan past in the play.[11] The first time that we, and

Pyrrhus, see her she is on her way to see her son: 'J'allais, Seigneur, pleurer un moment avec lui' (line 263) she tells him. The tears of Andromaque however are not just for a moment; they stand for past, present and future grief. They have their origin in Troy at Pyrrhus' instigation, but they do not stop there, as she makes clear when she asks him, 'Quels charmes ont pour vous des yeux infortunés/Qu'à des pleurs éternels vous avez condamnés?' (lines 303—4). They unite in an indissoluble tragic vision Andromaque, Hector, and Pyrrhus: 'Et vous n'êtes tous deux connus que par mes larmes' (line 362) she says to Pyrrhus in a reference to the murder of Hector by his father Achilles. Her tears also stand for the unbridgeable temporal and spatial gulf which separates her from Pyrrhus even in his presence:

> ...c'est un exil que mes pleurs vous demandent.
> Souffrez que loin des Grecs, et même loin de vous,
> J'aille cacher mon fils, et pleurer mon époux.
>
> (lines 338—40)

They separate Andromaque from Pyrrhus by linking her to her son, and through him, to Hector. Pleading with Hermione to intervene on behalf of her son's life, Andromaque tells her that Hermione must enjoy the spectacle of 'la veuve d'Hector pleurante à vos genoux' (line 860). Her great decision to remain faithful to her husband and to her son by marriage with Pyrrhus and immediate death is taken at the place which throughout the play is the focal point of her grief: 'Allons sur son tombeau consulter mon époux' (line 1048).

It is the tears of Andromaque which exert both a sadistic and masochistic fascination over Pyrrhus. In the opening scene Pylade informs Oreste that in his treatment of his captive Pyrrhus 'fait couler des pleurs, qu'aussitôt il arrête' (line 114). They are a symbol of his apparent God-like supremacy over her, the result of his emotional blackmail, and the source of his own renewed suffering. He has the power to provoke them, but in so doing he only strengthens past loyalties which he can never command. We see the remark of Pylade dramatized in Act I, Sc. 4, when Pyrrhus announces to Andromaque, not that he has just refused the request of the Greeks to deliver up her son, but that '...les Grecs, si j'en crois leurs alarmes,/Vous donneront bientôt d'autres sujets de larmes' (lines 265—6). Having provoked her tears anew, he can now use them to further his passion for her, informing her that 'Madame, mes refus ont prévenu vos larmes' (line 281).[12] In her tears, he reads all the brutality which he displayed at Troy and his subsequent remorse:

> Mais que vos yeux sur moi se sont bien exercés!
> Qu'ils m'ont vendu bien cher les pleurs qu'ils ont versés!
> De combien de remords m'ont-ils rendu la proie!
>
> (lines 315—17)

He displays a certain lucidity in his passion for Andromaque, sensing the power which her tears exert over him, but in the final analysis he is powerless to resist an influence which he has provoked against himself: his awareness of this is paradoxically a prelude to his return to Andromaque from Hermione: 'Oui, je sens à regret qu'en excitant vos larmes / Je ne fais contre moi que vous donner des armes' (lines 949—50).[13] His ultimate objective behind his alternating dependence upon Andromaque and his threats against her son is that of being accepted by her. Hence his obsession with her when she is present as he continually craves from her what he terms 'un regard moins sévère' (line 290), that is, a sign that his love for her is accepted in the present by overlooking the past.[14] Her 'regard sévère' results of course from her image of 'Pyrrhus, les yeux étincelants' who is the mass-murderer of her people.[15] It is 'sévère' for him both as regards its cause and effect: not only in its judgement of him at Troy, but also as it treats him as absent even when present by directing itself in his presence exclusively towards Hector, 'Le seul, où mes regards prétendaient s'adresser' (line 864) as she will say to Hermione.

When Pyrrhus moves from Andromaque to Hermione, he can see with retrospective clarity the dangers which marriage with his captive would have occasioned for him, and he contrasts the damage which he has averted with the potential cause of his downfall to Phoenix in Act II: 'Un regard m'eût tout fait oublier' (line 640). Even at this moment of insight, however, his underlying obsession with her emerges in the minute attention with which he examines every gesture and reaction of their last meeting and in his need to submit them again to the test of his blackmail: 'Ma colère à ses yeux n'a paru qu'à demi' (line 675), 'Je veux la braver à sa vue' (line 677). In his rationalization of his need to see again the absent Andromaque in terms which assert too stridently his vaunted superiority to her, there is more self-deception than insight, as he evinces the same unconscious determination to deceive himself as he does in his attempts to persuade the captive whom he has irrevocably alienated to marry him.

It is Céphise who is aware of the ascendancy of Andromaque's 'regard' over Pyrrhus and she urges her mistress to turn this to the advantage of her son: 'Un regard confondrait Hermione et la Grèce' (line 889) she tells her. Hermione has already refused to intercede on behalf of Astyanax with Pyrrhus, taunting Andromaque with the remark that 'Vos yeux assez longtemps ont régné sur son âme' (line 885), and urges her to use them to regain her ascendancy over Pyrrhus. Act III, Sc. 6 provides an excellent example of the way in which such a *précieux* commonplace as 'the power of the glance' is used by Racine with great dramatic and ironic effect. Hermione has just left the stage after her confrontation with Andromaque and Pyrrhus has just entered. Dramatically and scenically he is precisely mid-way between

Hermione and Andromaque. He makes a show of looking for Hermione, turning away from the disconsolate Andromaque who plaintively echoes the taunt of Hermione by saying to Céphise 'Tu vois le pouvoir de mes yeux' (line 892). Céphise urges her to break the obstinate silence with Pyrrhus, and she replies 'Non, non, j'ai beau pleurer, sa mort est résolue' (line 897). Pyrrhus in turn says to Phoenix 'Daigne-t-elle sur nous tourner au moins la vue?' (line 898). When eventually they speak, Pyrrhus renews the threat to kill Astyanax, and Andromaque contrasts this with his earlier promise to protect them from the Greeks; Pyrrhus replies in terms which explicitly assert his new-found lucidity, but which in reality reveal the depths of his cecity: 'J'étais aveugle alors: mes yeux se sont ouverts' (line 908). It is precisely at this point that Pyrrhus admits the power of her tears over him (lines 949—50) whilst pleading with her to look in his direction: 'Mais, Madame, du moins tournez vers moi les yeux:/Voyez si mes regards sont d'un juge sévère' (lines 952—3). The co-existence of lucidity and cecity in Pyrrhus is nowhere better illustrated than in his passionate plea to Andromaque to save her son's life and in the simultaneous renewal of the threat to his life by ordering her to come to the temple where her son will await them, and he uses Andromaque's presence in the temple as a means of intensifying both his promise and his threat: 'Et là vous me verrez, soumis, ou furieux,/Vous couronner, Madame, ou le perdre à vos yeux' (lines 975—6).

Although Andromaque does not appear on stage after her decision in Act IV, Sc. 1 to marry Pyrrhus and commit suicide, her presence continues to manifest itself in Pyrrhus' fascination with his vision of her. The final ascendancy of her glance over him makes itself felt in the subsequent reactions of Hermione to the fresh betrayal by Pyrrhus. In Act IV, Sc. 2 Cléone cannot understand the strange silence of her mistress who has learnt of the marriage of Pyrrhus and Andromaque: 'Vous qui sans désespoir ne pouviez endurer/Que Pyrrhus d'un regard la voulût honorer?' (lines 1135—6). It is the avowal of the ascendancy of Andromaque's glance over Pyrrhus as well as over herself, an ascendancy about which she has deluded herself for so long, which she finally and bitterly hears from Pyrrhus himself in Act IV, Sc. 5. He comes in person to break off formally his engagement to her, an engagement made by Menelaus and Achilles during the campaign against Troy, without Pyrrhus or Hermione having had the opportunity to see or consult each other about it. Pyrrhus describes in dispassionate terms her arrival in Epirus at the time when he was already in love with Andromaque and his efforts to remain faithful to the Greek princess:

> Et quoique d'un autre oeil l'éclat victorieux
> Eût déjà prévenu le pouvoir de vos yeux,
> Je ne m'arrêtai point à cette ardeur nouvelle.
>
> (lines 1291—3)

But such attempts have proved vain and love for Andromaque cannot be resisted. Pyrrhus tries to put an end to the vindictive and passionate recriminations of Hermione, to the effect that he has broken the agreement between them, by saying that it is their duty to themselves which demands that they separate. This occasions a renewed outburst from her as she rejects bitterly the implication that she did not love him. Her most bitter words however are provoked by her inability to nullify the power of Andromaque's glance over Pyrrhus:

> Mais, Seigneur, s'il le faut, si le ciel en colère
> Réserve à d'autres yeux la gloire de vous plaire,
> Achevez votre hymen, j'y consens. Mais du moins
> Ne forcez pas mes yeux d'en être les témoins.
> (lines 1369—72)[16]

Just as she requests him to delay his marriage for a day, perhaps in a last desperate effort to win him from her rival, she sees that his attention has wandered from what she is saying to him. Her passionate jealousy is aroused to the pitch of fury, as she understands in a flash the truth from which she has so long tried to escape by rationalizing it, namely, that Pyrrhus' gaze is directed towards no one except Andromaque. Dramatically, the moment marks the axis of the tragic action. Oreste, it is true, has already been dispatched on his mission to murder Pyrrhus (Act IV, Sc. 3). But Racine in this scene has created a pause in the ascending action as instigator of the murder and victim speak together. It is at a moment of potential mutual explanation that Pyrrhus' inattention to the woman who loves him passionately and his preoccupation with the woman who can never do so cause Hermione to explode with jealous rage:

> ...Perfide, je le vois,
> Tu comptes les moments que tu perds avec moi!
> Ton coeur, impatient de revoir ta Troyenne,
> Ne souffre qu'à regret qu'un autre t'entretienne.
> (lines 1375—8)[17]

He leaves Hermione, oblivious to her presence as to her absence, ignoring the warning of Phoenix that her fury may well seek to revenge itself through Oreste (lines 1387—91), as in fact he had ignored the same warning in Act I, Sc. 3. The final appearance of Pyrrhus is an intensified repetition of his first one: then he had ecstatically exclaimed to Phoenix, in answer to the latter's prudent counsel, 'Andromaque paraît' (line 258), and now, in a veritable state of trance, he can only utter the words 'Andromaque m'attend' (line 1392). In spite of his moments of apparent lucidity, he remains from beginning to end hypnotized by his vision of Andromaque, just as Orgon is hypnotized by the vision of Tartuffe in Molière's play. And the presence of Andromaque and Tartuffe is supremely apparent in the hypnotic state of Pyrrhus and Orgon.

It is Cléone who tells Hermione of Pyrrhus' arrival in the temple for his marriage. Intoxicated with his passion, 'd'un oeil où brillaient sa joie et son espoir' (line 1435), he shows no sign of remorse for his betrayal of Hermione, nor does he spare a glance for her *confidente* as Cléone tells her: 'Madame, il ne voit rien' (line 1449). This is of course true both on the literal and figurative levels. In his preoccupation with Andromaque and her son, he has thrown caution to the winds, and has given his own guards to Astyanax.[18] It represents the culmination of Pyrrhus' blindness which Andromaque has induced in him: after the murder Oreste recounts how Pyrrhus in front of the altar gave Andromaque power over his state and himself, promising to act as a father to her son and to defend the interest of Troy against all (lines 1507—12). In his blindness he explicitly renounces his past, Hermione, Greece, his deeds and his victory at Troy, and this is the precise signal for the enraged Greeks to attack him. Absence from consciousness is not however effacement of the past, which survives in the memory of others (Hermione and the Greeks) as an objective reminder to him of his historical role which he has created for himself but which he is not free to abolish. The supreme irony of Pyrrhus is that he, the maker of history in the sacking of Troy, is destroyed both as a man and as a hero by the past which he has created for himself, Greece and Troy, and that Andromaque, the symbol of his past victory, now becomes the instrument of his disintegration and finally his destruction.

The blindness of Pyrrhus in his love for his captive is in turn responsible for the blindness in which Hermione commissions Oreste to kill the man she loves; this is illustrated most strikingly in her poignant disavowal of Oreste as well as of her order to avenge herself, as she rounds on him in helpless frustration after the murder: 'Qui te l'a dit?' (line 1543). Her blindness in turn leads Oreste to murder someone whom he respects, and the 'épaisse nuit' of madness which subsequently engulfs him after his recognition of his true situation is a symbol of the dark forces lurking in all the characters except Andromaque, forces which have only awaited the framework of particular circumstances to produce the final cataclysm. These circumstances have been prepared by what Pyrrhus in retrospect regrets as the cruelty induced in the Greeks by the intoxication of victory during the night of the Trojan massacre and by what Andromaque experiences continually as a 'nuit éternelle' (line 998). The tragedy originates in the darkness of Troy and ends in the darkness of Epirus.

Only Andromaque survives the final catastrophe, as she survived the massacre of Troy. In the 1668 and 1673 variants of Act V, Sc. 3, she reappeared on stage to accuse Oreste and Hermione of the death of Pyrrhus, which in the present version is recounted to Hermione by Oreste, and to mourn Pyrrhus who, she said, had taken the place of Hector. Her re-appearance may have been tempting from a dramatic point of view in order to counter-balance the more extensive roles of Oreste and Hermione. But it would have changed the character of Andromaque herself beyond recognition, from the unswervingly faithful 'veuve d'Hector' to a coquettish and expedient woman, in flagrant contradiction to the character who refuses to accept the pragmatism of Céphise at the end of Act III and at the beginning of Act IV. In the present version we have merely the indication from Pylade that Andromaque is prepared to avenge the death of Pyrrhus on the Greeks (lines 1589—92). The death of Pyrrhus and the promised vengeance on his assassins harmonize finally for Andromaque the combat between the victor of Troy and the defeated Hector, a combat which has taken place in front of her eyes before the play and in her mind during it. Pyrrhus expiates his crimes of Troy, which in her eyes he compounded by marrying her, and by her vengeance on the Greeks Hector will obtain his posthumous revenge. The 'regard' of Andromaque, fashioned by Pyrrhus in the 'nuit éternelle' of Troy, is the means of his expiation for that night and the Trojan vengeance for the past. It survives as a symbol of the desolation of the past suffering projected into the present and the future.

4

Néron does not appear in the first Act of *Britannicus*, but the opening lines direct us to his sleeping presence.[19] Even though physically absent from the stage, he is the focus of attention of the other characters from the beginning. The principal theme is the awakening of what the *Seconde Préface* calls the 'monstre naissant'. Indeed, the nascent monster has begun to stir; behind his seizure of Junie, the perspicacious Agrippine perceives his attempt to free himself from her influence, which she has lent to Britannicus and Junie to counter-balance such an eventuality. She is acutely aware of what is at stake, hence her premonition of her imminent loss of power: 'Je sens que je deviens importune à mon tour' (line 14).[20] The erstwhile omnipresent and invisible manipulator of the Senate, the creator of Néron as man and Emperor, is able to date precisely the change in his attitude towards her: the day that she made as usual to take her place with Néron on the throne in the presence of his ambassadors 'Il m'écarta du trône où je m'allais placer' (line 110). This formal sign of independence has been followed by his estrangement from her person. In her presence, he is no longer her son. When he speaks, he does not communicate his thoughts to her. She is constantly under surveillance, as indeed he is in his turn.[21] His voluntary or imposed refusal to confide in her acts as an incitement to her to pursue him all the more relentlessly, just as her pursuit incites him to avoid her. Néron's evasiveness sustains the pursuing presence in his palace in such a way that the unnatural pursuer and pursued are virtually indistinguishable: '...je le poursuivrai d'autant plus qu'il m'évite' (line 123) expresses a clear-sighted determination to corner her quarry sooner or later which will be echoed shortly by Néron (line 510). At last the door of Néron's chamber opens to reveal one of her inevitable surveillants, Burrhus. Her strident call for Néron's emancipation from the tutelage of his advisors constitutes the ostensible theme of her outburst to him: 'Néron n'est plus enfant: n'est-il pas temps qu'il règne?' (line 159). Her argument however is double-edged, based as it is on the opposition between the counsel of the outsider and the counsel of the ancestor. Néron is not allowed to see through the eyes of the former, but the eyes of the latter, of which she approves, are the eyes of heredity and habitual obedience to Agrippine. Her argument in favour of Néron's freedom is in reality nothing more than a strong statement in favour of his total dependence on her instead. The growing emancipation of Néron is however a reality, acknowledged inwardly by Agrippine and outwardly by Burrhus as he defends the seizure of Junie. As a descendant of Augustus, Junie might choose as husband a potential rival to the Emperor: therefore

>...le sang de César ne se doit allier
>Qu'à ceux à qui César le veut bien confier;
>Et vous-même avoûrez qu'il ne serait pas juste
>Qu'on disposât sans lui de la nièce d'Auguste.
>
>(lines 241—4)

The 'sans lui' anticipates with unconscious irony the total encroachment of Néron on the liberty of others manifested in his visible and invisible pressure on Junie to marry him in the following Act. The assertion of power by the elimination of rivals is a tactic which Agrippine herself has used to become the wife of her uncle, Claudius, and to persuade him to adopt Néron into the imperial family as his successor. From the outset, she is only too aware of the fact that her son has inherited the same unscrupulous drive for power over others ('La fierté des Nérons qu'il puisa dans mon flanc' (line 38)) and is using her own tactic to relegate her to the periphery of power by his threat to the marriage of her protégés.

The entire debate between Agrippine and Burrhus points to the former's redundant state. She has not seen Néron, her lengthy discussion with his advisor has achieved nothing and symbolizes, by its sheer inconclusiveness, the distance between mother and son. In the following scene, however, she seems to reassert herself somewhat by promising cryptically to help the distraught Britannicus in his attempt to rediscover Junie, and to this end arranges to meet with him at the house of Pallas. But just at the point at which she reasserts her influence over events, she is overheard by the treacherous Narcisse, in whom both she and Britannicus trust.[22] From the start of the play, Néron will be aware through Narcisse of the schemes of Agrippine, which are, in spite of her commanding postures, doomed to failure. She is, with the exception of the last scene of the first Act, present throughout, and seems, by her powerful personality, to hold the centre of the stage. But she is a presence continually frustrated by Néron's elusiveness from the first lines of the play. Neither absent nor present at the beginning, he gradually encroaches onto the stage through Burrhus, in Britannicus' distracted search for everything which he has lost, and at the end, through the all-surveying eye of the Emperor's *confident*, whom J. Brody has well called 'Néron's vicarious stare'.[23]

Our first view of Néron at the beginning of Act II confirms him as the close observer of the conduct of others, who, invisible in Act I, has surveyed the actions of Agrippine and Britannicus. The order to banish Pallas from the precincts of Rome forthwith is his first action within the play designed to weaken his mother's influence. In banishing the powerful ex-slave of Claudius, Néron affirms his presence unequivocally at the expense of his past, for it was Pallas who engineered the incestuous marriage of Claudius and Agrippine and his own adoption into the imperial family. This act of independence from a past dominated by Agrippine is quickly followed by another, no less politically important to mother and son: Néron has fallen in love with his captive. In his attachment to a woman other than Agrippine, he is paradoxically made more aware than ever of the dreaded maternal ascendancy. In Junie's presence, he felt totally at a loss for words, just as he has been overcome so often in the past by the sheer presence of his mother: 'J'ai voulu lui parler et ma voix s'est perdue' (line 396). And he is simultaneously confronted by all the obstacles which separate him from Junie: 'Octavie, Agrippine, Burrhus,/Sénèque, Rome entière, et trois ans de vertus' (lines 461—2). Behind all these obstacles lurks the ubiquitous presence of 'l'implacable Agrippine' (line 483). Far from her dreaded presence, he can agree with Narcisse that he should live and reign for himself: 'Eloigné de ses yeux, j'ordonne, je menace' (line 496), but all his prepared resistance crumbles under the imperious stare of his mother: 'Mon génie étonné tremble devant le sien' (line 506). The elusiveness of Néron for his mother stems as much from his fear of his helplessness in her presence as from his desire to act independently. His paradoxical pursuit of her through flight is expressed in a line which counter-balances ironically the earlier vow of Agrippine to track him down, as he states to Narcisse that he thwarts her purposes obliquely 'Afin qu'elle m'évite autant que je la fuis' (line 510). The impression from our first view of Néron is that he is dominated by others, whilst appearing to dominate them. Until now, he has been dominated by the insidious flattery of Narcisse, by the power of the unseen Junie, and supremely by the absent Agrippine. In the following scene (Sc. 3) we see him dominated by his passion for Junie and by the absent Britannicus. Alone with the anxious Junie, Néron immediately tries to focus attention exclusively on his total control of the situation, as he asks her 'Lisez-vous dans mes yeux quelque triste présage?' (line 528). In spite of this, our attention is focused on his immaturity and insecurity as, following the earlier advice of Narcisse that his authority as Emperor is sufficient to command Junie's love, he stakes his claim to her in terms of his public office. In an attempt to forestall Néron's declaration of love, Junie evokes the name of his estranged wife, Octavie (lines 608ff) which he construes as a subterfuge to conceal her interest in Britannicus. Forced to admit her feelings for the latter, she does so in terms which evoke the superiority of the Emperor's rival. Britannicus has been deprived of throne, rank, and court, deprivations which unite Junie all the more to him, whereas the Emperor has all the resources of the world at his disposal. In contrasting the limitless pleasures of the Emperor with the tears of Junie which console the unfortunate Britannicus, she brings Néron to the point at which he must admit his inferiority: '... ce sont ces plaisirs et ces pleurs que j'envie' (line 659). His passion for her is composed of both possessiveness and sadism which come to the fore in his plan to coerce her to rid herself of his rival without indicating that Néron is jealous of him (lines 669—70). He wishes to possess Junie without the dependence on another implicit in jealousy, and he is sadistic in that he will witness the pain inflicted on Junie and Britannicus as just punishment for happiness enjoyed independently of himself. Before the interview which he is going to allow her to give Britannicus, he commands her: 'Renfermez votre amour dans le fond de votre âme' (line 680), a command which exemplifies pathetically the sadistic possessiveness that passes for love to him.[24] In this scene Néron claims the right to make up Junie's mind to love him and to forget his rival: but in fact he merely succeeds in revealing all the more clearly her love for Britannicus. His hidden presence in the scene in which he has commanded her to tell Britannicus that she no longer loves him takes this claim a stage further. He does not only claim the right to decide for his subjects, but also the right to control the way Junie speaks, thinks, and looks in front of his rival. The means of arriving at her enforced decision must please him as much as the decision itself: he warns her that

> Vous n'aurez point pour moi de langages secrets:
> J'entendrai des regards que vous croirez muets;
> Et sa perte sera l'infaillible salaire
> D'un geste ou d'un soupir échappé pour lui plaire.
>
> (lines 681—4)

Having played the role of the Emperor with supreme authority, Néron now attempts to play God in his universe, present everywhere and visible nowhere.

Néron is doubly present in the eavesdropping scene, both overlooking and overhearing the scene between Junie and Britannicus in secret, and present on the stage through the eyes and ears of the treacherous Narcisse. This double presence accounts for the different levels of dramatic tension and irony which the scene produces for the spectator and for Junie; the spectator is aware of both the hidden and vicarious presence of Néron on stage, whereas Junie is aware only of the hidden Néron. Néron surveys Junie, Britannicus and Narcisse from his position as the all-seeing omnipresent spectator; Narcisse in his turn surveys the meeting of Junie and Britannicus; and Junie surveys with anguish her looks, gestures, words, aware that any loss of control on her part will mean the death of Britannicus. Néron's presence however is mediated most strongly to us and to Junie by the character who is unaware of his presence, who, by his transparency of look and word forces Junie to assert that presence more than ever by denying her instincts, that is, Britannicus. He speaks of the joy which the sight of Junie gives him each day (line 698) and of the need to make best use of 'cette heureuse absence' of Néron (line 711). His expansiveness forces Junie to emphasize the ubiquity of the Emperor's hidden presence and their constricted situation:

Vous êtes en des lieux tout pleins de sa puissance.
Ces murs mêmes, Seigneur, peuvent avoir des yeux;
Et jamais l'Empereur n'est absent de ces lieux.
(lines 712—4)

When he tells her that Rome condemns the abduction, Junie, who at all costs must not speak her thoughts, nevertheless manages to convey them with great delicacy by attributing vicariously to Britannicus her own feelings: 'Sans doute la douleur vous dicte ce langage' (line 728). In her subtle circumvention of Britannicus' derogatory remarks about Néron, she indicates for all to understand, including Néron but not Britannicus, that the expression of deepest feeling transcends speech and gesture. The presence of Néron is overwhelmingly actualized by Britannicus' shocked reaction to the sudden change in her language and look: 'Qui vous rend à vous-même, en un jour, si contraire?' (line 735). The irremediable confusion of Britannicus is evidenced by his final words to Néron's vicarious presence, as he asks if there is anyone whom he can trust now. The apparent triumph of Néron also emerges in the drained flatness of Junie's remark to him when Britannicus has disappeared: 'Vous êtes obéi' (line 745). And he has been obeyed in look, gesture and word. But he has indeed understood full well the secret language which, as he had warned Junie, would not escape his attention, that unambiguous language which his presence made possible, as he admits to Narcisse that their love 'a paru jusque dans son silence' (line 748). His reaction takes the form of sadistic delight in inciting Britannicus' jealousy of him, but in fact prepares the way for his still more crushing defeat at the hands of his rival at the end of Act III.

Before the climactic clash with Britannicus, we have two separate testimonies in Act III to the increasing emancipation of the nascent monster from all restraint. The first is his disregard of Burrhus' advice to seek reconciliation with Octavie and to avoid Junie, and the advisor acknowledges his helplessness in the face of this sinister trend: 'Enfin, Burrhus, Néron découvre son génie' (line 800). The second is that of Agrippine, whose jealousy of the power which Junie will wield over her son intensifies that sense of imminent eclipse expressed at the outset: 'Ma place est occupée, et je ne suis plus rien' (line 882). Formerly, as Néron admitted, he took his instructions from '... le pouvoir/De ces yeux où j'ai lu si longtemps mon devoir' (lines 501—1).[25] Now Agrippine envisages the ascendancy of her glance as being transferred to Junie: 'Tout deviendra le prix d'un seul de ses regards' (line 890). As in Act I her presentiment of diminishing influence is followed by a promise to Britannicus to dominate Néron once more (Sc. 5). The promise is accompanied by her advice to avoid at all costs being seen by Néron, and given, ironically, as it was earlier, in the presence of his *alter ego* Narcisse, and thus nullified immediately.

But when Junie escapes from the clutches of Néron to see Britannicus (Sc. 7) the Emperor's all-seeing presence is momentarily avoided with the departure of Narcisse to inform him. This scene is the first one in which Junie and Britannicus are alone together; in all previous scenes in which they appear individually or together they are surveyed by Néron or Narcisse. The dramatic tension is heightened by Britannicus' lengthy misunderstanding about their previous meeting, as well as by the imminent confrontation of the rivals. Although absent, Néron looms large in the scene, in the anxiety of Junie ('Néron vous menace' she tells Britannicus breathlessly, line 985) and in her vivid description of the extent to which Néron's presence penetrated her gestures in the eavesdropping scene, even in her *avoidance* of Britannicus' glance: 'Je trouvais mes regards trop pleins de ma douleur' (line 1010).

The long-awaited confrontation is focused principally in the respective 'regards' with which the two claimants to Junie and the Empire seek to outdo each other. Britannicus denies boldly the authority of the all-seeing Néron to conceal Junie from him: 'Et l'aspect de ces lieux où vous la retenez/N'a rien dont mes regards doivent être étonnés' (lines 1033—4). Néron's 'regard', so recently submissive in front of Agrippine, seeks the reflection of its new-found authority in the unquestioning obedience of others. But the 'regard' of Britannicus penetrates beyond the present authority of the Emperor to a past as unwelcome as it is dangerous for that authority, since it does not view Néron in legitimate succession to Claudius. That past reminds Néron not only of his displacement of the rightful heir but also of the woman who achieved the succession for him. Just as his past is not to be exposed to the inquiring gaze of others, so too his means of sustaining his authority must remain hidden:

> Rome ne porte point ses regards curieux
> Jusque dans des secrets que je cache à ses yeux.
> Imitez son respect.
>
> (lines 1049—51)

His failure to achieve this here is seen in his increasingly crude and physical reactions to Britannicus' provocations which become more intangible as they make Junie's approval and not Néron's authority the supreme arbiter. By telling Néron that the presence which he aspires to possess is the one least likely to be impressed by intimidation, Britannicus forces him to concede publicly what he has already conceded privately to Narcisse — that if he cannot possess her love, he will compensate by punishment of his rival who does: 'Je sais l'art de punir un rival téméraire' (line 1060). Britannicus further exposes the vulnerable aspect of Néron by lifting the dispute onto an entirely figurative plane out of reach of the tyrant's threats: enmity with Junie is the only peril he, Britannicus, fears, pleasing her is his only objective. The omnipresent Néron is not merely a secondary presence to Junie in Britannicus' reckoning: he simply does not count at all. His final provocation is the most devastating for Néron, as he contrasts the manner in which he has been accepted by her with the way in which Néron has ensured his own rejection:

> Je ne sais pas du moins épier ses discours.
> Je la laisse expliquer sur tout ce qui me touche,
> Et ne me cache point pour lui fermer la bouche.
>
> (lines 1066—8)

Britannicus not only challenges Néron for Junie's love: by his triumphant openness of manner by which he loves and is loved he challenges Néron's burgeoning self-affirmation to its very core. He is a living denial of everything to which Néron aspires and which he is in the process of becoming, and so must die. Néron's simultaneous understanding of this and his reaction to it are reflected in his defeated rejoinder: 'Je vous entends. Hé bien, gardes!' (line 1069)

Néron's reaction to this fresh evidence of Junie's love for his rival is to see the hated influence of Agrippine at work to thwart him. His very lucidity leads him to conclude blindly that she has only delayed her confrontation with him in order to be able to savour more fully his total disintegration brought about by her latest master-stroke, 'ce ressort odieux' (line 1089). The outcome of the trial of strength has important implications for Néron's relationship with his mother. It brings him to the point in his thinking at which he contemplates more clearly than hitherto the final phase of his struggle with her (he places her under arrest in his palace), and closer to the moment at which the confrontation, so long delayed, must take place. With consummate dramatic skill Racine juxtaposes the hardening of his attitude towards her (Act III, Sc. 9) and their encounter (Act IV, Sc. 2). It is Britannicus who has been responsible for this reaction in Néron. In the light of the dramatic context, it does not seem accurate to say, as does Bernard Weinberg, for example, that 'his role is that of one who reacts more than he acts ... He is passive to Néron's activity'.[26]

It has taken Agrippine from the first scene of the play until the second scene of the fourth Act to obtain the interview with her son. The distance between the scene where she first expressed her fear for the loss of her influence over him and their belated encounter reflects structurally and temporally the deterioration of their relationship and the diminution of her influence. Its position heightens immeasurably the drama of the clash of two presences which a common heredity has rendered equally domineering. Agrippine's fury has been exacerbated by suppression through delay; Néron's independence has increased correspondingly, as Agrippine's catalogue of actions committed by him without her approval will soon underline. She has finally succeeded in tracking down her 'quarry', as she imagines; but to the spectator, who has had a less partial view of the action, quarrier and quarry are indistinguishable.

Her bold attempt to re-establish the supremacy of her presence over her son is initially conveyed by her regal gesture which precedes her imperious words to him: AGRIPPINE, *s'asseyant*: 'Approchez-vous, Néron, et prenez votre place' (line 1115), and subsequently by her massive speech of one hundred and seven lines. This speech falls into two distinct parts; three-quarters of it are devoted to a recapitulation of imperial history, which Agrippine has shaped to ensure her son's succession to the throne of her uncle Claudius. The rest is a bitter reminder of the signs of Néron's recent ingratitude towards her. In the first part, she begins by referring to the explanation she is about to give for her past deeds (lines 1115—18), then alludes briefly to the present ('Vous régnez'), a present rank which neither the imperial standing of son or mother could ever have achieved legitimately (lines 1119—22). The critical intervention of Agrippine came with the fall from favour of Claudius' wife, the mother of Britannicus. With the help of Pallas, she managed to persuade Claudius to marry his niece, and obtained the agreement of the Senate (lines 1123—37); then she persuaded Claudius to adopt Néron into the imperial family, and to marry his daughter to him (lines 1138—48). Claudius was persuaded to alienate Britannicus,

Andromaque, Britannicus and Bérénice

and accept Néron as his successor (lines 1149—72). The news of the death of Claudius, hastened by Agrippine, was held back from the people until she was sure of the army's support for Néron. The death of Claudius was followed swiftly by the reign of Néron as successor (lines 1173—94). The remainder of her speech is a coldly studied reproach to Néron for present ingratitude.

Néron's spirited defence of his actions is based on the fact that Rome is no longer satisfied with an Emperor who receives instructions from his mother. The bitter reproaches which concluded his mother's speech are answered by his equally bitter charges that she is plotting his removal from the throne in favour of Britannicus. This occasions Agrippine's passionate outburst that she, a dependant in the court of Néron, would be a convicted criminal in the court of his rival (lines 1258—68). Until now, accusation and counter-accusation have nullified each other. But the reassertion of her presence comes towards its climax when she rounds on him unequivocally: 'Vous êtes un ingrat, vous le fûtes toujours' (line 1270). This is followed by a highly emotional challenge to him to take her life, since he has already deprived her of liberty. She has seen that her studied recital of her benefits to Néron has been ineffective and that some stronger tactic must be brought into play if she is to regain the place of influence to which she has literally sacrificed herself, and without which she cannot live. Her emotional blackmail of Néron is designed to make his resistance crumble, or else to provoke her total eclipse.

Néron's reaction is different from the cold insolence of his first speech, as he seems to wilt under the verbal and emotional onslaught. Agrippine dictates her conditions for reconciliation with him in answer to his question about what she wishes him to do in the situation. They amount to a complete reversal on his part of all his actions from the seizure of Junie onwards and culminate in her demand to have freedom of access to his counsel at any time (lines 1288—94). His consequent *volte-face* is apparently complete, but within the scene there are warning signs that he is feigning reconciliation with her. The new-found tone of respect in his reply to her demands (lines 1295ff) is in total contrast with the studied irony with which he has just asked her to specify the measures she would like him to take to remedy her grievances, as are his unexpected show of magnanimity towards Pallas and Britannicus and his compliance to Agrippine with what we have already seen of his deep-seated resentment of each trace of her influence.

This is confirmed in the following scene, where he says to Burrhus that Britannicus' death is going to free him from the fury and constricting presence of his mother: 'Tant qu'il respirera, je ne vis qu'à demi' (line 1317). Polite acquiescence to her demands in her presence provides him with the necessary cover for his own actions and is essentially the same tactic which he has employed throughout the play in his efforts to erode her influence: formal deference expressed through his advisers and avoidance of her or 'reculer pour mieux sauter'. Agrippine's demand for surrender on his part to her will has brought him finally to the point where he will either destroy her influence completely or regress to her total control over him. Racine conveys exactly the equipollent nature of the alternatives facing him by the juxtaposition of this scene with Burrhus with the following one with Narcisse, both of which come after his encounter with his mother. So delicately balanced are the opposing courses of action in his mind that either adviser may influence him in his own particular way. Burrhus seems to persuade Néron to renounce his plan to murder his rival and to be reconciled with him instead, by a powerful speech which stresses the crucial nature of his present decision: Néron will either project his past virtue into the future, or blight it for ever by plunging into an unending cycle of violence and counter-violence: 'Vertueux jusqu'ici, vous pouvez toujours l'être' (line 1340). The appeal to past virtue is a powerful one, but in Néron's case the past is ambivalent, for Narcisse returns with the poison for Britannicus, prepared by Locuste, whose services, according to Tacitus, had helped Agrippine rid herself of Claudius. The amazed Narcisse hears of the intended reconciliation and unsuccessfully taunts Néron with sacrificing Junie to his rival. His evocation of Agrippine's hated presence is however a more successful stratagem: she has boasted

> Qu'elle n'avait qu'à vous voir un moment:
> Qu'à tout ce grand éclat, à ce courroux funeste
> On verrait succéder un silence modeste;
> Que vous-même à la paix souscririez le premier,
> Heureux que sa bonté daignât tout oublier.
>
> (lines 1418—22)

Fresh uncertainty is induced in him, but he is still held back by fear of public judgement, his own scruples, and Burrhus. Racine subtly maintains the dramatic oscillation between the courses of action until the end of this scene with Narcisse, whilst indicating the inevitable unfolding of Néron's nature. The most powerful check to it, Agrippine's influence, has been eroded, the monster is about to assert itself at the expense of the monster who spawned it.

Néron only appears once in the final Act, after the murder of Britannicus, and in all speaks not more than eight lines. Physically, the monster is absent, as it was in the first Act, yet by its very absence Racine succeeds in creating the idea of its monstrous presence which, after the removal of Britannicus, is about to crush everyone else. This sinister presence is conveyed principally through the deep dramatic irony of the Act and the reaction of Néron to Britannicus' death.

In the final Act the actions of the other protagonists take place against the background of uncertainty created by the ambiguous ending to the previous Act. It opens with Britannicus declaring to Junie that he is going to effect the reconciliation with Néron. His trust in Néron's sincerity is perhaps less important in the creation of the dramatic irony than the form in which it is expressed: 'Dans son appartement [Néron] m'attend pour m'embrasser' (line 1482). Every element in this line, as well as the invitation, has been shaped by Néron long before Britannicus articulates it. To Burrhus Néron had intimated his intention after the scene with Agrippine: 'J'embrasse mon rival, mais c'est pour l'étouffer' (line 1314) and had issued his order to Burrhus to summon Britannicus: 'Dans mon appartement qu'il [Britannicus] m'attende avec vous' (line 1390). The irony derives from the multivalent meanings of the verbal elements common to the lines of Néron and Britannicus. The first statement by Néron to Burrhus is hostile to his rival, the second apparently amicable, judging from his words to Narcisse at the beginning of the following scene, and the line spoken by Britannicus amalgamates unconsciously both statements. It is at once a transparent reflection of Néron's verbal and literal expression and the most ingenuous misinterpretation of his possible intentions. For Britannicus, the 'reconciliation' betokens a sudden reversal of Néron's attitude towards him, nothing less than 'un coup d'Agrippine' (line 1511) which, ironically, is truer than he could ever imagine. For the basis for Néron's feigned reconciliation with him has indeed been laid in the clash with his mother in Act IV, subsequently to be undermined by Burrhus and finally relaid by Narcisse's reminder of her vindictive gloating over her undiminished power to sway her son. His presence is evoked everywhere in the first scene, in Britannicus' confidence and words, as well as in Junie's universal sense of foreboding:

> Tout m'est suspect: je crains que tout ne soit séduit;
> Je crains Néron; je crains le malheur qui me suit.
> D'un noir pressentiment malgré moi prévenue,
> Je vous laisse à regret éloigner de ma vue.
>
> (lines 1537—40)

and in Agrippine's words to Britannicus which betray her own eagerness to enjoy the evidence of her reasserted influence over her son as much as the monster's impatience to commit the act which will at last end the irritation of self-restraint: 'Néron impatient se plaint de votre absence' (line 1564).

The dramatic irony of the last Act is most sharply focused in the character whose presence is ostensibly responsible for the reconciliation between the rivals — Agrippine. Her triumphant description to Junie in Scene 3 of the change which has been brought about in Néron's conduct begins at the point at which the encounter with him ended in Act IV, Sc.

2. She speaks of his 'caresses' and his 'embrassements' (lines 1587—9), terms of natural endearment which can only be emptied of normal content in the 'reconciliation' between the unnatural mother and son. Just as she proclaims stridently the primacy of her presence over her son ('Il suffit, j'ai parlé, tout a changé de face' (line 1583)) Néron's encroaching presence is overwhelmingly manifested in the sudden clamour which interrupts her speech of triumph. His presence emerges most strikingly in the contrast between the long lull of false security and the seismographic reaction of Junie: 'O ciel, sauvez Britannicus!' (line 1610).

The final phase in the evolution of Néron's monstrous presence is conveyed by his initial and subsequent reactions to the death of Britannicus. In Burrhus' account of the poisoning, he notes that some of the guests at the banquet of 'reconciliation' were stricken with terror on seeing the dramatic way in which Britannicus dies. But Néron's impassive features show no trace of emotion or reaction: '... sur son lit il demeure penché; / D'aucun étonnement il ne paraît touché' (lines 1637—8). The courtiers who have been longer accustomed to Néron's ways assume the same inscrutable mask of indifference: 'Mais ceux qui de la cour ont un plus long usage/Sur les yeux de César composent leur visage' (lines 1635—6). Only the perfidious Narcisse betrays his malignant pleasure. This pattern of expressionless reaction to horror is further set by Néron's brief exchange with Agrippine in Scene 6. His reply to her accusation that he is the murderer of Britannicus is evasive in a coldly mechanical way: his death is merely one of 'des coups de destin' (line 1656) for which he is not responsible. As was seen in his scene with Britannicus in Act III, Néron is not so much concerned with covering up his crimes as with bringing others to the point already reached by his courtiers where totalitarian control of mind and gesture is reflected in complete acquiescence to horror. He relies on Narcisse to provide the flimsy pretext of *raison d'état* for the murder. It is above all the eyes of Néron which finally mirror his inward change and predict the course of the future. There are three witnesses who underline his metamorphosis into the incarnation of cruelty, tyranny, and finally of madness. Agrippine is transfixed by the chilling vision of the future which his look mediates to her:

> Burrhus, avez-vous vu quels regards furieux
> Néron en me quittant m'a laissés pour adieux?
> C'en est fait: le cruel n'a plus rien qui l'arrête;
> Le coup qu'on m'a prédit va tomber sur ma tête.
> Il vous accablera vous-même à votre tour.
>
> (lines 1697—1701)

Burrhus, who witnessed the poisoning of Britannicus, retains the vivid recollection of Néron's soulless look, which signifies not only his inhuman presence and future, but an inhuman past as well:

Néron l'a vu mourir sans changer de couleur.
Ses yeux indifférents ont déjà la constance
D'un tyran dans le crime endurci dès l'enfance.
(lines 1710—12)

The dehumanization of Néron is completed with the news that Junie has escaped to the temple of the Vestal Virgins, thus depriving him of the object of his passion and finally unhinging his mind. Albine describes the vacant stare which has replaced the Emperor's all-seeing glance: 'Il marche sans dessein; ses yeux mal assurés/N'osent lever au ciel leurs regards égarés' (lines 1757—8).

The murder of Britannicus has apparently freed Néron from the habitual tyranny of Agrippine's presence; but in reality it has only bound him all the more firmly to their common nature and heredity, from which, as Agrippine's long catalogue of her crimes committed to secure the imperial succession for her son has amply indicated in Act IV, Sc. 2 and the ending of the play underlines, there is no deliverance — only a relentless regression into depravity unmatched even by his mother.

5

The famous simplicity of action in *Bérénice* has for so long been the principal focus of admiration for students of the play that we have perhaps tended to overlook the extremely rich historical background which sets it in relief. Yet the play provides us with constant and vivid reminiscences of critical happenings in Roman history, such as the hatred of the Romans of the Tarquin kings and the decision to exile them, the crimes of Nero and Caligula, the love of Antony for Cleopatra and the disastrous consequences for Rome, the unscrupulous scheming of the freedman Pallas, and the immorality of his brother, Antonius Felix.[27] Racine continually evokes for us the might of imperial Rome, with its ever-expanding Empire beyond the borders of Palestine and including Arabia and Syria, the resounding military triumphs of the son of the Emperor Vespasian, and his campaign against the Jewish insurgents, culminating in the capture and destruction of Jerusalem, the arrival of the struggling and forlorn Jewish captives in the Capitol. Everything in the play takes place within the framework of the grandeur that is Rome which is reflected effulgently in the burning torches, the imperial insignia of the fasces and the eagles, and the purple of the Caesars.[28] In addition, Racine lets us catch sight of the Roman *cives* as they move about like shadowy figures in the background, as well as the consuls and the Senate and, most important of all, the rebellious *plebs* whom he endows with an invisible but tangible presence in the play. The wealth of detail and the variety of colour in Racine's picturesque evocation of imperial Rome give to it far greater importance than that of a mere historical or poetic background to the drama. It is also more than just a source of noble or evil influence on the characters, as for example Troy had been on Andromaque and Rome on Néron.[29] In *Bérénice*, on the other hand, Rome acts as a complex of dynamic and mysterious forces, now inspiring in Titus the decision to leave Bérénice, now confronting him with the agonizing choice between his love for her and his Roman *devoir*, and eventually triumphing over him in spite of all his efforts to decide for himself. As a powerful psychological and dramatic force in the play, it serves to create in the minds of the characters both certainty and uncertainty, and thus constitutes a rich source of peripety which Racine utilizes with great dramatic skill.

The presence of Rome in the play manifests itself in the first instance in the influence of the Roman people on Titus and this has led Lucien Goldmann to remark perceptively that 'la pièce se joue entièrement entre Titus et Bérénice d'une part et, d'autre part, entre Titus et le Peuple Romain toujours absent et toujours présent à la fois'.[30] However, it seems more exact to say that the influence of the people is exerted on Titus, and through him, consciously and mostly unconsciously on Bérénice. Moreover, the people of Rome, who symbolize both the heritage and the prejudices of the city, are absent and present at the beginning of the play, manifesting themselves as a dynamic presence as events proceed towards their climax. The absent Rome, which in the course of the play's events is in the process of becoming a tangible presence, serves both as the historical framework to the tragedy and as the means by which Racine can give dramatic expression to the affinity and the distance between the Jewish Bérénice and the heir to the Roman Empire, and to the conflict between the person of Titus and his persona.

In the first Act Rome appears to us through the eyes of Bérénice as the background to recent past events in imperial history and to her own personal situation in relation to Titus. To Antiochus she describes the grief of Titus and Rome for the death of Vespasian his father, the divinization of the dead Emperor by the Senate and its first convocation by Titus (Sc. 4); her description of the grief-stricken son of Vespasian is soon effaced by her image of the all-powerful Emperor whom she loves and who will have no difficulty in obtaining the Senate's permission for their marriage, which is due to take place that day (lines 259—60). Her total confidence in Titus makes her intolerant of the doubt expressed by her *confidente*, Phénice, who reminds her of two obstacles to their marriage: Roman laws of marriage only allow marriage between citizens of Rome, and Rome's traditional dislike of kings bodes ill for the marriage of the Queen of Palestine with its Emperor (lines 295—6). Bérénice, however, is oblivious to such objections, and replies with a paean of praise to the glory of Rome, a glory which derives all its splendour and brilliance from Titus himself:

> De cette nuit, Phénice, as-tu vu la splendeur?
> Tes yeux ne sont-ils pas tous pleins de sa grandeur?
> Ces flambeaux, ce bûcher, cette nuit enflammée,
> Ces aigles, ces faisceaux, ce peuple, cette armée,
> Cette foule de rois, ces consuls, ce sénat,
> Qui tous de mon amant empruntaient leur éclat;
> Cette pourpre, cet or, que rehaussait sa gloire,
> Et ces lauriers encor témoins de sa victoire.
>
> (lines 301—8)

The tragic irony of Bérénice does not lie far beneath the surface of her rhapsodizing here, for the Queen of Palestine is as alien from the Roman notion of *gloire* as she is passionately in love with Titus. (In the final scene of the play she admits that she has never aspired to the title of Empress, and that all the trappings of imperial power, such as the purple of the Caesars, have no intrinsic attraction for her (lines 1475ff).)

If Bérénice is certain of the decision which Rome will give about her impending marriage with Titus, her certainty is based upon the knowledge that Titus loves her; but it is the very uncertainty of Rome which absorbs the mind of Titus as he unburdens himself to Paulin at the beginning of the second Act: '... de mes desseins Rome encore incertaine/Attend que deviendra le destin de la Reine' (lines 339—40).

When he speaks of Rome here, Titus is not thinking of the courtiers in the Emperor's entourage or of the ruling patricians in the Senate. He chooses quite deliberately 'un plus noble théâtre' (line 356) as the public arbiters of his decision regarding his marriage with Bérénice, who are to be none other than the *plebs*. In so doing, he hopes that he will avoid falling victim to the insidious flattery of the court, which tolerated the most atrocious crimes to please Nero. But his very anxiety not to succumb to the same danger leads him to go farther than that tyrant had ever dared to go. The only law which the inhuman Nero was afraid to flout was the one which forbade marriage with a foreigner, the same law which the humanity of Titus seeks to circumvent! It is not difficult for his *confident* Paulin to ennumerate the many examples in Roman history which demonstrate the wisdom of this law and the beneficial effects which it has conferred on the government of the Republic (lines 371—419). His detailed account of its importance in Roman history has the effect of a catalyst on Titus' thoughts, inducing in them first despair and then almost immediately complete lucidity about his situation. His dejected admission 'Hélas! à quel amour on veut que je renonce!' (line

420) is followed by a much more surprising reaction on his part. The answer which Paulin has given to Titus' query about the attitude of the Roman people to his proposed marriage corresponds exactly to his own painful conclusion which he reached privately, at the moment of his accession to the throne a week ago, and which he utters now for the first time:

> Pour jamais je vais m'en séparer.
> Mon coeur en ce moment ne vient pas de se rendre.
> Si je t'ai fait parler, si j'ai voulu t'entendre,
> Je voulais que ton zèle achevât en secret
> De confondre un amour qui se tait à regret.

(lines 446—50)

Titus has been able to align his decision with the Roman *raison d'état*, and it only remains now for him to effect the actual separation from Bérénice which he has already accepted in his mind. The remainder of his speech to Paulin tells us of the stages through which Titus has passed before coming to his critical decision not to marry Bérénice. While his father was still Emperor, Titus was able to view the prospect of marriage to her with equanimity. But with the death of his father, the responsibility of safeguarding the heritage of Rome has devolved upon the son. But Titus has not merely undergone a change in his formal status; in succeeding his father, he has become aware of his historical function and his public role. Having accepted the fact that he is the one chosen by the gods to succeed Vespasian, he has emerged from the shadow of his father, where he was able to enjoy his liberty, to place himself under the gaze of the public and of history where he can never belong completely to himself. It is his misfortune to find himself at the point where the traditions of the past and the present interlock most firmly. As the first magistrate of the Empire, whose duty it is to inculcate in his subjects a proper respect for the laws, he owes it to himself and to them to set the example by his scrupulous observation of each detail. It is therefore misleading in the extreme to view the situation of Titus as consisting simply in the mere contradiction between love and duty. It is rather the infinitely more complex (and tragic) conflict in the mind of a character who has accepted once for all the obligations which his imperial title lays upon him (and in so doing the destruction of his personal happiness) and who at the same time continues to love Bérénice in the same way that he did before becoming Emperor. The final acceptance on his part of his tragic fate will be determined as much by his Roman sense of *devoir* as by the circumstances which elevate him above the rest of mortals. If the imperial decision at the beginning of the play is seen in the light of the historical and ethical framework of Rome which encloses it, it may well appear to be much less gratuitous than has been supposed, notably by

P. F. Butler, who has suggested that this was in fact Racine's intention: 'Is it not rather as if Racine was at pains to make it as gratuitous as possible and deprive it of all substance?'[31] Titus' decision to part from Bérénice seems rather to bear the stamp of authentic tragedy, for it is the lucid way in which he accepts it in the scene with Paulin which can only prepare and increase the final tragedy of their separation. His lucid attitude to his own fate and to that of Bérénice which he is going to determine (an attitude which deserts him momentarily in Act IV, Sc. 4, 6, Act V, Sc. 5) is as tragic and as destructive for himself as is Bérénice's illusion about their marriage, an illusion which he nevertheless undertakes to dispel at the beginning of Act II. It is his full knowledge of their mutual position which imposes on him the strain of acting and speaking to Bérénice in a manner completely alien to his nature (Act II, Sc. 4, Act IV, Sc. 5) and which he cannot sustain for long. The final collapse of his resolve to separate from Bérénice (Act V, Sc. 5) will be as complete and as overwhelming as is his awareness of the situation.

In the first scene between Titus and Bérénice (Act II, Sc. 4), she is at a loss to understand the reason for his formal attitude towards her, particularly since he has assured her so many times that there is no basis for her concern about the rigorous Roman laws on marriage. When she asks him anxiously if he still loves her, he answers that he has never loved her so much, but his reply immediately tails off as he attempts to tell her his decision: 'Rome ... l'Empire ...'(line 623). His incoherence in no way diminishes the lucidity with which he had reached his decision, for in spite of his manifest disarray, he is more lucid than ever before. Titus, who formerly was able to close his eyes to the obstacles in the path of their marriage, is now only too painfully aware both of the demands of the Roman ethic which he has chosen to obey and of the totally vulnerable woman whom he has chosen to hurt.

After his first failure to tell Bérénice of his decision, Titus turns to Antiochus and entrusts him with the task of breaking the news to her (Act III, Sc. 1). The fact that he makes use of a third party to carry out what he himself is unable and ultimately unwilling to do might seem to indicate at first sight cowardice or even insincerity on his part; the truth is that it reveals nothing so much as his own inner turmoil and his regard for the feelings of Bérénice, which he is so anxious to spare as much as possible in the circumstances that we see him rush with apparent indecent haste to accomplish his distasteful task. This is amply borne out by the argument which he uses to convince Antiochus of the urgency with which Bérénice must be informed of the decision and dispatched from Rome:

> Si le peuple demain ne voit partir la Reine,
> Demain elle entendra ce peuple furieux
> Me venir demander son départ à ses yeux.
>
> (lines 732—4)

But the people of Rome have not evinced the smallest sign of discontent in relation to the presence of Bérénice and the marriage to Titus! Has not Titus himself stated that Rome was still awaiting the imperial decision? His reasoning in this scene is indeed specious but dictated solely by honourable motives on his part and is repeated to Bérénice on his behalf by Antiochus several scenes later: 'Une reine est suspecte à l'empire romain./Il faut vous séparer, et vous partez demain' (lines 901—2). The first change of mind in Titus takes place between Antiochus' revelation of the decision to Bérénice in Act III, Sc. 3 and the second scene between Titus and Bérénice in Act IV, Sc. 5. In his lengthy soliloquy which forms the fourth scene in Act IV, we see Titus pondering his decision, then momentarily reversing it, only to come back to it with more resolution and urgency at the end. Rome's silent neutrality with regard to Bérénice holds out to him the illusion that marriage to her would prove acceptable:

> Car enfin Rome a-t-elle expliqué ses souhaits?
> L'entendons-nous crier autour de ce palais?
> Vois-je l'Etat penchant au bord du précipice?
> Ne le puis-je sauver que par ce sacrifice?
>
> (lines 1001—4)

The ephemeral illusion of freedom which he enjoys is all the more bitterly ironic because, if Rome has not yet spoken objectively within the play, it has nevertheless spoken with commanding authority through the inward subjectivity of the successor to the Roman Empire. For the acute lucidity of the new Emperor overrules the freedom of action which Titus was able to cherish formerly:

> Titus, ouvre les yeux!
> Quel air respires-tu? N'es-tu pas dans ces lieux
> Où la haine des rois, avec le lait sucée,
> Par crainte ou par amour ne peut être effacée?
> Rome jugea ta reine en condamnant ses rois.
>
> (lines 1013—7)

The second meeting between them (Act IV, Sc. 5) is thus preceded by Titus' fresh awareness of the impossibility of his marriage to a foreign queen, and the outcome of it is an apparent stiffening of his resolve to let Bérénice leave Rome. But in fact it only renders him more emotionally vulnerable than ever as he attempts to explain the reasons for the decision to the shocked and wounded Bérénice. It is she who seizes the initiative in their scene, accusing him of constituting the sole obstacle to their marriage, not Rome. And she finds evidence of the clearest kind to support this charge in the fact that Rome has hitherto remained silent (line 1084). With unconscious cruelty, she directs the very argument against him which he had considered and eventually rejected in the preceding scene. The bulk of her argument centres on the *devoir* which Titus has alleged as his reason for his decision (lines 1062—86). When she points out to him that he has fallen back on his *devoir* too belatedly for it to pass as a convincing reason for his decision not to marry her, it cannot be denied that her argument at this point carries great cogency: her life has found its fulfilment in her love for Titus, and her predicament is therefore most poignantly expressed in her pertinent question to him: '... Ignoriez-vous vos lois,/Quand je vous l'avouai pour la première fois?' (lines 1065—6). Has he not had opportunity enough to send her away from Rome, before their relationship came to this pass? But she can never appreciate the full measure of the pressure which Roman history exerts on Titus; he struggles truthfully to tell her of his painful pilgrimage from unclouded optimism to imperial responsibility:

> Mon coeur se gardait bien d'aller dans l'avenir
> Chercher ce qui pouvait un jour nous désunir.
> Je voulais qu'à mes voeux rien ne fût invincible;
> Je n'examinais rien, j'espérais l'impossible.
> Que sais-je? J'espérais de mourir à vos yeux,
> Avant que d'en venir à ces cruels adieux.
> Les obstacles semblaient renouveler ma flamme.
> Tout l'Empire parlait; mais la gloire, Madame,
> Ne s'était point encor fait entendre à mon coeur
> Du ton dont elle parle au coeur d'un empereur.
> (lines 1089—98)

In the ears of the Semitic queen Titus' words about his awakening to the imperative of imperial *gloire* can have but a hollow ring, unaware as she must be of the deep inner change which has taken place in his mind since his accession to the throne. To her at this moment his 'problem' consists in nothing more intractable than the modification of laws which are so patently unjust. To say this is not at all to undervalue the sense of anguished betrayal which Bérénice feels so keenly and which is expressed movingly in this scene. One may be sensitive to her helpless distress whilst disagreeing with the reasoning used to articulate that distress. P. F. Butler, on the other hand, considering the tragedy from the standpoint of Bérénice, writes as follows of the reasons which Titus has given her for rejecting the marriage: 'Cette opinion publique, à laquelle Titus est si anxieux déférer, n'est que l'aveugle préjugé contre l'étrangère, un absurde tabou qu'il est assez fort pour braver s'il le veut. Enfin cette loi, à laquelle il sacrifie Bérénice, et qu'il revêt d'un caractère sacré, n'est ni raisonnable ni juste.'[32] One might say that to summarize his dilemma in this fashion is to be unfair to him, for the premise of this thesis is that Titus has the necessary authority to change the laws of Rome if only he wished to do so. His problem however is not just one of external constraint but of inner necessity. Titus recognizes the injustice of this law against marriage with foreigners, and much of his personal suffering results from it. In this respect he is a poor Roman citizen, but this does not prevent him from being a good Roman Emperor. As Emperor, he has accepted the responsibility of upholding the law of Rome whilst foreseeing with apprehension the suffering he will cause to Bérénice and sharing fully in it. If he makes mention to Bérénice of the harrowing trials which his predecessors have had to face unflinching in the name of Roman patriotism, he does not display the cold indifference of the zealous patriot to human distress: he seeks rather in the abstract notion of patriotism a strong support for his vacillating will and purpose (lines 1155—68). He resembles his predecessors in bowing inevitably to the will of Rome, but differs from them in one respect: '... le malheureux Titus/Passe l'austérité de toutes leurs vertus' (lines 1169—70). His reference here to the cruel way in which he treats Bérénice is not a shallow attempt to save face in front of her or to salve his conscience: there is no doubt about the depth and genuineness of the inner conflict which he experiences as he openly revokes his decision for the first time in the following scene, the decision which he has just upheld in front of Bérénice. He confesses to Paulin:

> ... Non, je suis un barbare.
> Moi-même je me hais. Néron, tant détesté,
> N'a point à cet excès poussé sa cruauté.
> (lines 1212—14)

At no point in the play's action is Racine's mastery of dramatic technique more admirable as he makes Titus' great *volte-face* coincide with the most important peripety of the play: for it is precisely at this moment that Rome breaks its silence to pronounce on the situation of the characters. Titus, whose decision to send Bérénice away from his court has been inspired by Roman tradition, now stands helplessly by as that tradition rebounds ironically upon him in the present, as Paulin informs him that

> Déjà de vos adieux la nouvelle est semée.
> Rome, qui gémissait, triomphe avec raison;
> Tous les temples ouverts fument en votre nom;
> Et le peuple élevant vos vertus jusqu'aux nues,
> Va partout de lauriers couronner vos statues.
> (lines 1220—4)

The pressure of Roman opinion, so long contained, is now about to manifest itself explosively on the stage in all its forms:

> ... tous les tribuns, les consuls, le sénat
> Viennent vous demander au nom de tout l'Etat.
> Un grand peuple les suit, qui, plein d'impatience,
> Dans votre appartement attend votre présence.
> (lines 1241—4)

The end of the fourth Act marks the climax of the tragic action and irony in the play. Titus decides to act for himself at the very moment that Rome decides to claim him totally and Antiochus implores him urgently to go to Bérénice again. Trance-like, he gives way to the irresistible pressure which Rome exerts on him from the level of the *plebs* to that of the Senate, and in so doing appears to seal his own fate and that of Bérénice. The intervention of Rome can only serve to heighten his tragedy in the final Act, since the all-important decision has been wrenched from him and made public as he is in the act of retracting it. The nature of the *dénouement* seems in no doubt from this point onwards, but the final Act produces two more dramatic reversals in the situation which give rise, fleetingly, to the hope that a non-tragic solution may yet be possible. Titus, in a state of shock, allows himself to be borne along by the collective enthusiasm of the crowds and the Senate, and in so doing commits himself irrevocably to the will of Rome, according to the report which Arsace gives us:

> Le peuple avec transport l'arrête et l'environne,
> Applaudissant aux noms que le sénat lui donne;
> Et ces noms, ces respects, ces applaudissements
> Deviennent pour Titus autant d'engagements,
> Qui le liant, Seigneur, d'une honorable chaîne,
> Malgré tous ses soupirs et les pleurs de la Reine,
> Fixent dans son devoir ses voeux irrésolus.
>
> (lines 1271—7)

All the pathos of the inner conflict which Titus undergoes in his final meeting with Bérénice emerges once he is viewed in the light of his involuntary servitude to Rome. For Titus, the unwitting actor who has been unaware of what has transpired between the Emperor and Rome in public, now advises Bérénice not to heed 'une foule insensée' (line 1319), the same crowd which he earlier chose as 'un plus noble théâtre' (line 356) for his decision, and which he has twice mentioned to her as the reason for their separation! Once again, it is easy but no less understandable for Bérénice to point out the cruel inconsistency in his attitude to her (lines 1320—6, 1328—34).

The second reversal in the attitude of Titus, which Racine reserves for the penultimate scene in the final Act, has the effect of bringing the situation of the characters to its greatest pitch of dramatic intensity, as the Emperor describes to Bérénice his stupefied reaction to the frenzied adulation of Rome, Rome which in spite of all appearances is *still* uncertain of the outcome of their relationship:

> J'ai vu devant mes yeux Rome entière assemblée;
> Le sénat m'a parlé; mais mon âme accablée
> Ecoutait sans entendre, et ne leur a laissé

Pour prix de leurs transports qu'un silence glacé.
Rome de votre sort est encore incertaine.

(lines 1375—9)

Racine has kept an even greater paradox in surprise for us, as Titus simultaneously underlines his total independence of the pressure of Roman opinion and his unshakeable resolve to separate from Bérénice. The tension between the rigid Roman law on marriage and his love for Bérénice, which Racine has increased to a degree at which Titus must either bend to it or triumph over it by a supreme act of will, has led him to examine past examples of imperial fortitude; in the Stoic examples of his predecessors he has found a source of moral inspiration which teaches him how to align his will with an apparently adverse destiny:

Lorsque trop de malheurs ont lassé leur constance,
Ils ont tous expliqué cette persévérance
Dont le sort s'attachait à les persécuter,
Comme un ordre secret de n'y plus résister.

(lines 1411—14)

Thus Rome finally exerts a dual influence upon Titus, since it creates at the same time his greatness as an Emperor and his misery as a man. On the one hand, it teaches him how to avoid the ignominious fate of being 'Un indigne empereur, sans empire, sans cour, / Vil spectacle aux humains des faiblesses d'amour' (lines 1405—6) and on the other it forces him to admit to Antiochus 'toute ma faiblesse' (line 1427). He had come to see Bérénice for the last time, he tells her, with one purpose in mind: 'Pour me chercher moi-même, et pour me reconnaître' (line 1384). Rome is the implacable mirror into which he has looked and which has provided him with bitter self-knowledge. He came to look for himself not knowing 'Si je suis empereur ou si je suis Romain' (lines 1381) and he has discovered that he is indeed both, being bound by his Roman nature and heredity to the glorious past and present of the Empire, as well as to its future maintenance. At the beginning of the play he had lucidly recognized the unbridgeable distance which he now accepts between himself and Bérénice, the Semitic queen so foreign to the Roman conception of *gloire* and who confesses to him in her last lines that

Mon coeur vous est connu, Seigneur, et je puis dire
Qu'on ne l'a jamais vu soupirer pour l'Empire.
La grandeur des Romains, la pourpre des Césars
N'a point, vous le savez, attiré mes regards.

(lines 1475—8)

Rome has brought Titus face to face with the demands of his duty, but it also makes him fully aware of his humanity. For in choosing to leave Bérénice he also rejoins her in the loneliness of tragic suffering. Both characters are aware at the end of the play of the bitter fact which they have refused to acknowledge completely hitherto, that is, that they love and will love each other and that they cannot marry each other.[33]

3 Person and Persona in the *raisonneurs* of Molière's *Ecoles*

1

The long-standing debate about the function and meaning of the role of the *raisonneur* in Molière's theatre is still as alive and as unresolved today as it ever was. Since F. Brunetière first used the word to identify and isolate a particular kind of recurrent character in the plays, the *raisonneur* has made a considerable contribution to the critical literature surrounding Molière.[1] By this term Brunetière designated Cléante (*Le Tartuffe*), Philinte (*Le Misanthrope*), Ariste (*L'Ecole des Maris*), Chrysalde (*L'Ecole des Femmes*), and Béralde (*Le Malade Imaginaire*). These *raisonneurs* had for Brunetière the function of articulating at least partially Molière's own thought on the topics treated in the plays, and later they came to represent for E. Faguet the ideas of the author.[2] It was G. Michaut who developed these views of the *raisonneur* in more systematic form by the elaboration of the philosophy of the *juste-milieu* which Molière was thought to express through them in each play.[3] R. Fernandez initiated the reaction to this line of thought by questioning the explicitly didactic relationship which Michaut established between Molière and his *raisonneurs*. Thus Molière became not just a thinker or philosopher but a comic dramatist as well, who was not to be identified solely with one of his characters but who animated all of them in and through a poetic vision of incompatibility.[4] The new criticism begun by W. G. Moore and R. Bray, whilst rejecting the biographical method of Fernandez, nevertheless owes much to his critical insights. Henceforth the *raisonneur* forfeited his didactic function as the mouthpiece for Molière's ideas and his *raison d'être* was seen to be purely aesthetic and dramatic.[5] The notion of the *raisonneur* as the character who expresses the author's views has tended to disappear from contemporary criticism but there is still no general agreement about the meaning of the enigmatic role which he assumes in the comedies. He has been viewed as providing a mere dramatic counterpart to the more forceful comic character, the *imaginaire*;[6] as the representative of a certain kind of wisdom and at the same time as a dramatic creation;[7] more recently, as reflecting the attitudes of society

The raisonneurs *of Molière's* Ecoles

whilst meriting the scorn of the audience, since Molière rejects both the values of his *imaginaire* and of his *raisonneur*.[8] In fact the character has kept his secret so well that it has even been suggested that the *raisonneur* might not exist at all as a type in Molière's theatre.[9] The wheel of interpretation has come full circle regarding this character, and it therefore seems appropriate to look afresh at the controversial question. In this chapter I should like to examine in some depth the roles of two characters who, it is generally agreed, may be termed authentic *raisonneurs*, that is, Ariste and Chrysalde of *L'Ecole des Maris* and *L'Ecole des Femmes* respectively. The choice of these characters as a means of focusing the question comprises in my view definite advantages for the study of the *raisonneur* as a whole. They are prototypes of the more famous characters whom Molière creates in later plays — Cléante, Philinte, Béralde — and the *Ecoles* provide us with a microcosm of the more complex comic situations in which their successors find themselves. In the cases of Ariste and Chrysalde we see the character of the *raisonneur* in his intermediate stage of development — between the first sketchy outlines of the role as played by Le Parent in *Sganarelle ou Le Cocu Imaginaire* and Elise in *Dom Garcie de Navarre* and his more ambiguous successors, who, nevertheless retain the essential characteristics of the so-called *raisonneurs* of the *Ecoles*.[10]

2

L'Ecole des Maris (1661) sets in comic opposition the brothers Ariste and Sganarelle who are the guardians of the sisters Léonor and Isabelle respectively. We see the clash of two well-defined approaches to life which are so different from each other as to appear irreconcilable. The quadragenarian Sganarelle, who is twenty years younger than his brother, clings to the customs and ideas of his far-distant youth. Like his more famous comic successor, Alceste, he stubbornly opposes everything which is modern and intends to cut off his ward from all contact with society in order to mould her into a wife who will be ideally submissive to the authority of her future husband, who is none other than himself. Although his brother is a sexagenarian, he espouses readily contemporary ideas and fashions. He is also in favour of an extremely liberal attitude towards Léonor, permitting her to behave as she pleases and to choose the husband whom she prefers.

The introspective and aggressive Sganarelle initiates the debate between these conflicting ideas by throwing down his anti-social challenge to his brother. He is aware that society condemns his behaviour, but far from taking this to heart, he rejoices in its opposition to him. In his eyes, he stands alone as the self-sufficient wise man, able to dismiss peremptorily all views contrary to his own as emanating from '... des fous comme vous,/Mon frère' (Act I, Sc. 1, lines 9—10).[11]

Yet the fact remains that society exerts the same paradoxical fascination over him as it does over the other *imaginaires* who profess so plangently to scorn it, for he delights to hear each detail of what people say about him in order to galvanize and prolong his resentment of them. Conforming to the perverse comic psychology of Molière's comic heroes, he is only too glad to hear Ariste say that he possesses the well-established reputation of being a 'loup-garou', for he has now the pretext he so avidly desired to launch into a tirade against society and its attitudes. He delivers himself of a biting satire, accumulated no doubt over a long period of misanthropic solitude, against those people who persist in following the fashions of the day without due consideration of the cost and the discomfort involved. He at least intends to continue to wear his warm doublet and his old-fashioned hose which is ample enough to let him move with comfort! In passing, he cannot forbear to make several acerbic allusions to his elder brother who endeavours to dress himself in the height of fashion, making great play with the discrepancy in their ages. The fury of Sganarelle is kindled and fuelled by his evident desire to suppress the different ideas and fashions of his brother and beyond him the attitudes of the society he represents, attitudes which Sganarelle views as threatening the existence of his own extremely rudimentary approach to life and people. In this opening debate with the ranting *imaginaire* Ariste has scarcely the time or the opportunity to speak a word. Even when he is silent, his very presence on the stage serves to act as a catalyst to the diatribes of his brother. From the first comic conflict of the play, one may conclude that far from being a mere dramatic foil for the more colourful comic character, the presence of Ariste is necessary to Sganarelle's comic development as the former, consciously or unconsciously, allows Molière to shape the anti-social trends of Sganarelle within the overall design of the comedy.

From a dramatic point of view, the first scene presents us with the seemingly irreconcilable clash of temperament and personality. One might think that this would be duplicated inevitably by the irreconcilable clash of opposing ideas as well. Such a conclusion however does not at all follow from a study of the roles, which rather allows us to see that the relationship between *imaginaire* and *raisonneur* may indeed be more complex than has sometimes been suspected. The interpretation of G. Michaut, for example, and the critics who adopted his approach to the question of the *raisonneur*, distorted the meaning of the role by concluding that dramatic opposition of the characters was tantamount to opposition of their ideas. For this *Moliériste*, the very fact that the *imaginaire* was cast in the role of the principal comic character made it axiomatic that Molière could not possibly share his aberrant ideas; and conversely, by the very fact that the *raisonneur* was his dramatic counterpart, his opinions were the opposite of ridiculous and thus said to represent the mind of his creator. There is a certain logic in the equation of dramatic with ideological opposition, on the one hand, and opposition by the author to what is apparently ridiculous with agreement with what is apparently not ridiculous on the other. But on closer examination, it will be seen that the dramatic function of Ariste does not correspond to this clearcut schema. In his reply to the tirades of his brother, Ariste begins by enunciating the principle which underlies his behaviour in society: 'Toujours au plus grand nombre on doit s'accommoder,/Et jamais il ne faut se faire regarder' (lines 41—2). At first sight this gnomic line seems to be nothing more than a mere platitude about conformity to the *juste-milieu* in everything, yet it entails a commentary on his part which makes it somewhat more complex. In order to practise such moderate advice, one must, Ariste says, follow prevailing fashion without alacrity and affectation and without wishing to draw attention to oneself by extravagant dress (lines 43—50). On the one hand, it is necessary to detach oneself from society in order to be able to discern the values of the customs practised; but on the other, one must not detach oneself from it to the extent of becoming a recluse and of imagining oneself wiser than one's contemporaries (lines 51—4). All this means in effect is that Ariste refuses to adopt the anti-social behaviour of his brother whilst agreeing with him in ridiculing people who cultivate fashion to the point of impoverishing themselves in order to shine in society. Under the diffuse ideas of Ariste there lies an area of concordance between the views of the brothers, which perhaps has not been sufficiently pointed up. Ariste however may very well agree with some of Sganarelle's opinions, but takes as his guiding principle the notion that the individual has never the right to presume that he can act independently of society, however rational or logical his opinions may be. In other words, Sganarelle may after all be right to deride all the ridiculous fashions of the day, but he will always be wrong in flaunting his independence of the society which moulds them. Even if criticism of social attitudes is fully justified, the fact remains that '. . . il vaut mieux souffrir d'être au nombre des fous,/Que du sage parti se voir seul contre tous' (lines 53—4).

Thus runs the exposition of Ariste's nuanced views on the individual in relation to society. One may now ask to what extent can he be termed a *raisonneur*? The central speech examined above shows that he chooses precisely to suspend his opinions about social attitudes and *not* to reason about them. Nevertheless one general conclusion seems to emerge from his cautious words about the contrary excesses which should be avoided in balanced social conduct, and this may be summarized as follows: if one analyses social attitudes and practices rationally, one will have no difficulty in concluding that there is much in them which is absurd and irrational, for example, squandering one's means in order to follow the latest fashions bears no logical relationship to the essential purpose of clothes, that of personal comfort. Reason may well propose however, but custom and fashion will in the end always dispose.

The anti-rational approach of Ariste echoes much of Montaigne's attitude to the same question: 'Qui voudra se desfaire de ce violent prejudice de la coustume, il trouvera plusieurs choses receues d'une resolution indubitable, qui n'ont appuy qu'en la barbe chenue et rides de l'usage qui les accompaigne.' And the author of the *Essais* likewise assures us that 'La société publique n'a que faire de nos pensées'.[12] The wheels of society only turn smoothly when lubricated by the flexibility of the individual. To introduce reason as a criterion for the accepted norms and values of society would be to impose the arbitrary law of individual wisdom in place of the wisdom consecrated in its collective folly. Ariste is content to play out his role on the stage of society all the while retaining what Montaigne terms his *arrière-boutique*, that is, the innermost sanctuary of his most intimate convictions which he does not divulge to others. In this sanctuary of reason and only there is the primacy placed on reality and not on appearances. Once under the public gaze however, the sprightly sexagenarian employs all the cosmetic and sartorial aids to repair the ravages of time; he wears a black wig and dresses in youthful styles, so enraging his younger brother, in whose opinion 'La vieillesse devait ne songer qu'à mourir' (line 62). Such is the stark rational viewpoint of the anti-actor and the natural man who, anticipating Alceste, delights to tear away the mask and embellishments of polite society to expose the naked truth of its real and infirm condition. Confronted with the unmasking and iconoclastic Sganarelle, Ariste is not just an actor; he is also the ironic spectator of his brother, just as the latter is in his turn of society, as well as the spectator of himself who is fully aware of the extent to which appearances have come to be his second nature.

In the first scene of the play the debate revolves around the theoretical aspect of the disagreement between the characters, before coming to the crux of the matter in question in the following scene, as is so often the case in Molière's comedies.[13] We progress to the topic of the marriages of Isabelle and Léonor and the decisions of the brothers. In Molière's theatre, marriage constitutes the comedy within the comedy, the point at which the comic fixation of the character is most personally, intensely and ludicrously focused. To Sganarelle, Isabelle must never be more than a mere extension of his own ideas and personality. Accordingly, the best method for ensuring that she does not cuckold him is to keep her fully occupied with the menial household tasks. This view of marriage would be rational enough if he were dealing with circumscribable chattels which could be secured under lock and key, but it is somewhat simplistic with regard to the unpredictability of a human being. As for Ariste, he maintains intact his attitude of total indulgence to Léonor, who is free to marry him or not according to her wishes.

In this scene, unlike the first one, the dramatic and ideological opposition of the characters is total. This double opposition is seen in the triple movement of the scene: in the first phase of this movement, the divergent views on marriage are expounded (lines 75—212); in the second, the way in which a married woman should behave in society is debated (lines 213—34); and the final one constitutes one of the comic apexes of the play and anticipates the *dénouement* (line 235 to the end of the scene). In the initial phase of this comic movement, Ariste expounds his progressive and liberal ideas on the education of women, and gradually provokes the irascible Sganarelle into dismissing his fine theories as completely impracticable in the trust which they place in infirm human (i.e. feminine) nature. In the subsequent phase, Sganarelle's exasperation with his brother's misguided liberal outlook is intensified by Ariste's series of ironic rejoinders. When the former hears the full extent of Ariste's permissiveness, he is lost in amazement that anyone could be so irrational, and can only question him about the various activities in which he is prepared to let Léonor engage. The more incredulous his questions become the more laconic and nonchalant the replies of Ariste, as he blandly answers 'Et pourquoi la [sa manière de vie] changer?' 'Sans doute', 'Oui, vraiment', 'Et quoi donc?' 'Cela s'entend' (lines 217—30). The frustration of Sganarelle is of the same order as that of the person who, thinking himself eminently reasonable, is continually confronted with flagrantly unreasonable attitudes, and who, having exhausted his powers of comprehension and reason on his obtuse interlocutor, can only expostulate in defeat 'Allez, vous êtes un vieux fou' (line 230). A ballet-like rhythm animates the movement of this scene, which, like so many others in Molière's theatre, could be entitled 'un ballet des incompatibles'.[14] Sganarelle goes through the scene with unwieldy gait, whilst Ariste lightly dogs his steps, provoking him gradually to the point where he unleashes the dreaded word which for so long has haunted his thinking, as he says with reference to his brother 'Que j'aurai de plaisir si l'on le fait cocu!' (line 234). Only retrospectively does one see how skilfully this dialogue has been contrived by Molière to make Sganarelle crystallize his comic phobia and lay bare (vicariously!) his innermost soul, and that the drollery of the elusively ironic Ariste is the instrument used to bring the *imaginaire's* obsession to its fullest pitch of development. In the final part of the scene Ariste is used to exploit dramatically his brother's manifest disarray, as he increases his psychological pressure with the dire warning that it is Sganarelle who contributes most powerfully to the realization of the fate predicted for himself. In return, Sganarelle can only parry this calculated thrust by alluding yet again to his brother's age. His insults however cannot conceal his frustrated rage at his inability to unsettle Ariste's *sang-froid*, which enables the latter to contemplate even the possibility of cuckoldry with philosophic serenity. The pent-up frustration of the reforming Sganarelle, who tries to redress the illogicality of others and finds himself ridiculed blatantly at each moment by a world impervious to reason, finally and formally renounces what is patently an impossible mission:

... non, la Sagesse même
N'en viendrait pas à bout, perdrait sens et raison
A vouloir corriger une telle maison.

(lines 256—8)

Beside the energetic and boorish Sganarelle, it must be admitted that Ariste may seem a somewhat insipid character in the opening scenes of the play. Yet we see here the undramatic emergence of a character with well-defined characteristics which may be essential to the role of the *raisonneur*:

(1) Ariste stands in an ambiguous relationship to his brother and society, for he is at once an actor in the comedy with him and a spectator of the comedy of his behaviour. Ariste can agree with Sganarelle to the extent that the latter points out the evident defects in accepted social usage. But it is a provisional and partial agreement, of the kind which says 'yes' to his rational strictures and immediately appends its qualifying 'but'. The 'yes' originates from Ariste the individual, the 'but' from his socialized and socializing persona. And of course the same ambiguity obtains in his outward social attitude. On the stage of society, his flexibility enables his individuality to merge chameleon-like into the prevailing social customs. Once he has left this stage, however, he can leave off the mask if he so wishes and become himself again. Through the careful scrutiny of others and himself, he has learnt to master the art of self-disguise. In this art, it is of paramount importance to know when and how to adjust one's appearances (the mask) in order to play the appropriate role perfectly. The description of Ariste as a comic actor characterizes most appositely his essential activity. Of course he reasons in his own fashion, as does every other character in Molière's theatre. But the essence of the role does not consist at all in the fact that he reasons, rather in the various degrees and levels of comedy provided for him by Sganarelle, society, and by his own participation in the social comedy. For the basic indispensable premise underlying all his reasoning is supplied by his perception of this triple comedy. To view him as nothing more than a mere *raisonneur* is not only to reduce a lively and charming character to the spokesman for sententious and

mediocre platitudes, but also to choose to overlook a fundamental feature of his role as comic actor of which he shows himself to be supremely aware.

(2) With such a finely-tuned sense of his vocation as a comic actor it is inevitable that Ariste should wish to play the appropriate part at all times, and fulfil himself by shaping the comic situation towards a certain end. He does this by countering the reactionary ideas of his brother with the exposition of his own liberal attitude to life. By acting *deliberately* as a dramatic counterpart and not as a mere mechanical foil he contributes greatly to the progressive downfall of the comic hero.

(3) He acts as a kind of aesthetic intermediary between the author of the comedy, who is not after all Ariste in spite of his natural penchant for comic acting, and the audience. In this privileged position, does he not invite us to place and keep Sganarelle in comic perspective, a perspective which must, at least partially, have been shared by Molière also as the creator of the total comedy? He does so explicitly for example when admonishing his brother wryly regarding the dangers of cuckoldry:

J'ignore pour quel sort mon astre m'a fait naître;
Mais je sais que pour vous, si vous manquez de l'être,
On ne vous en doit point imputer le défaut,
Car vos soins pour cela font bien tout ce qu'il faut.

(lines 235—8)

From this point onwards our expectation of Sganarelle's comic deflation by the fateful event evoked here is keenly aroused. But Ariste does more than create a perspective in which the comic phobia of Sganarelle may be fully enjoyed. He also prompts us discreetly and playfully to place ourselves within its focus. Life, he seems to suggest undidactically, delights to overturn the most elaborate projects of those who deem themselves to be wise. It is better then to live as a fool, ridding oneself of the absurdity of fixed and preconceived ideas and thus making oneself adaptable to any situation, whether it is favourable or not. Ariste is not just content to play out his vocation as a comic actor — he also makes it into the most elementary and cavalier of 'philosophies' able to accommodate any event.

After the first two scenes he disappears and only reappears towards the end of the play. His role is episodic in its nature, but this does not detract from the fact that its *raison d'être* is dramatic. Molière uses the irony of the character to excite Sganarelle's imaginary fear of cuckoldry to such a pitch that all the latter's consequent precautions inevitably contribute to his downfall at the hands of Valère and Isabelle. In the mistaken belief that it is Léonor who secretly marries Valère, Sganarelle invites his brother to their marriage which will provide irrefutable proof for all to see of the soundness of his own educational principles (Act III, Sc. 5). The misunderstanding between the brothers (for 'Léonor' is of course none other than the jealously guarded Isabelle) is extended over three scenes, and Sganarelle is kept in ignorance of his fate until the last lines of the play, so that the spectator may savour fully the climax of the comedy with the *comédien-raisonneur* Ariste, as the latter imparts to him with discreet irony the fact that he, Sganarelle, has narrowly failed to achieve — through no fault of his own — the dreaded fate of being a *cocu*. His final gloss on the matter, made from the periphery of the comedy, bears out his earlier prediction about Sganarelle's discomfiture, which his role as *agent provocateur* has done so much to bring about, and underscores the deep unity between his status as detached commentator and his dramatic involvement in the play.

3

The comedy of *L'Ecole des Maris* revolved around a rigid and outdated attitude to fashion and marriage. As the focus of the play shifted from the first to the second topic, the farcical role of the hero offered far greater potential for comic effects ranging from the most grotesque to the most pathetic. The subject of fashion placed at stake only the theories and the vanity of the character, whereas that of marriage challenged most directly his most cherished ideas of honour and of himself. Whenever Molière's *imaginaires* are faced with the question of marriage, they have the acute presentiment that both their persons and personas are at risk, their reputations as well as their very existence. One might say that they find themselves involved in a game of double or quits, of all or nothing, if this image did not devalue what they place at stake. In *L'Ecole des Femmes* (1662) Molière adds a further comic dimension to the situation of his earlier play as he endows Arnolphe with the calculating instinct of the gambler in addition to an extremely vulnerable sensitivity. Arnolphe's ideas may well be in direct line with those of his comic predecessor; his character has nonetheless quite a different comic depth and human tonality, to which Dorante points in *La Critique de L'Ecole des Femmes* (1663) when he says in defence of Molière's characterization of his comic hero that '...il n'est pas incompatible qu'une personne soit ridicule en de certaines choses et honnête homme en d'autres' (Sc. 6).

In the first scene Arnolphe displays all the breadth and richness of his comic presence. The ribald bachelor who belatedly decides to marry reveals that for thirteen years he has been contemplating an ambitious scheme designed to safeguard him from all the risks of cuckoldry of which he is supremely aware. To this end, he has superintended the upbringing of his prospective wife Agnès since she was four years old, isolating and insulating her from the world to such an extent that she believes that children are born through the ears. Having made a lifetime study of all the cuckolds in his town, Arnolphe imagines that he is in possession of the secret method for ensuring a safe marriage, like a gambler who has calculated the risks to an infinitesimal degree and can finally play for the highest stakes. There is in fact a marked propensity for 'intellectualizing' his situation in his character. If events happen to run counter to his scheme of things, as for example when Horace falls in love with Agnès, he is able to rationalize his position so brilliantly that evident failure on his part is converted into the most resounding triumph for his methods.

Just as Arnolphe has more depth and colour than Sganarelle, so too Ariste's successor, Chrysalde, is less monochromatic and more burlesque. In his counsel to the *imaginaire*, he is less circumlocutory as he advises Arnolphe at the outset of the comedy not to countenance the prospect of marriage: 'Prendre femme est à vous un coup bien téméraire' (line 8). His advice is dispensed in earthy jocular tones and enables us to evaluate the full extent of Arnolphe's comic situation. According to Chrysalde, no-one has less right to deride cuckolds than their great detractor, Arnolphe, on the principle that '...qui rit d'autrui / Doit craindre qu'en revanche on rie aussi de lui' (lines 45—6). Like the *comédien-raisonneur* of the earlier play, he too sets up carefully the comic perspective in which the events may be fully appreciated by the spectator. But he differs from Ariste in opening up this perspective on the comic hero in more explicitly ironic fashion. Through the medium of his *pince-sans-rire* Chrysalde, Molière inserts into his comedy an ironic dimension lacking in his previous plays. Thus Chrysalde does not confine himself to suggesting obliquely to Arnolphe that he may well fail in his scheme of marriage, as Ariste had done to Sganarelle; his ironic counsels take a much more extensive and yet intangible form, consisting in the ostensible acceptance of cuckoldry as the most normal and natural occurrence in the world which should not evoke the slightest comment from anyone, and in discoursing on the best way of comporting oneself in such an eventuality. His argument is less designed to contradict the grandiose scheme outlined to him by Arnolphe, to which he alludes perfunctorily, than to elaborate a 'philosophy' to palliate the misfortune of cuckoldry. He enunciates the guiding principle of this 'philosophy' at once to Arnolphe, which is that one should never trumpet abroad the misfortunes of other husbands. If he agrees with his friend in stigmatizing the indecent tolerance evinced by many cuckolds, he himself opts for a more discreet line of conduct. One never knows when cuckoldry could befall oneself, still less the way in which one would be likely to react to the event (lines 49—58). If it were to overtake him, then he would hope to benefit from his accumulated credit in the opinion of others by his refusal to laugh at their misfortune.

The same dichotomy of person and persona, action and thought is visible here as in the role of Ariste, underlining the double function of actor and spectator which make up the role of the *comédien-raisonneur*. Chrysalde is as aware as Arnolphe of the ridiculous aspects of cuckolds, but he is also aware that he is under the gaze of society and therefore an object of its approval or disapproval and that he cannot afford to rid himself of either. In the interest of his person, the persona must be carefully protected from social blame. It may be noted in passing that both characters pursue the same end, the maintenance of their *amour-propre* from injury, and both try to insure against this in vastly different ways. The individualistic and aggressive Arnolphe does so in a way intended to challenge openly social attitudes to marriage and cuckoldry, and Chrysalde in a way which conforms outwardly to them whilst reserving the right to criticize them in private. The ironic counsel of Chrysalde in the first scene seems however to fall on deaf ears, but in fact it roots Arnolphe all the more firmly to his obsession and allows us to anticipate with the former the probable *dénouement*. In order to convince Chrysalde of the certain success of his project, Arnolphe enters into an enthusiastic description of it: 'Epouser une sotte est pour n'être point sot' (line 82) summarizes both the plan and the confidence which sustains it. Chrysalde in turn becomes more precise in his objections: a stupid wife may well prove unfaithful without realizing the implications of her infidelity, but an educated wife, of whom Arnolphe has such pathological dread, must at least have the courage to wish to do so (lines 107—16). Arnolphe is cut to the quick by this thrust and the bonhomie of the opening lines disappears: he adopts his magisterial tone, whereas Chrysalde takes refuge behind replies which are intentionally laconic: 'Je ne vous dis plus mot', 'J'y consens', 'Je me réjouis fort' (lines 123—65). His remaining remarks are provoked by his failure to remember the title of nobility which Arnolphe has just assumed (M. de la Souche); although he can see no reason for the change, he knows that his opinion is of no importance whatsoever, since the tetchy Arnolphe obeys the logic by which he lives, that is, his own: 'J'y vois de la raison, j'y trouve des appas;/Et m'appeler de l'autre [nom] est ne m'obliger pas' (lines 185—6).

Chrysalde at once changes tack, since he knows that Arnolphe is impenetrable, choosing to indulge the new whim and remaining the ironic spectator of his folly. The 'dialogue' tails off into complete incomprehension, as Chrysalde tells himself that Arnolphe is irremediably mad and Arnolphe reflects on the ways in which people (i.e. others!) are indissolubly wedded to their prejudices.

Is the role of Chrysalde more than a foil to offset Arnolphe's absurdity, or is he merely an episodic character whom Molière uses conveniently for the exposition and *dénouement* of the play but who remains otherwise detached from the intrigue?[15] On the evidence of this scene he seems to fulfil a fundamental dramatic function without which neither plot nor a full-blooded Arnolphe would be scarcely conceivable. For he does not merely serve to point up Arnolphe's fixation, but to enclose the *imaginaire* more hermetically than ever within it by the series of pointed provocations which Molière has carefully graduated to bring him to the paroxysm of his comic folly.

It is not until Act IV, Sc. 8 that Chrysalde makes his second appearance in the play, and it is not surprising to find contemporaries of Molière, such as Donneau de Visé, anticipating modern criticism by commenting on the supernumerary nature of his role. In his comedy *Zélinde* (1663) the latter makes one of his characters say that 'Chrysalde est un personnage entièrement inutile; il vient, sans nécessité, dire six ou sept-vingts vers à la louange des cocus, et s'en retourne jusques à l'heure du souper, où il en vient dire encore autant pour s'en retourner ensuite; sans que ses discours avancent ou reculent les affaires de la scène.'[16] Unfortunately Molière tells us nothing of the way in which he wished the role to be played in *La Critique de l'Ecole des Femmes*, performed at the height of the controversy surrounding the play and in which we see him hard-pressed in his defence against the supposed immoral nature of some passages, as well as justifying his conception of comic drama and the comic hero. In the absence of such indications, several conclusions seem to emerge from a close study of the role. The first is that Chrysalde's disappearance from the stage after the opening scene is motivated by Arnolphe himself, who says to him 'Ce soir je vous invite à souper avec elle [Agnès]' (line 152), which leads one to suppose that this dialogue takes place either in the morning or early in the afternoon. In the period of time which elapses between the first scene and Act IV, Sc. 8, Arnolphe has to return to his home from which he has been absent for some time, suffer three defeats at the hands of his youthful rival Horace, each one of which is more mortifying than the last, have two lengthy tête-à-tête with Agnès, in one of which he pontificates on the interminable *Maximes du Mariage*, arrange the contract for their wedding, involve himself in several slapstick routines with his servants. The progression of the intrigue which Arnolphe initiates necessitates Chrysalde's prolonged absence from the stage and is not simply in order to 'faire voir la durée de sa pièce' as another of the characters of *Zélinde* objected to Molière.[17] The return of Chrysalde is equally as justified on dramatic and psychological grounds as is his departure. Since his first meeting with Chrysalde, Arnolphe has suffered ever more humiliating defeats at the hands of his rival. But another factor which is just as alien as Horace's rivalry to his scheme has intruded into his consciousness — love for Agnès. At the beginning of the play his elaborate theory of a perfect marriage promised to ensure the fidelity of his prospective wife by reducing her to the status of an object. He would thus avoid the fate of those cuckolds ridiculed so much by him who are so emotionally dependent on their wives that they remain blissfully unaware of their state (lines 21—45). Love, which at that time did not and could not at all enter into Arnolphe's reckoning, makes its presence felt powerfully in his mind at the very moment that he sees Agnès escaping from his clutches:

> J'étais aigri, fâché, désespéré contre elle:
> Et cependant jamais je ne la vis si belle,
> Jamais ses yeux aux miens n'ont paru si perçants
> Jamais je n'eus pour eux des désirs si pressants;
> Et je sens là-dedans qu'il faudra que je crève
> Si de mon triste sort la disgrâce s'achève.
>
> (lines 1020—5)

His love for Agnès is of course more a crude wish to possess her by dispossessing Horace than a wish to cherish, but the fact remains that he loves for the first time in his life and in the only way possible to a character of his emotions and temperament. This means that the second meeting between Chrysalde and himself is situated at a focal point of the action and the development of the hero. Earlier the detached Arnolphe had dismissed loftily Chrysalde's jocular remarks about the dangers of marriage for him. In Act IV, Sc. 8 however the shrewd Chrysalde immediately locates the Achilles' heel of the comic character as he wryly interrogates him:

> Quels chagrins sont les vôtres?
> Serait-il point, compère, à votre passion
> Arrivé quelque peu de tribulation?
> Je le jurerais presque à voir votre visage.
>
> (lines 1221—4)

Now that the *pince-sans-rire* has found the chink in Arnolphe's armour, he zestfully sets to the task of knocking down all the elaborate defences with which Arnolphe has hedged around his vulnerable ego. To Arnolphe's tormented mind, these remarks must seem a thousand times more diabolical in intent than the earlier jesting, for far from appearing to sympathize with his plight Chrysalde takes it upon himself to eulogize that fate which is to Arnolphe worse than death:

> Mettez-vous dans l'esprit qu'on peut du cocuage
> Se faire en galant homme une plus douce image,
> Que des coups du hasard aucun n'étant garant,
> Cet accident de soi doit être indifférent,
> Et qu'enfin tout le mal, quoi que le monde glose,
> N'est que dans la façon de recevoir la chose.
>
> (lines 1244—9)

Within its comic context, this burlesque apologia for cuckoldry can have no other function than that of puncturing Arnolphe's inflated ego at its most sensitive point.[18] Having sweetened the bitter pill of cuckoldry Chrysalde comes back again to an ironic exposition of the virtues of circumspection in such contingencies. Like Ariste in his attitude to society, Chrysalde counsels Arnolphe to avoid all extreme approaches to the matter: he must not emulate the conduct of husbands who delight in the number of admirers surrounding their wives or of husbands whose indiscreet reaction to cuckoldry focuses all the more attention on it (lines 1250—75). In between these extremities lies the method of controlling one's external attitude in spite of one's inner feelings on the subject, that of the *juste-milieu*. This finely nuanced speech produces the effect which Molière's comic vision doubtless intends it to of enraging Arnolphe still farther, for in the matter in question he makes not one whit of distinction between the word and the event which it describes. Chrysalde however goes still farther in his paradoxical apology, as he claims that the concomitant pleasures of cuckoldry are preferable to many marriages (lines 1288—1305). His increasingly penetrating taunts finally bring Arnolphe to a point where, for the first time, he is confronted with the imminent spectre of cuckoldry and he swears solemnly that this will never happen to him! Molière uses Chrysalde here to drive Arnolphe to the comic climax of this scene as the *comédien-raisonneur* sees a fresh opening for attack: 'Mon Dieu! ne jurez point, de peur d'être parjure./Si le sort l'a réglé, vos soins sont superflus' (lines 1309—10).

At once Arnolphe visualizes the realization of the obsession which has haunted him from the outset of the play and ripostes incredulously 'Moi! je serais cocu?' (line 1312). This is the stupefied reaction of the man who sees the impossible coming to pass in front of his eyes and it is underlined by his involuntary change of expression, which Chrysalde of course is not slow to remark on: 'Vous voilà bien malade!' (line 1312). Arnolphe hastily brings this disastrous scene to an end, in which Chrysalde and Molière have orchestrated his phobia to such a pitch that it becomes reality in his mind's eye. Consequently, he has recourse to his famous precautions, redoubling them and barricading himself in his house (Act IV, Sc. 9). The psychological pressure exerted by Chrysalde on Arnolphe leads directly to the comic disintegration of his pretended coherence. As a true *imaginaire*, subjective obsession is so overwhelming that it is liable to become fact at any given moment. Molière through Chrysalde supplies the shrewd insight into the character which makes this comic transformation as evident as it is predictable. In other words, Chrysalde is at once the producer, causally as well as theatrically, of the last phase of Arnolphe's comic evolution, as well as a participant in it. In spite of this, his triple role as comic actor, *raisonneur* and producer comes effectively to an end with this scene (Act IV, Sc. 8) which anticipates Arnolphe's downfall. Chrysalde does appear in the *dénouement*, but only to tie up the loose ends of the plot, by explaining that Agnès is really the daughter of his sister and promised previously in marriage to Horace in any event. As many of his contemporaries were well aware, Molière did not concern himself overmuch about giving the illusion of probability in his *dénouements*.[19] But the all too evident facility and rapidity of the *dénouement* in this play provides an ironic counterpoint to the precipitate deflation of the comic hero.

4

From this study of the roles of Ariste and Chrysalde I conclude that they do not fit at all naturally into the narrow psychological confines set for them by tradition. The description of them as *comédiens-raisonneurs* would appear to account more appropriately for their function in their respective comic and dramatic contexts. In particular three features characterize in varying degrees Molière's conception of the characters:

(1) The *comédien-raisonneur* is both a self-conscious actor and the ironic spectator of the principal character.

(2) He fulfils a precise dramatic function without which the hero cannot achieve his full comic status. The view has been expressed that the character finds himself on the periphery of the plot.[20] On the contrary, he is intimately, if not at first sight evidently, bound up with it, even to the extent of shaping it by the special influence which he brings to bear on the comic hero, who is himself the dynamic centre of the action.

(3) The *comédien-raisonneur* transcends the temporal and spatial restrictions of a role within a play as he offers the audience a means of evaluating the comic fixation of the hero at the outset of the play and subsequently enables it to measure the comic excesses to which he will goad the *imaginaire*. This is by no means to infer that his views are to be identified with those of Molière, or that he is made the mouthpiece for any philosophy of the *juste-milieu* or of reason. Within the comedy he provides a perspective upon it and not upon life as we know it beyond the threshold of the theatre. He beards the choleric and authoritarian wisdom of the *imaginaire* with a debonair and cavalier attitude which is the antipode of all sermonizing about prudent behaviour and the golden mean. The guiding principle of this attitude, which inspires the part he acts out as well as the ideas he speaks, is above all else that of comic disengagement. This signifies that one must not take oneself seriously, that is, to the extent of reducing life to the proportions of a fixation or of narrowing it to an exclusively subjective focus. Hence his perennial liking for *badinage* by which he hopes more to unwrinkle the puckered and frowning brow of the comic hero by reminding him that

the egotistical fantasies with which he battles intensely and which close his horizons are not the unique criteria for interpreting life on the comic stage, rather than to catechize him.[21] The essential *raison d'être* for his actions and words is to be found in the role which he acts out. His attitude may crystallize in comic form, but it constitutes nevertheless a philosophy within the framework of the comedy. The role which he knowingly plays expresses that philosophy, just as the philosophy in its turn presupposes at each moment the role. The unity of role and idea in the character accounts for the perfection with which he plays his allotted part with the result that the mask and the person appear as one. It is this unity which enables him to traverse the comic stage with an air of supreme nonchalance, unencumbered with leaden moralism.

4 The Triumph of Art over Nature in the *Maximes*

1

In a letter of 1664 to Père Thomas Esprit La Rochefoucauld discusses the reactions of the first readers of his *Maximes* and avers that his objective is to show that without religious faith, the apparent virtues of man in general and the philosophers of antiquity in particular are false.[1] The latter part of this objective is confirmed by the frontispiece of the first edition of the *Maximes* on which a winged child who symbolizes 'L'Amour de la Vérité' strips the smooth mask of benign reason and smiling virtue from the bust of Seneca to display the scowling human features. In this way the *Maximes* explicitly align themselves against writers such as Père Sirmond and La Mothe Le Vayer who, in order to refute the doctrine of Jansenius as embodied in the *Augustinus* (1640) had written respectively *Défense de La Vertu* (1641) and *De la Vertu des Payens* (1642). Both argued in favour of the merits of good works performed without the aid of supernatural grace which the Jansenists considered fundamental to salvation. La Rochefoucauld's attack on antique philosophy places him on the same side of the theological divide as the Jansenists. But in spite of the letter quoted above and the passage in La Rochefoucauld's *Avis au Lecteur* (1666) stating that he had viewed man in his natural state of sin, the *Maximes* point up the contradictions lurking under the mask of reason and virtue without reference to the need of divine grace. They do not seek to affect what Pascal called 'ce vilain fond de l'homme, ce *figmentum malum*', which to the Jansenists rendered good works morally null and void.[2] Maxims in the manuscript versions referring to theological concepts such as charity, original sin, the devil, etc., disappeared from the first edition as did the *Discours de la Chapelle-Bessé* with its theological justification of the author's intention from the second.[3] In spite of the background of the *Maximes* and their basic agreement with the Jansenist analysis of unregenerate human nature, it is clear that they were not written from a specifically Jansenist or Christian standpoint, but confine themselves to a view of man within a human perspective. The comment of Sainte-Beuve is pertinent in this connexion: 'Les *Maximes* de La Rochefoucauld ne contredisent en rien le christianisme, bien qu'elles s'en passent.'[4]

The Triumph of Art over Nature in the Maximes

Begun as a game within the *salon* of Mme de Sablé, the *Maximes* were not intended to give a comprehensive or dogmatic view of human nature. To do so would have offended the amateur spirit of the *honnête homme*.[5] In 1664 La Rochefoucauld described them as 'un ramas de diverses pensées' without order, beginning or end. There is some attempt to group them thematically, but it is by no means systematic, for one finds maxims treating a particular theme scattered throughout the volume. Nor is there a leitmotiv as seems at first glance to be the case. In 1665 this seems to be *amour-propre*, and we are warned in the *Avis au Lecteur* against its subtle influence on our judgement of the contents. The long reflection here on *amour-propre* was however omitted from subsequent editions. The first sentences of the fifth edition (1678), the last to be published during the author's lifetime, directs our attention instead to our capacity to be deceived by virtuous appearances. *Amour-propre* is not a theory or a thesis in the sense of being a key to the understanding of human motivation in the *Maximes*; it is rather one of the means by which the author invites us to explore the tangled skein of man's psychology, and provides us with more questions than answers about the nature of our actions, suggesting rather than defining. It is one of a number of concepts which serve to reinforce repeatedly the view of the irreducible contradictoriness and diversity of man.[6]

The word *amour-propre* appears in only a dozen or so maxims, less frequently than other common words such as 'amour', 'amitié', 'fortune' etc. In spite of the deletion of the long reflection on *amour-propre* in the first edition of the *Maximes* three of the first four maxims portray it in general terms and as having universal properties. In two of these maxims it is personified in ways which point to its infinite capacity for subtle deception: it is 'le plus grand de tous les flatteurs', and 'plus habile que le plus habile homme du monde' (Nos. 2 and 4). The other maxim describes it in terms of a country in which the discovered and the unexplored territory are never coterminous (No. 3). In other words, from the beginning of the *Maximes* a fundamental paradox emerges which resides in the fact that the apparently closed, elliptic and final form of the maxim's expression, so necessary for the effects of surprise and shock on the reader, is totally out of proportion to the thought which underlies it. For beneath this form, the maxim points to the conscious and mostly unconscious extents to which *amour-propre* may be present in human motivation and the protean-like forms in which it is capable of presenting itself. The maxims suggest and describe the activity of *amour-propre*, but do not at all attempt to define it. It does not admit of definition because it is something elemental, primordial in man, which precedes language; language can merely describe it approximately, but inevitably fails to coincide with its essence. The hiatus which the first maxims suggest between the description of *amour-*

propre and comprehension of its essence points to a nominalist understanding of language which places the author in the tradition of Montaigne and therefore diametrically opposed to any 'esprit de système'. For the descriptions of the activity of *amour-propre* seem to bear out the understanding of the role of language as revealed in a sentence of the author of the *Essais*: 'Il y a le nom et la chose; le nom, c'est une voix qui remerque et signifie la chose; le nom, ce n'est pas une partie de la chose ny de la substance, c'est une piece estrangere jointe à la chose, et hors d'elle.'[7]

The best way to glimpse something of the universal scope and indefinable nature of *amour-propre* is not to attempt to define it in the abstract, but to scrutinize, as La Rochefoucauld prompts us to do, its multifarious effects on our behaviour. Its name implies that it is adjacent to the qualities of love and friendship, and it is in these areas of human relationships that La Rochefoucauld seems to locate it most visibly; but it is the motivating factor which predates these relationships, being at once part of, and separate from, them. It is the principle behind the illusion that one loves one's mistress for her sake alone (No 374); it makes us happier in experiencing love than in inspiring it (No. 259); in love, it seems to watch over its own interests with totalitarian zeal, to the point where it is prepared to jettison the peace of mind of the person loved in order to salvage its own (No. 262). But its nature is not at all that of all-devouring Racinian passion which renders human relationships intolerable. Although it is a principle of conduct which acts primarily for its own ends, it paradoxically unites those who are in love in a blissful euphoria based on nothing more than individual self-preoccupation. As in Molière's *Le Misanthrope*, *amour-propre* likewise provides the basis of friendship, making social and individual interests coincide; friendship thus becomes a mutually practised deception for individual and social gain, 'un commerce où l'amour-propre se propose toujours quelque chose à gagner' (Nos. 83, 85).[8]

Amour-propre is not merely a quality which underlies love and friendship and which is seen on closer inspection to reside beneath the surface. It is rather inevitably a part of, but by no means synonymous with, them, co-existent with variable degrees of apparent selflessness: 'Nous ne pouvons rien aimer que par rapport à nous, et nous ne faisons que suivre notre goût et notre plaisir quand nous préférons nos amis à nous-mêmes; c'est néanmoins par cette préférence seule que l'amitié peut être vraie et parfaite' (No. 81). Initially, *amour-propre* is the biological condition which determines relationships with our fellows, and may manifest itself in a narrowly self-directed fashion which recalls the opening phrase of the first of the *Maximes Supprimées*, or, as in the present maxim. in a less ostensibly selfish way. Altruism and selfishness necessarily blend in the act of preferring others to ourselves, since our nature disposes us to take pleasure in our preference. Enlightened self-interest seems too low and cynical a description to apply to this highest form of friendship in which one's own pleasure is an inescapable biological constituent and likely frequently to be not at all a conscious or calculating factor.

The clear implication of this maxim and of others is that terms like self-interest and self-preservation are too narrow and restrictive to be equated with *amour-propre*. They are more accurate in describing the causes and ends of our actions than in accounting for the unselfish positive effects which the principle of *amour-propre* produces. *Amour-propre* is an ambivalent principle, embracing negative and positive elements, and our evaluation of it depends largely on whether our attention falls on its cause or on its effect. The necessarily elliptic form of the maxim should not be taken to imply cynical dismissal by La Rochefoucauld of friendship and other qualities. Maxim No. 88 draws attention to the fact that we esteem our friends to the extent that they prove useful to us, whilst concealing the implication that *amour-propre* promotes friendship. It may be true that we forgive easily mistakes which do not concern us, but *amour-propre* stimulates the potentially positive value of forgiveness (No. 428). *Amour-propre* may create mutual trust between people as a means of increasing its own importance. Yet it cannot be denied that by the same token it creates an harmonious basis for co-operation (No. 247). Maxim No. 236 expresses well this dislocation of ends and means which characterizes the activity of *amour-propre,* and which results in the paradox that we can at the same time serve ourselves and others:

Il semble que l'amour-propre soit la dupe de la bonté, et qu'il s'oublie lui-même lorsque nous travaillons pour l'avantage des autres. Cependant c'est prendre le chemin le plus assuré pour arriver à ses fins; c'est prêter à usure sous prétexte de donner; c'est enfin s'acquérir tout le monde par un moyen subtil et délicat.

The shattering of first impressions by the sharp triple reassertion of the reality of *amour-propre* should not be allowed to hide the fact that what for La Rochefoucauld is an ever-present principle in human conduct can lead to effects of self-forgetfulness in the service of others.

The deep ambivalence of *amour-propre* is seen strikingly in the paradoxical effects which it produces in ourselves and in others. If the bulk of the maxims concentrate our attention on the extent to which *amour-propre* deceives the observer by its hidden role in our actions, the effect on the subject is more complex and subtle, and is compounded simultaneously of self-deception and self-enlightenment: No. 303 seems to place the emphasis on the way in which self-interest illuminates our awareness of our own qualities: 'Quelque bien qu'on dise de nous, on ne nous apprend rien de nouveau.' But it illuminates only the area of self which we find praiseworthy, whilst blinding us carefully to the less flattering truth about ourselves. It is *amour-propre* which makes us alive to the exquisite pleasure to be gained from talking about ourselves to others, whilst closing our eyes to our capacity to bore them (Nos. 314, 304). It rationalizes the fortunes and misfortunes which happen to us so that they square with our interests (No. 339); it sharpens our memory of all that has happened to us, and hides from us the fact that we have told the same things many times to the same audience (No. 313); it brings us to the point of supreme self-delusion where we actually imagine that we have no faults, but paradoxically does not give us the courage to say so publicly (No. 397); it renders us unable to see the truth about ourselves, as our enemies can, and perhaps provides the hidden reason for our dislike of them (No. 458). The paradoxical nature and effects of *amour-propre*, with its bewildering capacity to blind and illuminate us alternately and simultaneously, attain their fullest expression in the first of the *Maximes Supprimées*, which is an admirable commentary on, and supplement to, our understanding of *amour-propre* in the *Maximes* proper.

The first of the *Maximes Supprimées* is not at all a maxim, but an extended reflection on *amour-propre*. It also differs from the maxims in that, apart from its opening sentence, it is not an epigrammatic statement about *amour-propre* in the context of a specific situation, or as it is seen more generally to underlie apparent virtue. The reflection begins with a deceptively simple statement about *amour-propre* which is archetypal of the *Maximes*: 'L'amour-propre est l'amour de soi-même, et de toutes choses pour soi.' This is an apparently fixed definition with no qualifications, but it is followed by a long poetic development which is not at all a supplement to the 'definition' but in the nature of a lyrical description of the scope and activity of the subject. From the first description of *amour-propre* as 'l'amour de soi-même', it becomes the dominant motivating force in the individual, but also something universal which is not limited to a particular form, time, or place, a mysterious life-force, everywhere evident at least through its myriad properties and effects and nowhere definable. It finally transcends the powers of reason and rational expression, and is capable of being understood by appeal to the poetic imagination alone.

Self-love or the idolatry of self is the power-centre of *amour-propre*, and thence it radiates its desire to possess for, and subjugate to, itself, all that is outside its own orbit. In its outward activity, it is ever-restless in its attempts to attract what is to its benefit: 'Rien n'est si impétueux que ses désirs, rien de si caché que ses desseins, rien de si habile que ses conduites; ses souplesses ne se peuvent représenter, ses transformations passent celles des métamorphoses, et ses raffinements ceux de la chimie.' The ternary structure of each part of this finely balanced sentence conveys an impression of authoritative finality belied in fact by the unique and extraordinary qualities of the subject. Having depicted its unique qualities in the only way possible, that is, by the representation of what they are not, La Rochefoucauld describes the natural habitat in which it flourishes. To achieve his desired effects of surprise and mystery, he uses the extended and graphic image of a loathsome creature which carries on its foul activity in the unfathomable pit of night. In his description there is deep unity between the subject, object and background. The darkness serves as a fitting setting for the imperceptible twisting and turning of the beast, where it is able to spawn its monstrous designs, so monstrous in fact that when they come to fruition it either disavows or affects to ignore them. The blackness of the habitat is accompanied by the internal cecity of the monster; the sinister image of the bottomless pit is thus intensified by the superimposing of a still more intangible level of darkness, as exemplified in 'les ridicules persuasions qu'il a de lui-même', 'ses erreurs, ses ignorances, ses grossièretés et ses niaiseries sur son sujet'. Nor must it be thought that the blackness of self-delusion is a mere metaphorical conceit by a writer whose pen has carried him into a flight of poetic extravagance. It is rather the literal expression of that very conceit and unawareness of self-limitation which *amour-propre* in the maxims induces so subtly in us.

As many of the maxims imply, however, the internal and external darkness which covers *amour-propre* does not in any way impair its extreme acuity of vision which it brings to bear on objects outside itself; it is at this point, says the author in one of the few sentences in the reflection which has the quality of a maxim, that it resembles the faculty of sight in that it is capable of discovering everything outside itself, yet incapable of seeing itself. Yet this impression of self-blindness is at once contradicted and confirmed: in matters important to itself, it is able to coordinate and concentrate in quasi-magical fashion the senses, imagination and intuition: 'il voit, il sent, il entend, il imagine, il soupçonne, il pénètre, il devine tout'. Whenever *amour-propre* focuses its attention strongly on an object, however, it cannot desist, even if it perceives the disadvantages of its design. Its only limitation seems to reside in the very strength with which it covets its object, for the subject is seen to replace the object as it reveals itself as a self-igniting, self-motivating and ultimately self-desiring force. Centre and circumference of this force are coterminous, as it is depicted as a super-universal personality encompassing all the contradictory attitudes of the mind: 'Il est tous les contraires: il est impérieux et obéissant, sincère et dissimulé, miséricordieux et cruel, timide et audacieux.' It depends on relative factors such as temperament and feeling, and its objectives vary according to age, fortune and experience. In spite of this dependence, it remains self-consistent and constant in its inconstancy.

The final movement in this symphony of paradox is characterized by a paradoxical crescendo. *Amour-propre* penetrates every stratum of life, living off everything and nothing, using whatever it finds at its disposal yet flourishing by its own resources. Self-sufficient, it nevertheless requires everything, it is self-hating in that it follows designs which are self-destructive. The only fixed element in this paradoxical vortex is the ground of its being: 'Enfin il ne se soucie que d'être, et pourvu qu'il soit, il veut bien être son ennemi.' It fulfils itself by simply existing, finding its *raison d'être* in the tensions generated by its conflicting activities. Thus self-immolation in one instance signifies self-resurrection in another, just as self-denial and self-defeat in one place imply self-indulgence and self-victory elsewhere.

La Rochefoucauld ends his bravura passage with the significant words 'Voilà la peinture de l'amour-propre'. Its role in human personality and motivation cannot be analysed, still less defined, only represented by a succession of images. Its activity is likened to bees drawing nectar from flowers, to protean-like metamorphoses, to chemical transmutations, to a beast in its lair, to a presence with extra-sensory perception, to the sum total of the diverse facets of personality. The sea is finally selected as the image most expressive of this seminal force, symbolizing, with its eternal ebb and flow, the incessant mobility and permanence of *amour-propre* in man, and pointing to the essential mysteriousness of human nature: 'la mer en est une image sensible, et l'amour-propre trouve dans le flux et le reflux de ses vagues continuelles une fidèle expression de la succession turbulente de ses pensées, et de ses éternels mouvements'.[9] Scintillating though the prose-poem is as an extended image of *amour-propre*, La Rochefoucauld was right to remove it from the *Maximes* after the first edition. For the maxim is not a poem, and aims for its effect chiefly through concentration and ellipsis, not through mystification, though the former by no means exclude the latter.

2

Amour-propre may be the most extensive growth in our personality according to the author of the *Maximes,* but there are various other subsidiary growths which flourish in its shade. One of the most important of these is *orgueil*, which, as one of the *Réflexions Diverses* makes clear, is inseparable from the parent-plant.[10] Although it serves frequently to reinforce in a minor key the leitmotiv of *amour-propre,* it has an identity and role peculiar to itself. Like *amour-propre,* it is a primordial element in human personality, but is more easily quantified, in spite of its variety of self-expression: 'L'orgueil est égal dans tous les hommes, et il n'y a de différence qu'aux moyens et à la manière de le mettre au jour' (No. 35). It complements *amour-propre* admirably in its wish to maintain the self-sufficiency of the ego in front of other people; indeed, one might say that whereas *amour-propre* is the basic principle which seeks self-advantage, *orgueil* implements it externally by refusing to show dependence on others: 'L'orgueil ne veut pas devoir, et l'amour-propre ne veut pas payer' (No. 228). Whereas the basic aim of *amour-propre* is self- affirmative, that of *orgueil* is self-demonstrative. It invariably repairs the dents in our reputation, and continues its course undiminished and undaunted whatever its misfortunes may be: 'L'orgueil se dédommage toujours et ne perd rien lors même qu'il renonce à la vanité' (No. 33).[11] It is impervious to the loss of prestige and vanity because, unlike *amour-propre* which is capable of extreme vision and blindness, it is permanently unaware of reality: 'Il semble que la nature, qui a si sagement disposé les organes de notre corps pour nous rendre heureux, nous ait aussi donné l'orgueil pour nous épargner la douleur de connaître nos imperfections' (No. 36). This endemic blindness makes it more resistant to correction than *amour-propre*, and is the most harmful of its effects on our personality: 'L'aveuglement des hommes est le plus dangereux effet de leur orgueil: il sert à le nourrir et à l'augmenter, et nous ôte la connaissance des remèdes qui pourraient soulager nos misères et nous guérir de nos défauts' (*Maximes Supprimées*, No. 19). It is *orgueil* which renders our self-improvement so ironically self-defeating: 'Notre orgueil s'augmente souvent de ce que nous retranchons de nos autres défauts' (No. 450). It is this blindness to our imperfections which makes *orgueil* the antithesis of *bonté,* rendering our relationships with others so sterile: it is *orgueil* not *bonté* which leads us to commiserate with our enemies when they experience misfortune in order to demonstrate our superiority over them (No. 463) and incites us to reprove other people: 'L'orgueil a plus de part que la bonté aux remontrances que nous faisons à ceux qui commettent des fautes; et nous ne les reprenons pas tant pour les en corriger que pour leur persuader que nous en sommes exempts' (No. 37). It is the sensitivity of our own *orgueil* which prompts us to complain about the *orgueil* of others (No. 34). *Amour-propre*, though irremediably self-centred, is at least capable of producing effects in social relationships which are of a positive nature. *Orgueil* is more thoroughly negative, always measuring itself with other people in order to demonstrate its superiority. Like *amour-propre*, on the other hand, it is not predictable in its reactions, but follows its own internal contradictory logic. It inspires in us so much envy of others, but also helps us to diminish it (No. 281). It makes us ashamed to admit that we are jealous, and yet provokes us to pride for past and present jealousy (No. 472). It is capable of making us doubly blind to ourselves by our double standards of criticism: 'Le même orgueil qui nous fait blâmer les défauts dont nous nous croyons exempts, nous porte à mépriser les bonnes qualités que nous n'avons pas' (No. 462).

Another word in the *Maximes* which is analagous to *amour-propre* and *orgueil* is *intérêt,* of which La Rochefoucauld wrote as follows in the *Avis au Lecteur* in the second edition of the *Maximes* in 1666: '... par le mot d'*Intérêt* on n'entend pas toujours un intérêt de bien, mais le plus souvent un intérêt d'honneur ou de gloire'. *Intérêt* is the advantage or gain coveted by *amour-propre,* the end-product of its activity, and therefore a stimulus in activating it. As La Rochefoucauld wrote in one of his *Maximes Posthumes*:

> L'intérêt est l'âme de l'amour-propre, de sorte que, comme le corps, privé de son âme, est sans vue, sans ouïe, sans connaissance, sans sentiment et sans mouvement, de même l'amour-propre séparé, s'il le faut dire ainsi, de son intérêt, ne voit, n'entend, ne sent et ne se remue plus. (No. 26)[12]

It is the watershed which marks the difference between the febrile self-interested activity of the man who crosses the seas for his own gain and the sudden inertia which afflicts him whenever it is a question of the advantage of others; it induces the same inertia in others to whom we tell our business and accounts for their sudden resurrection to hear something about themselves.

Like *amour-propre,* but unlike *orgueil, intérêt* is ambivalent in its nature. On the one hand the smallest *intérêt* suffices to quench our good nature, which preens itself on being sympathetic to others (No. 275); on the other, it is responsible for actions which are more positive than the source which produces them: 'L'intérêt que l'on accuse de tous nos crimes mérite souvent d'être loué de nos bonnes actions' (No. 305). It achieves this paradoxical effect because, like *amour-propre,* it is both polyglot and virtuoso: 'L'intérêt parle toutes sortes de langues, et joue toutes sortes de personnages, même celui de désintéressé' (No. 39). Since it is generally in the fabric of human nature, like *amour-propre,* we need not be surprised to discover it beneath qualities which in appearance are totally divergent from it, as the first of the *Maximes* warns us. It is the inevitable and natural end of our virtues: 'Les vertus se perdent dans l'intérêt, comme les fleuves se perdent dans la mer' (No. 171); the word virtue is as useful to its designs as vices (No. 187); 'L'intérêt met en oeuvre toutes sortes de vertus et de vices' (No. 253). More specifically, friendship is merely an agglomeration of collective interests (No. 83); *intérêt* lurks beneath the surface of the praise we give and receive, and dispenser and recipient each obtain self-satisfaction from it (No. 144); similarly, it underlies the advice which we give and affect to take (No. 116) and the tribulations we bear (No. 232). What appears to be generosity is often the spurning of small interests for greater ones (No. 246), and we are extra-lucid in seeing through trifling advantages to ourselves (No. 302). Conversely, avarice is sometimes nothing more than the turning of one's back on substantial future advantage for present small gain (No. 492). Our professed respect for the rights of others is often fear for our own interest (*Maximes Supprimées*, No. 14). Military victory is often not the triumph of some grand overall strategy, but rather the coincidence of innumerable individual interests with the general interest (*Maximes Supprimées*, No. 41).

In spite of the extent to which *intérêt* seems to penetrate apparent virtues, qualities, and achievements, it does not seem to be as endemic an element in human personality as *amour-propre* or *orgueil*. This is the implication for example of the maxim which suggests that *intérêt* is not as universally prevalent as envy: 'Il y a encore plus de gens sans intérêt que sans envie' (No. 486); and we are more willing to renounce it than our preferences or opinions (No. 390). Such remissions on its part however ought not to induce us to underestimate its subtlety or our capacity to ignore its presence and nature. It may overtake us imperceptibly, making us lose sight of our objectives which we thought we had kept firmly in mind, like negotiators who forget about the interests of their friends which they are supposed to represent for the sake of the glory accruing to them from a successful negotiation (No. 278). We are apt to overlook the fact that *intérêt* is subtly present in our passions, persuading us that they are perfectly reasonable, thus rendering them all the more dangerous for us to follow (No. 9). And a maxim on curiosity points up almost by chance one of the ways in which *intérêt* differs from *orgueil*: the curiosity of the former incites us to learn what will be of use to us, whereas the curiosity of the latter emanates from the wish to know what others do not (No. 173). Unlike *orgueil*, but like *amour-propre, intérêt* is capable of inducing in us either cecity or clear-sightedness (No. 40).[13] It is the latter presumably which helps the more intelligent person to regulate the order in which he is going to pursue his various goals, thus avoiding unnecessary expenditure of energy on trifles (No. 66). In this case *intérêt* is clearly of positive value, since it inculcates a degree of self-knowledge and a sense of perspective necessary to self-fulfilment. This enlightened and creative self-interest would seem to be free of hypocrisy, unlike the *intérêt* which may inspire others to spend their lives castigating deceitfulness in their neighbours whilst all the while lying in wait for the opportunity to employ their cunning in the service of great self-gain (No. 124).

3

Amour-propre, orgueil, and *intérêt* are just three of the forces which the *Maximes* see as underlying the appearances of virtue, reason and will. Following Montaigne, La Rochefoucauld points to other unseen influences which serve to increase the fragility and the mutability of our judgement and other qualities. At each moment our conduct is dependent on the unconscious working of our physiology: 'La force et la faiblesse de l'esprit sont mal nommées; elles ne sont en effet que la bonne ou la mauvaise disposition des organes du corps' (No. 44). Our will is no less exposed to this physiological influence than our reason:

> Les humeurs du corps ont un cours ordinaire et réglé, qui meut et qui tourne imperceptiblement notre volonté; elles roulent ensemble et exercent successivement un empire secret en nous: de sorte qu'elles ont une part considérable à toutes nos actions, sans que nous le puissions connaître. (No. 297)[14]

The main channel through which we are influenced by the state of our physical constitution is that of our *humeur*. La Rochefoucauld takes over without question the common seventeenth-century notion of the four *humeurs* which formed the basis of current medical knowledge and practice handed down from Galen and Hippocrates. This theory allowed for four principal substances in the body: blood, phlegm, choler, melancholy. All four *humeurs* were held to be present in the body, but usually one predominated and constituted the temperament of the person in question, who was accordingly either of sanguine, phlegmatic, bilious, or melancholic temperament.[15] An excellent contemporary example of the way in which the prevalent *humeur* controls subtly one's judgement of things is provided by Philinte and Alceste in Molière's *Le Misanthrope*. The former is ruled by a phlegmatic *humeur*, which inclines him to view events with detachment, whereas the latter's *bile* makes him into an ardent critic of social life. In Molière's play, however, the dramatic conflict springs from the consistency of the characters' behaviour with their respective *humeur*; La Rochefoucauld in this respect goes further than his contemporary as he stresses the sheer inconsistency of *humeur*: 'Le caprice de notre humeur est encore plus bizarre que celui de la fortune' (No. 45).It is less a key to the understanding of human nature than another indication of man's complexity: 'On peut dire de l'humeur des hommes, comme de la plupart des bâtiments, qu'elle a diverses faces, les unes agréables, et les autres désagréables' (No. 292). It is not therefore surprising that our judgement should oscillate so much since we have such an inconstant criterion as one of its guides. The arbitrary nature of our actions is intensified by the fact that La Rochefoucauld makes *humeur* depend on fortune: 'Notre humeur met le prix à tout ce qui nous vient de la fortune' (No. 47). Nor is the interaction between fortune and *humeur* as simple as one might suppose from such maxims: for there would seem to be a total lack of proportion between the state of *humeur* and the significance of events which influence it from outside: 'Le calme ou l'agitation de notre humeur ne dépend pas tant de ce qui nous arrive de plus considérable dans la vie, que d'un arrangement commode ou désagréable de petites choses qui arrivent tous les jours' (No. 488).[16] It is entirely typical of the *Maximes* that, whilst implying so strongly that we are in the grip of the external and internal contingency of fortune and *humeur*, we should also find a maxim like No. 414 ('Les fous et les sottes gens ne voient que par leur humeur') which could only be written by someone who still held some belief in the possibility of the exercise of judgement.

Fortune then is the great external force acting jointly with and on *humeur* to produce our fluctuations in mood, temperament, and circumstances: 'La fortune et l'humeur gouvernent le monde' (No. 435) is the general conclusive truth of the *Maximes* even for the wisest among us. Happiness and unhappiness alike, praise and blame, lofty deeds, all originate from chance (Nos. 58, 61, 57). Fortune is a capricious goddess capable of turning every circumstance to the advantage of those people on whom she smiles (No. 60) and of remaining obstinately blind to those on whom she wishes to turn her back (No. 391). Yet, paradoxically, she is also capriciously democratic to all, compensating erratically with her favours and disappointments (No. 52). It is she who discovers the hidden qualities in men (No. 344), showing up virtue and faults as light lays bare objects (No. 380), sometimes using our defects to gain advancement for us (No. 403), sometimes revealing aspects of ourselves to others but especially to ourselves (No. 345). Fortune can use sudden elevation of our status as a means of revealing to us our inability to assume such a position (No. 449). As with the maxims on *humeur*, those on fortune seem to leave little scope for the practice of our reason and foresight. We lavish praise on wisdom, but it cannot make us certain of the most insignificant event (No. 65); 'Notre sagesse n'est pas moins à la merci de la fortune que nos biens' (No. 323). Yet the *Maximes*, without losing sight of our dependence on arbitrary fortune, point to the possibility of channelling events to our own advantage: 'Pour être un grand homme, il faut savoir profiter de toute sa fortune' (No. 343). The wisest profit from fortune not by anticipating it, which is plainly impossible, but in knowing how to accommodate themselves to it *après coup*. The ability to use and turn events to one's own advantage distinguishes the intelligent man, rather than the events which he experiences: 'Il n'y a point d'accidents si malheureux dont les habiles gens ne tirent quelque avantage, ni de si heureux que les imprudents ne puissent tourner à leur préjudice' (No. 59).

With *humeur* and fortune, the passions represent another powerful contingent force hostile to man's control of life and of himself. Unlike the Jansenists, who viewed them as evidence underlining the corrupt state of human nature and of man's need of divine grace, La Rochefoucauld accepts them as integral to human nature. In his self-portrait, he writes that although the effects of 'les belles passions' may be opposed to a rigid conception of wisdom, '... elles s'accommodent si bien d'ailleurs avec la plus austère vertu que je crois qu'on ne les saurait condamner avec justice'.[17] It is in his attitude to the passions that the author of the *Maximes* places himself most fully in the succession of the humanism of Erasmus and Montaigne, as he sets his intention within their anti-Stoic tradition. For the Stoics, the passions were 'perturbationes animi', contrary to right reason and emanating from the baser levels of man's nature, thus interfering with the operation of his divine faculty which linked him to God himself. In their claim to eradicate the passions, Erasmus perceives their intention to create a new god, who does not and can never exist, 'marmoreum hominis simulacrum', devoid of intelligence and emotion.[18] Montaigne, considering the philosophers' conception of man, can only exclaim in amazement 'Tant sage qu'il voudra, mais en fin c'est un homme: ... *Humani a se nihil alienum putet*'.[19] Contrary to the Stoics, the *Maximes* at once remove the control of the passions completely from our will: 'La durée de nos passions ne dépend pas plus de nous que la durée de notre vie' (No. 5). Their intrinsicalness to human nature is suggested by the range of effects which they produce, consciously and unconsciously in our actions, great and small. Our emotional and imaginative faculty, the heart, is seen as the theatre for 'une génération perpétuelle de passions, en sorte que la ruine de l'une est presque toujours l'établissement d'une autre' (No. 10). It is not the reason of the Stoics which controls man, but rather nature's art, the passions, 'les seuls orateurs qui persuadent toujours' (No. 8). It is they, not the unwavering exercise of reason, which operate the most astonishing metamorphoses in man: 'La passion fait souvent un fou du plus habile homme, et rend souvent les plus sots habiles' (No. 6). They in fact usurp the right of reason to such an extent that they may appear as eminently reasonable, and therefore most dangerous for our judgement (No. 9). It is at this point that they cause us to overlook the real causes of great actions: 'Ces grandes et éclatantes actions qui éblouissent les yeux sont représentées par les politiques comme les effets des grands desseins, au lieu que ce sont d'ordinaire les effets de l'humeur et des passions' (No. 7).[20] Their capacity to deceive us is increased by the fact that they are able to produce passions directly opposite to themselves: thus avarice may beget extravagance, weakness firmness, and vice versa (No. 11). They bring powerful reinforcement to La Rochefoucauld's vision of the irreducible contradictoriness of man, and betray all attempts to conceal them: 'Quelque soin que l'on prenne de couvrir ses passions par des apparences de piété et d'honneur, elles paraissent toujours au travers de ces voiles' (No. 12). Molière, within several years of the publication of this maxim in its original form, provides comic evidence for its theory, as his hypocrite Tartuffe ('l'âme de toutes la plus concertée' according to the *Lettre sur la comédie de l'Imposteur* (1667)) is shown to be quite incapable of hiding his lustful passion for Elmire behind his appearances as a holy man.[21] In addition, they inspire in us a strange mixture of blindness and lucidity about ourselves, as do *amour-propre* and *intérêt*. We often boast about the most criminal kind of passion, but are lucid enough not to mention the shameful passion of envy (No. 27). La Rochefoucauld would seem to regard this last passion as one of the most harmful, more inequitable than jealousy (No. 28), outlasting hatred itself (No. 328) and proving ultimately self-destructive by outliving the happiness of those whom we envy (No. 476). In general, the stronger our passions, the more harmful is the effect upon us, as is the case with enduring hatred: 'Lorsque notre haine est trop vive, elle nous met au-dessous de ceux que nous haïssons' (No. 338). Nowhere is the potentially destructive nature of the passions for the person who nourishes them more clearly seen than in the maxims which mark the different gradations of jealousy. In its origin, it may be just and reasonable, wishing only to preserve its legitimate possessions (No. 28). Its development is unpredictable, since it feeds on our doubts, but it either transforms itself into fury or else disappears (No. 32); it begins with love, but does not always die with it (No. 361); it survives because there is more *amour-propre* in it than love (No. 324). Perhaps this is the reason for La Rochefoucauld writing in his final maxim that jealousy is the greatest of all evils (No. 503): deprived of its objective, does it not finally turn in on itself and feed on its own self-torturing? Strong passions like envy, hatred, and jealousy manifest themselves to us in ways which are often spectacular. But we deceive ourselves, writes La Rochefoucauld in a maxim of great penetration, if we think that so-called violent passions, such as ambition and love, subjugate all the others. There are 'passive' passions too, which can take possession surreptitiously of all our other passions and energies: 'La paresse, toute languissante qu'elle est, ne laisse pas d'en être souvent la maîtresse; elle usurpe sur tous les desseins et sur toutes les actions de la vie; elle y détruit et y consume insensiblement les passions et les vertus' (No. 266). Another maxim is more specific about the activity of this passion: it impairs seriously our ability to extend our knowledge by persuading us to do what we find easy or pleasant and the thrust of the maxim conveys forcefully its paralysing effect on our minds: '.... et jamais personne ne s'est donné la peine d'étendre et de conduire son esprit aussi loin qu'il pourrait aller' (No. 482). Another of these 'passive' passions is vanity, whose influence on our nature is more deep-seated and subtle than that of the more violent ones (No. 443).

Complementary to the anti-Stoic intention of the maxims asserting the influence and permanence of the passions in human nature are the maxims on wisdom and folly. Far from viewing our condition as one of potential or natural wisdom, La Rochefoucauld uses the word *folie* as the one which most aptly characterizes our human endeavours. By it he simply reinforces the central idea of his maxims in yet another paradoxical way to remind us that, try as we may to mask ourselves with the appearances of reason and virtue, we cannot finally be other than our nature and circumstances decree that we should be. *Folie* crystallizes all the contradictions implicit in our proud resolve to dominate our circumstances and in our rationalizations of our actions so that they are made to harmonize with our highest idea of ourselves, as well as in our attempts to close our eyes to the extent to which we are at the mercy of fortune, our *humeur*, and our passions. *Folie* thus expresses the full range of our human weakness, inability, self-deception, and is to be equated with nothing less than our human condition itself. Once we have an insight into the essential *folie* of our condition, we see that so-called 'wise' conduct is merely conscious or unconscious concealment of that condition: 'La folie nous suit dans tous les temps de la vie. Si quelqu'un paraît sage, c'est seulement parce que ses folies sont proportionnées à son âge et à sa fortune' (No. 207). All our highest wisdom is merely the well-knitted appearances of pretence to cover this universal and individual condition. To overlook this is to deceive oneself doubly into thinking that one is wiser than one's fellows, as one compounds one's natural *folie* with the *folie* of presumption: 'C'est une grande folie de vouloir être sage tout seul' (No. 231) and 'Qui vit sans folie n'est pas si sage qu'il croit' (No. 209). Such maxims go far in explaining the deep-rooted nature of the comedy of Alceste in Molière's *Le Misanthrope* which was performed for the first time several months before the publication of the second edition of the *Maximes* in September, 1666.[22] Since *folie* is but the compendium of our human failings, the longer we live the more we experience it — and consequently the wiser we become, not of course in the Stoic sense of leading a rationally directed life, but in our increasing awareness of our individual and collective condition: 'En vieillissant on devient plus fou, et plus sage' (No. 210). The *Maximes* therefore see no danger of man suppressing his inner contradictions since the mind may continually propose, but the *coeur* inevitably disposes (Nos. 43, 102). Perhaps the best comment on the impossibility of living according to absolute reason and theory is contained in the lapidary maxim which reads 'Nous n'avons pas assez de force pour suivre toute notre raison' (No. 42).

A prey to innumerable *puissances trompeuses* both from within and without his own nature, man's condition seems habitually to alternate between deception and self-deception. Like Montaigne, La Rochefoucauld sees in his condition more weakness than evil design, since our deception of others invariably leads us to deceive ourselves (No. 120):[23] 'Nous sommes si accoutumés à nous déguiser aux autres qu'enfin nous nous déguisons à nous-mêmes' (No. 119). We live in a world where we all wish other people to accept the image that we have of ourselves ('... le monde n'est composé que de mines' (No. 256)) but our vision remains largely monocular for all that. Hence the antithetical structure common to many maxims, as they illustrate as invariably and as satisfyingly as does Molière's theatre the multiple variations on the theme of *le trompeur trompé*. We dislike being deceived by our enemies and betrayed by our friends '... et l'on est souvent satisfait de l'être par soi-même' (No. 114). It is as easy to deceive ourselves without noticing it as it is difficult to deceive others without them noticing it (No. 115). We employ consummate subtlety to avoid being deceived by other people and yet '... on n'est jamais si aisément trompé que quand on songe à tromper les autres' (No. 117). In such cases, we appear more worthy of ridicule to ourselves than those whom we have duped (No. 407). Such maxims have in them a ring of finality, as though they were enunciating an elementary natural law, not at all a moral one but rather one ingrained in the weakness of human nature, and which continually operates to ensure that 'On peut être plus fin qu'un autre, mais non pas plus fin que tous les autres' (No. 394) and 'Le vrai moyen d'être trompé, c'est de se croire plus fin que les autres' (No. 127). Unlike Molière's comic law adumbrated in the *Lettre sur la Comédie de l'Imposteur*, according to which the nature of the *trompeur* is sooner or later destined to pierce through all attempts to disguise it, La Rochefoucauld sees the design of the *trompeur* as leading less to self-exposure than to inevitable self-deception.[24] Man is perfectly capable of introducing all kinds of refinements into his deception of himself, such as that of doing good in order to be able to commit evil with impunity (No. 121); or we may indulge in the contrary self-deceptions of believing on the one hand that we can do without the help of others, and on the other in the myth of our own indispensability (No. 201).

4

As each fresh accretion to virtue is remorselessly stripped off in the *Maximes*, it becomes easier to understand how some of the first and many of the subsequent readers concluded that they were negative and destructive in effect, if not in intention. Yet if there were no virtues left intact by the *Maximes*, there could scarcely be any counterfeit ones, and vice would not pay its homage of hypocrisy to virtue (No. 218). La Rochefoucauld is not undermining the existence of man's qualities and virtues, as the *Discours de la Chapelle-Bessé* rightly if somewhat inexpertly argued in the first edition of the *Maximes*: he simply points relentlessly to the fact that our negative and positive attributes are inextricably bound up together. Again and again his description of this impure admixture in our nature comes close to Montaigne's view of man as 'rapiessement et bigarrure... [la] mixtion humaine', or as in the sentence of self-description: 'je trouve que la meilleure bonté que j'aye a de la teinture vicieuse' or as in the moral paradox which he finds underlying our best actions: 'l'estrangeté de nostre condition porte que nous soyons souvent par le vice mesmes poussez à bien faire'.[25] This paradox is discerned in all aspects of our nature by La Rochefoucauld, and is fundamental to the series of maxims on vice and virtue (Nos. 182—97); it represents the limits of vice and virtue which nature has fixed in each person (No. 189); it means that great men have great faults (No. 190), that our vices are unavoidable stopping-places along the road of our lives (No. 191), and that, finally, we do not leave them behind us, but it is rather they who leave us (No. 192).

In his view of man as being a mystery even to himself he echoes again one of the main themes of the *Essais*, that of the unanalysable diversity of the individual: 'On est quelquefois aussi différent de soi-même que des autres' (No. 135).[26] Pascal also takes up Montaigne's great theme, and the vision of the innumerable contradictions in man impels him to exclaim in astonishment that 'l'homme passe l'homme'.[27] And the voice of La Rochefoucauld tells us, with its own particular accent, that our contradictions surpass anything which imagination could invent: 'L'imagination ne saurait inventer tant de diverses contrariétés qu'il y en a naturellement dans le coeur de chaque personne' (No. 478). Man is an arena of contesting and bewildering paradoxes, defying an analysis of his actions even in terms of the famous *vice-vertu* paradox: the evil we do does not attract so much hatred as our good qualities (No. 29), it is more dangerous to do too much good to most people than evil (No. 238), there are evil men who would be less dangerous if they possessed less goodness (No. 284), we please often better by our faults than by our qualities (Nos. 90, 155, 354, 468), in unimportant occupations we can appear important, and in important ones unimportant (No. 419), even stupid people may employ their stupidity with dexterity (No. 208).

This vision of the elusive nature of man, with his self-multiplying contradictions, is just beneath the surface of the *Maximes*. Behaviour and emotions which we think of as being familiar to us are never so simple as they appear on the surface. Four examples may be given of well-known attitudes which, on closer inspection, are not just seen to be different from appearances: their reality is found to be as rare as it is indefinable in man. The first maxim on love (No. 68) begins with a neat tripartite 'definition': in the soul it is a passion to rule, in the mind a sympathy, and in the body an unavowed desire to possess what one loves after much mystery. La Rochefoucauld does not go beyond such generalities, and the following maxims on love tell us the reason. There is only one sort of love, but a thousand copies (No. 74); it is like the appearance of ghosts, of which everyone speaks, but which few have seen (No. 76); again, it is invoked in innumerable instances where it has as little effect as the doge in the affairs of Venice (No. 77). Similarly, the subject of courage is seen to undergo the same process of mystification. It is sometimes thought that the *Maximes* are in this respect mainly destructive of heroic values.[28] But this does not seem to be borne out by an analysis of the maxims on courage and heroism. It is true that La Rochefoucauld frequently sees as causes of valour vanity, fear of shame, individual temperament, etc. (Nos. 219, 220). But it is also true that his vision of man and of courage embraces many kinds of valour. Indeed he sees the gamut of the actions commonly said to be of a courageous nature as extending from valour to cowardice, with innumerable shades of bravery between these extremes: 'L'espace qui est entre-deux est vaste, et contient toutes les autres espèces de courage: il n'y a pas moins de différence entre elles qu'entre les visages et les humeurs' (No. 215). Then he lists no fewer than eight kinds of courage, all of which reveal varying mixtures of motivations under the surface. Some men are brave at the beginning of a battle, and lose heart subsequently. Others are satisfied when they have fulfilled the minimum requirements of worldly honour, fear cannot always be kept under control in some, whilst others openly give way to panic, and some are so frightened that they actually rush into battle, etc. The conclusion to this maxim seems to be that courage has no existence at all: 'Tous ces courages de différentes espèces conviennent en ce que la nuit augmentant la crainte et cachant les bonnes et les mauvaises actions, elle donne la liberté de se ménager.' But several maxims further on, there is a passage of unqualified and unstinted praise of courage which must be set against the more sceptical evaluation (No. 217). La Rochefoucauld evidently perceived that the motivations of heroism were too complex and diverse to be circumscribed in a generalized fashion; true courage can only be recognized when we have understood that there are many counterfeit copies. The same process of qualification can be observed in the maxims which describe our motives for our attitudes in tribulation and grief. One states baldly that often self-interest and vanity are our reasons for grieving (No. 232). The following extended maxim on the same subject however is rather more complex in its conclusions, although its basic premise is simple enough: 'Il y a dans les afflictions diverses sortes d'hypocrisie' (No. 233). Three examples of hypocritical grief are given; the first two neatly detect self-interest and vanity as causes, but the third example of hypocrisy in grief lifts the subject out of the range of such facile categorizing and points to more complex motivations: 'on pleure pour avoir la réputation d'être tendre, on pleure pour être plaint, on pleure pour être pleuré; enfin on pleure pour éviter la honte de ne pleurer pas'. To say that one finds here another manifestation of *amour-propre* is simply begging the question of motivations in the *Maximes*: for *amour-propre*, as we have seen, is the mysterious omnipresent yet invisible force which defies all efforts to analyse it. A last example of the complexity underlying the *Maximes* may be seen in the maxims on humility. On the one hand, it is merely 'un artifice de l'orgueil' demeaning itself in order to exalt itself (No. 254, cf. No. 327). On the other hand, La Rochefoucauld is not totally dismissive of all humility: in a maxim introduced, it is true, in the fourth edition of the *Maximes* in 1675 but which must be quoted in any overall view of his treatment of the topic, he allows for a humility without which we retain all our faults and which is the true proof of Christian virtue (No. 358).[29]

5

The constant movement of the maxims from the appearances of our virtues to their underlying reality is the instrument which La Rochefoucauld employs to challenge the reader's faculty of judgement by stimulating it out of complacency to self-reflection. Not the least of the innumerable paradoxes of the *Maximes* is that amid all the questioning of appearances a norm of judgement is seen to emerge gradually. This norm is not at all in the nature of a rigid moral category, but is rather a flexible and sinuous means whereby a civilized man may come to terms with the infinite contradictoriness of his nature and of life. Because it is more difficult to know one man than men in general (No. 436) such a norm of judgement implies above all the choice of a correct focus on each person and event: 'Les hommes et les affaires ont leur point de perspective. Il y en a qu'il faut voir de près pour en bien juger, et d'autres dont on ne juge jamais si bien que quand on en est éloigné' (No. 104).[30] And because of the contradictoriness of both subject and object, correct judgement will also contain contradictions: if 'la souveraine habileté' consists in knowing the value of things (No. 244), it can also consist in knowing how to conceal one's judgement (No. 245); good judgement need not mean that one is correct in one's evaluations, but may rather be vindicated in being deceived by skilful deception (No. 282). This is necessarily so because even our best judgement is always lacking in that knowledge of infinitesimal detail required for sound conclusions (No. 106).[31] If our judgement habitually reflects inadequate knowledge of the situation, too much penetration of mind also makes us miss the mark (No. 377). In the *Réflexions Diverses* we read that some people display good judgement in matters which do not concern them, and others poor judgement in those which relate to themselves.[32] Judgement, which is so paradoxical in nature and effect, is however a positive qualitative value in the *Maximes* and in the

Réflexions Diverses, to be sharply distinguished from the superficiality of *esprit*: 'On est quelquefois un sot avec de l'esprit, mais on ne l'est jamais avec du jugement' (No. 456).[33]

It is this paradoxical norm which provides the link between the necessary negativism of many of the maxims and the positive standards of conduct to which they point, that is, the socially acceptable ideal of *honnêteté* which anticipates and prepares for the *Réflexions Diverses*. The *Réflexions* are not at all a simple addendum to the *Maximes*, but grow from and exemplify the outline of *honnêteté* which the latter trace.[34] In the *Maximes* the true *honnêtes gens* are those people who know and admit their faults as opposed to the false *honnêtes gens* who dissemble to others and to themselves (No. 202). This maxim implies a considerable degree of self-knowledge and lucidity, in view of the potentially disruptive force of our *amour-propre*: this is, as the *Réflexions* repeatedly insist, the arch-enemy of sound judgement, blinding us to our own qualities and making us strive after attributes which are alien to our temperament and nature. Those people who manage to control their *amour-propre* are as rare in the *Réflexions* as in the *Maximes*, but they achieve that harmony of thought and action, instinct and behaviour, person and persona, which is evidently the individual and social ideal of the author:

> Il y en a qui, par une sorte d'instinct dont ils ignorent la cause, décident de ce qui se présente à eux, et prennent toujours le bon parti. Ceux-ci font paraître plus de goût que d'esprit, parce que leur amour-propre et leur humeur ne prévalent point sur leurs lumières naturelles; tout agit de concert en eux, tout y est sur un même ton. Cet accord les fait juger sainement des objets, et leur en forme une idée véritable; mais, à parler généralement, il y a peu de gens qui aient le goût fixe et indépendant de celui des autres; ils suivent l'exemple et la coutume, et ils en empruntent presque tout ce qu'ils ont de goût.[35]

In the second of the *Réflexions, De la Société*, the socially destructive effects of our natural tendency to prefer ourselves to others is fully recognized, as is also the possibility of controlling it in one's own nature and in turn directing it towards social ends which may be advantageous to all: 'Il faudrait du moins savoir cacher ce désir de préférence, puisqu'il est trop naturel en nous pour nous en pouvoir défaire; il faudrait faire son plaisir et celui des autres, ménager leur amour-propre, et ne le blesser jamais.'[36]

The *honnête homme* knows how to accommodate himself to the mind and *humeur* of his interlocutor, how to circumvent subjects which are likely to offend the sensitivity of others. He is not a rigid Alceste in society, but rather a flexible Philinte, who enters into the vanities and foibles of all: he is

> Un esprit adroit, facile, insinuant, [qui] sait éviter et surmonter les difficultés; il se plie aisément à ce qu'il veut; il sait connaître et suivre l'esprit et l'humeur de ceux avec qui il traite; et en ménageant leurs intérêts il avance et établit les siens. Un bon esprit voit toutes choses comme elles doivent être vues; il leur donne le prix qu'elles méritent, il les sait tourner du côté qui lui est le plus avantageux, et il s'attache avec fermeté à ses pensées parce qu'il en connaît toute la force et toute la raison.[37]

The art of social living described in the *Réflexions* is prepared in the *Maximes* by the cultivation of one's natural qualities and judgement and by moulding them to suit society's ends. At first sight there may appear to be something of a contradiction between the emphasis of the *Maximes* that we should let ourselves be seen as we are, rather than as we are not (No. 457) and the flexible social ethic of the *Réflexions*. If, as the *Maximes* state, one is never as ridiculous with the qualities one has as with those one affects to have, Alceste at first sight may appear less ridiculous than Philinte in proclaiming

> Je veux que l'on soit homme, et qu'en toute rencontre
> Le fond de notre coeur dans nos discours se montre,
> Que ce soit lui qui parle, et que nos sentiments
> Ne se masquent jamais sous de vains compliments.
>
> (*Le Misanthrope*, Act I, Sc. 1, lines 69–72)

La Rochefoucauld however would seem to provide the thought which underlies Molière's comic portrayal of Alceste as the man who sets his heart on appearing to be natural as he writes that 'Rien n'empêche tant d'être naturel que l'envie de le paraître' (No. 431). It is not at all a question of nature in the raw ruling our behaviour; nature provides us with our temperament and disposition, but in the *honnête homme* they must come into a felicitous blend with art:

> Il y a de bonnes qualités qui dégénèrent en défauts quand elles sont naturelles, et d'autres qui ne sont jamais parfaites quand elles sont acquises. Il faut, par exemple, que la raison nous fasse ménagers de notre bien et de notre confiance; et il faut, au contraire, que la nature nous donne la bonté et la valeur. (No. 365)[38]

This theme of the blend of natural and acquired qualities is developed further in the *Réflexion De l'Air et Des Manières*: after stressing the importance of encouraging natural inclination and talent, La Rochefoucauld adds that he is not saying that we must not acquire qualities which nature has not given us. The question is not to seek qualities for their own sake, but to discern and acquire those which are appropriate to us: '... ces qualités acquises doivent avoir un certain rapport et une certaine union avec nos propres qualités, qui les étendent et les augmentent imperceptiblement'.[39]

La Rochefoucauld agrees with other theoreticians of *honnêteté* such as Faret and Méré that to be natural in one's conduct is the fruit of long study: Faret in *L'Honneste Homme* (1630) writes that the *honnête homme* must 'user partout d'une certaine négligence qui cache l'artifice' and Méré enjoins his readers to regard *honnêteté* as 'un art consommé'.[40] The lucid self-conscious and apparently natural art of social living of the *Réflexions Diverses* is everywhere implicit in the *Maximes*: by the insight which the latter provide into his nature the *honnête homme* is led to that detachment from himself which is both condition and sign of the cultivation of the art of appearing natural: 'Le vrai honnête homme est celui qui ne se pique de rien' (No. 203).[41] The final and greatest paradox of the *Maximes* is that the most permanent element in man's nature — *amour-propre* — can be fashioned by judgement into the construction of the *honnête homme*, and that they represent, in spite of appearances, the triumph of art over nature.

5 The Paradox of Pascal's *Pensées*

1

One of the striking features of the *Pensées* is the fact that they do not begin their apology for the Christian religion with any of the classical Christian proofs of the existence of God and the truth of Christianity. The reader cannot fail to notice the absence of such traditional scholastic arguments as those based on cosmology, teleology, the rational ordering of the universe, and the moral consciousness of man which leads him to accept a metaphysical source for his value-judgements. Pascal likewise refuses to employ ontological arguments, such as Descartes' proof of God's existence derived from the presence in his mind of the idea of perfection.[1] Arguments drawn from history and prophecy, as well as from the comparative study of other religions, are used in the second part of the *Pensées*, but they serve a secondary function in the overall design of the apology.

The absence of such proofs is all the more surprising since the first chapter underlines the importance of demonstrating the intellectual respectability of the Christian religion: '... il faut commencer par montrer que la religion n'est point contraire à la raison. Vénérable, en donner respect' (No. 12). But this intention forms but a part of Pascal's starting-point, which is explicitly paradoxical: faith is different from proof, the first being a gift of God and the second of human origin, although proof may often be the instrument which leads to faith (No. 7).[2] Pascal affirms simultaneously the relative power of reason to help the unbeliever come to faith in God and the absolute power of faith alone to convert from unbelief. The paradox which consists of believing at the same time in the power of reason and in its transcendence by faith is by no means peculiar to Pascal the apologist for the Christian religion, for it provides the connexion between his approach to Christianity and his method as a geometrician. In *De l'esprit géométrique* he states that the highest form in which truth may be demonstrated is to be found in geometrical reasoning, which advances no proposition without proof. Yet if one adopts its rigorous method of defining each term used, one comes ultimately to the first principles on which its reasoning is based, such as those of time, space, the infinity of numerical progression, etc., which are impossible to define by reason. Geometry does not therefore attempt to define them, not only because they are indefinable, but also because they present themselves with great clarity to everyone without the intermediary of reason. The principles which underlie our knowledge are guaranteed not by our intelligence but by the certainty which nature gives us instinctively that they are true. The highest form of reasoning is based on belief in the truth of principles which are taken for granted by us, and without this belief all the excellent secondary reasonings of geometry would be useless. Pascal thus avoids any dichotomy involving belief in first principles and the method of scientific reasoning by making the former sustain the latter. To attempt to define first principles would only introduce obscurity and diversity into an area of truth which is universally accepted as such even though it is imperfectly understood.

The second stage in the outline of the projected apology is also closely bound up with this basic paradox. After having shown that religion is not contrary to reason, Pascal proposes to 'la rendre ensuite aimable' (No. 12). The stress on the importance of making the argument for religion 'aimable' is prompted by man's complex attitude towards truth. In *De l'art de persuader*, Pascal writes that we receive truth by one of two ways, either by understanding, which is the more natural, or by will, which is the more usual, since we are almost always persuaded by 'agrément' rather than by proof. He adds that the method of persuasion by 'agrément' is not worthy of use in the argument for divine truths, for it is not man who can make them attractive: 'Dieu seul peut les mettre dans l'âme, et par la manière qu'il lui plaît'.[3]

Between reason and belief in God, truth and the will to believe it, there is a gap unbridgeable by any other influence than that of God himself. At one fell swoop the *raison d'être* of the apology falls, rendered superfluous by the primacy of God's act in inclining the unbeliever towards belief, in spite of, or because of reason, and by means of the method which he alone deigns to use. The aims of making religion intellectually respectable and attractive reflect the paradox of the *Pensées*, which consists in attempting to promote belief in God and in recognizing at the same time that this is solely the prerogative of God. The existence and argument of the *Pensées* are compelled by Pascal's acute awareness of what Hugo Friedrich in an excellent article has termed his 'Daseinsparadox', expressed most lucidly at the end of fragment 110:[4] those people who believe the truth of religion without need of proof are truly persuaded indeed 'mais ceux qui ne l'ont pas nous ne pouvons la donner que par raisonnement, en attendant que Dieu la leur donne par sentiment de coeur, sans quoi la foi n'est qu'humaine et inutile pour le salut'. It is this overwhelming sense of God's primacy in stimulating faith in the unbeliever and in bringing him to conversion which gives the *Pensées* the character of an existential wager long before Pascal confronts the unbeliever in the famous fragment of the *Pari*. His arguments may after all not succeed in bringing the unbeliever to the place where he will find faith in God or even in making religion an attractive proposition to him. In *De l'art de persuader* Pascal emphasizes that it is easier for the apologist to find 'l'art de convaincre' than 'l'art d'agréer' on account of the extreme diversity in the ways in which people find different subjects attractive.[5] The argument of the *Pensées* then is Pascal's own lucid response as a Christian to the existential paradox whereby God's truth, which is wholly different from man's condition, must be articulated by human reason; the consequence is that he is led to acknowledge the sheer impossibility of mediating faith through reason, whilst seeking through the unrelenting force of his logic as a mathematician to bring man to the point where faith will follow.

This paradoxical premise provides the *raison d'être* of the argument, which is based on two fundamental principles apparently in contradiction but in fact complementary. In No. 6 Pascal uses them to summarize his plan first on a psychological and then on a theological level in two sets of statements:

(1) Partie. Misère de l'homme sans Dieu.
(2) Partie. Félicité de l'homme avec Dieu.
               autrement
(1) Part. Que la nature est corrompue, par la nature même.
(2) Partie. Qu'il y a un Réparateur, par l'Ecriture.

In the first set reason's evaluation of the human condition is implied, and in the second, that of faith, and both evaluations are complementary. For reason perceives man's misery without God all the while aware however dimly that true happiness is only to be found in God (this emerges more clearly with the establishment of the paradox *misère-grandeur* in man's nature in Chapter VI and its explanation in Chapters VII—XI). In the second, faith transcends but does not contradict the evidence of reason with the still more paradoxical Biblical evaluation of man as a fallen but redeemable creature embodied in the person of Jesus Christ (Chapters IX,XIII,XIV). The explanation of the human paradox of *misère-grandeur* by Jesus Christ is the supreme validation of the Christian religion and the touchstone by which other faiths are to be tested (Chapter XVI). The argument develops between the apparently distant but always co-terminous bounds of this paradox, drawing on a multitude of observations from experience, philosophy, theology, science and history. But its powerful coherence and relevance come from the concentric character with which these bounds invest it. From paradox all proceeds, to paradox all returns.

2

The two terms of the paradox *misère-grandeur* are the concepts used to create and sustain Pascal's 'art de persuader'. It is reason which establishes relentlessly the first term, the reality of man's misery: it does so however by discovering at each level of his experience its own capacity for irrationality. The first term of the paradox therefore is made up of many layers of paradox, and the cumulative effect is to prepare the mind and the will for the second. The more reason perceives the misery in ourselves and our condition, the more it stimulates itself and the will to seek an answer to the human dilemma outside our nature. The second term *grandeur* seems to promise relief from the spectacle of our misery: in fact it makes our misery self-perpetuating by revealing our paradoxical awareness of the truth of our condition and of our inability to change it, thus intensifying still more the will to find a solution outside our experience.

Reason's paradoxical diagnosis of our condition begins with the description of man without God. *Vanité* is the term which Pascal uses to designate the universal inability of man to achieve a rational basis for his attitude to himself and to others. Following Montaigne's sceptical onslaught on man's reason in his *Apologie de Raimond Sebond* by which he presumes to elevate himself above the rest of the animal kingdom, Pascal invokes some of the innumerable factors which combine to make man's judgement of himself, of others and of life contingent, both self-deceived and self-deceiving. No consistent criteria of judgement are possible, for they vary with age, time and place. It is possible to view paintings in perspective, but no perspective exists on questions of truth and morality (No. 21). Nor can intellectual knowledge provide man with a stable inner balance (No. 23); his judgement is exposed to the effects of the most insignificant phenomena (No. 22). He can give no rational account of his actions, whether great or small: 'Deux visages semblables, dont aucun ne fait rire en particulier font rire ensemble par leur ressemblance' (No. 13), 'Un bout de capuchon arme 25 000 moines' (No. 18); we admire a painting because of its resemblance to an object which we do not at all admire in reality (No. 40). The belief in the divine right of kings derives from the custom of seeing monarchs with their imposing retinue and of imagining that such trappings are the natural attribute of greatness (No. 25). The respect paid to the upper classes has no rational relationship to intrinsic merit, ability or function (No. 30). Man's nature is as variable as the course of a fever (No. 27); yet his condition remains one of 'Inconstance, ennui, inquiétude' (No. 24).

Of all the *puissances trompeuses* which undermine man's ability to establish a rational connexion between the cause and effect of his actions the principal one is his imagination. Montaigne's *Apologie* had already followed the arguments of the theoretician of Greek scepticism, Sextus Empiricus, to underline in devastating fashion the deceptiveness of our reason and senses, which are responsible for different impressions in our judgement according to changes in our bodily and emotional conditions, so that what we judge to be true at one moment we deem false at another. Since the sources of all our judgements are influenced by factors which are constant only in their variability, all our reasoning about ourselves and the external world can have no necessary correspondence to reality. The result is that man is removed from any claim to establish truth and enclosed in a dream-like world of subjective circularity:

> Or, nostre estat accommodant les choses à soy et les transformant selon soy, nous ne sçavons plus quelles sont les choses en verité; car rien ne vient à nous que falsifié et alteré par nos sens. Où le compas, l'esquarre et la regle sont gauche, toutes les proportions qui s'en tirent, tous les bastimens qui se dressent à leur mesure, sont aussi necessairement manques et defaillans. L'incertitude de nos sens rend incertain tout ce qu'ils produisent.[6]

Pascal weaves many of Montaigne's remarks about the unreliability of our reason and sense experience into his fragment on the power of the imagination, but at the same time he gives to them a systematic development and purpose which have no place in his source. The factors which Montaigne suggests as undermining our judgement are welded together by Pascal into a powerful entity called imagination, unfailingly present in the mind as the supreme faculty of error: 'C'est cette partie dominante dans l'homme, cette maîtresse d'erreur et de fausseté, et d'autant plus fourbe qu'elle ne l'est pas toujours, car elle serait règle infaillible de vérité, si elle l'était infaillible du mensonge' (No. 44). Imagination is presented as a universal protean concomitant of our judgement, capable, like *amour-propre* in the *Maximes* of La Rochefoucauld, of infiltrating each action and thought. *Amour-propre* weaves its way, for the most part invisible, through all the fabric of human motivation. Imagination on the other hand does no less than establish a second nature in man, with its own activities and objectives; this substitute for reality is so much a product of self-deception that man experiences it as entirely natural and satisfactory. In one crucial respect only does it fail to duplicate man's original nature and its very failure is for Pascal the criterion of its consummate power to deceive us: 'Elle ne peut rendre sages les fous mais elle les rend heureux, à l'envi de la raison qui ne peut rendre ses amis que misérables. . . .' Reason is a commodity which we willingly barter in exchange for the illusion of happiness which imagination holds out to us.

Imagination does not only play a decisive role in creating the value-judgements of individuals; it also provides the basis for the respect for

The Paradox of Pascal's Pensées

laws and authority on which society operates. Its control of our minds, as complete as it is arbitrary, is focused sharply both in the respect which we have for the venerable magistrate with his look of gravity and in the lessening of that respect if we perceive that he is less well shaved than usual. The power of imagination is so great that the most perspicacious observers of the social scene utilize it as the firmest foundation for their influence and profit. Pascal reinforces doubly the power of imagination as he views it both in its cause and in its effects: it flourishes on account of our ineradicable wish to blind ourselves to the reality of our situation, endowing our activities with a reality more real than reality itself.

Our inability to achieve inner harmony and stable judgement from within our own resources is borne out by our attitude towards time. Situated temporally between the past and the future, we nevertheless insist on turning our gaze towards time which we cannot experience in any meaningful sense. Just as imagination provides us with an escape from reason's evaluation of our condition, so too we seek to escape from the present consciously or unconsciously. Even though our experience of the present may be pleasant, we try to prolong it by projecting it into the future. As in the depiction of the ways in which imagination infiltrates its own reality into each conscious and unconscious level of our mind, the effect of the fragment on our attitude to time comes from the mathematical precision with which the abstract concept of thought is divided between past, present and future, and the stringently logical manner with which the existential position of man, one of self-deception, illusion and escapism, is delineated. Preoccupied with the past and the future, imagination fills our thoughts with fantasies which we pursue so avidly that we are provided with a second and more vital reality responsible for the supreme paradox whereby we continue to live in a biological sense, whilst failing to establish any meaningful connexion with the reality of our existence: 'Ainsi nous ne vivons jamais, mais nous espérons de vivre, et, nous disposant toujours à être heureux, il est inévitable que nous ne le soyons jamais' (No. 47).[7]

The inner disharmony of man (*misère*) results from the conflict between the complex nature of his self and the equally complex reality which confronts it, from the disparity between his real needs and the unreal ways in which he seeks to fulfil them. Balance and harmony cannot be restored to his nature without first understanding his dissonances and contrasts: 'Ce sont des orgues à la vérité, mais bizarres, changeantes, variables.... Il faut savoir où sont les [touches]' (No. 55). The complex nature of the self and reality is seen in the diversity of reactions to the same phenomenon: 'Les choses ont diverses qualités et l'âme diverses inclinations, car rien n'est simple de ce qui s'offre à l'âme, et l'âme ne s'offre jamais simple à aucun sujet. De là vient qu'on pleure et qu'on rit d'une même chose' (No. 54). We can only take pleasure in an activity when we know that we shall become angry if we fail (No. 56). *Inconstance,* which is also endemic to humanity, stems at once from our knowledge that the pleasures of the present are false and the fact that we know nothing of the triviality of pleasure which we strive to obtain (No. 73). In other words it is a product, like *vanité* and *misère,* of our wish to escape from thinking about our present condition into future happiness of our own making.

The necessity for balance between our aspirations and the way in which they are fulfilled is illustrated by its absence in *Tyrannie* (No. 58). Each human quality has its own peculiar laws and form through which it comes to perfection, which must be followed if it is not to lose its natural harmony and effect. When it leaves its natural path to follow another way, it aborts, degenerates, and becomes unnatural tyranny. When for example beauty and strength seek to vie with each other by the same means, they overreach themselves by moving into spheres which do not belong or correspond to their natures: 'La tyrannie est de vouloir avoir par une voie ce qu'on ne peut avoir que par une autre. On rend différents devoirs aux différents mérites, devoir d'amour à l'agrément, devoir de crainte à la force, devoir de créance à la science.'

Man, unable to obtain truth and harmony within himself, seeks to find them outside his nature in the concept of justice. If such a concept existed, it would be practised universally, but this lofty ideal is fashioned in practice by contingent factors such as time and topography: 'Plaisante justice qu'une rivière borne. Vérité au-deçà des Pyrénées, erreur au-delà' (No. 60).[8] But if justice varies with country and custom, is there not a principle of natural law common to mankind in general? Pascal follows Montaigne in stating that no principle of law or justice is more intrinsically natural or just than any other.[9] Custom is canonized as the highest principle of justice for the very reason that it is custom. To submit such principles of justice to rational analysis is to overthrow all the foundations which custom gives to the law of a state, for custom, initially without rational basis, acquires such a basis through its longevity. It is therefore dangerous to tell people that the laws are not just: in order to keep the peace, it is important to tell them that the laws must be obeyed because they are laws. It is at this point that Pascal's divergence from Montaigne's use of scepticism begins to emerge. The latter thought that to question one social principle was necessarily to endanger the whole social structure, and that there was no advantage to be gained by the individual placing his own relative ideas above the relative ideas of society as a whole. Pascal on the other hand takes over his sceptical principle about the diversity and relativity of laws not to advocate nominal adherence to the laws of one's country but to reinforce the argument of the first part of his apology that the customary value-judgements of men have no correspondence to truth and reality. The demolition by Pascal of the

The Paradox of Pascal's Pensées

received ideas about 'reality' and 'truth' is not a sceptical end in itself, but rather a stimulus to search for the higher reality provided by the Christian explanation of man's condition. The application of reason to man's condition is not therefore to be discouraged, as Montaigne advised sceptically; it is to be encouraged, as it leads man to ask the existential question of why he as an individual should occupy for a brief span of time a space in the immense infinity, and thus become aware of the apparent contingency of his existence at a particular time and place: '...car il n'y a point de raison pourquoi ici plutôt que là, pourquoi à présent plutôt que lors. Qui m'y a mis? Par l'ordre et la conduite de qui ce lieu et ce temps a [-t-] il été destiné à moi?' (No. 68).

Beneath the actions of men there lurk the apparently opposing motivations of *orgueil* and *ennui*. *Orgueil* stimulates man to seek the unfamiliar situation, and *ennui* persuades him to accept the *status quo*. They are different in the actions to which they give rise, but both fulfil complementary needs in man's nature: one satisfies his need for regularity and custom ('dépendance') and the other his need to change his surroundings ('désir d'indépendance') (No. 78), and thus represent variations on the themes of 'inconstance' and 'le mouvement perpétuel' of Chapters II and III.

In Chapter V, *Raisons des Effets*, Pascal returns to the theme of justice, which he has mentioned briefly in previous chapters. Like Montaigne, he concludes that true justice does not exist among men, and sees proof for this in the fact that our ideas of what are just and unjust are derivative in their origin. But Montaigne was content to accumulate evidence for the diversity in the concepts and practices of justice before counselling sceptical submission to the laws of one's particular society. Pascal goes further, by asking the question: how have men created their ideas about justice? The answer is rooted in the central moral supposition about man which underlies the first part of the *Pensées*. Since man is unable to put the concept of justice into effect, his concupiscence leads him to replace the idea of justice, which is 'une qualité spirituelle', by its opposite quality, force, which is 'une qualité palpable' and thus capable of disposing of justice as it pleases: 'On l'a mise [la justice] entre les mains de la force et ainsi on appelle juste ce qu'il est force d'observer' (No. 85). Man's corrupt reason ('cette belle raison corrompue a tout corrompu' (No. 60)) finds no difficulty in metamorphosing the idea of incorruptible justice into human 'justice' based on coercion. The apparent success of this paradoxical conversion of moral principle into pragmatism only conceals the failure of man's corrupt nature to ground justice in anything other than crude authoritarianism: 'Et ainsi ne pouvant faire que ce qui est juste fût fort, on a fait que ce qui est fort fût juste' (No. 103).

The presumption of man's reason in seeking to order his life on his own terms is confounded by the paradoxical effects which true wisdom ought to induce in us. Wisdom in fact sends us back to the simplicity and trustfulness of childhood (No. 82); the two extremities of knowledge, the lack of knowledge with which we are born and the acquisition of great knowledge, converge at the point where both reveal an ignorance which is different in degree but not in kind. For the first extremity of ignorance is the natural one, and the second 'une ignorance savante qui se connaît' which is akin to the 'ignorance doctorale' of Montaigne and the 'ignorance louable' of his successor, La Mothe Le Vayer.[10] The half-baked pedants find themselves situated between the two ignorances, since they know more than those who are naturally ignorant and have insufficient knowledge to perceive the limitations of human knowledge (No. 83). Whereas they despise the opinions of the people, the wise man acknowledges that such opinions are often closer to the truth than those of the rest of society. The people are generally right in honouring established laws and aristocratic rank. But they too are no more exempt from error and illusion than the rest of mankind, for they venerate institutions which cannot claim to be more intrinsically rational or true than those of any other country (No. 92). The wise man however shares their opinions whilst retaining his own 'pensée de derrière', that is, his own critical faculty of judgement unimpaired by custom and appearances (No. 91). Pascal comes here to the same position as Montaigne, as the latter advocated a rigid separation of public attitude and private opinion: 'Mon opinion est qu'il se faut prester à autruy et ne se donner qu'à soy-mesme'.[11] This separation of opinion and belief, person and persona, is however as permanent a feature of the *Essais* as it is temporary in the *Pensées*. This is illustrated in fragment 90, where Pascal outlines in hierarchical form the diverse effects which aristocratic rank produces on men: the people venerate those who are born with great privilege, and the 'demi-habiles' despise them, whereas the more intelligent men (the 'habiles') combine both attitudes, honouring them, but 'par la pensée de derrière'. Christians who are more zealous than enlightened judge them adversely according to their narrow ideas of piety, but true Christians alone honour them correctly, viewing them within the Christian perspective on society.

Chapter VI, *Grandeur*, seems to offer reason and will the way out of the sceptical morass of ethical relativism and self-contradiction as Pascal discovers intact in the mind the residue of self-knowledge and awareness of our condition. But this knowledge is paradoxical in nature, having something in common with those dogmatic philosophers who claim that there is a source of ultimate truth which can be known by man as well as with the Pyrrhonists whose doubt of all branches of knowledge leads them to suspend judgement regarding the possibility of obtaining an unimpeachable source of knowledge. The 'clarté naturelle' available to man is at once able to withstand Pyrrhonic doubt and the efforts of our reason to plumb its depths (No. 109). In other words, in our clarity we still have areas of darkness, in our knowledge, doubt. The paradoxical quality of this knowledge is attributable to the two ways in which truth may be mediated to man, through the *coeur* and the reason, as the following fragment makes clear. The *coeur* is the faculty which assures us instinctively of the knowledge of first principles, space, time, movement, the infinite progression of numbers. Reason on the other hand is unable to prove first principles, and its demonstrations are ultimately founded upon those principles whose certainty is guaranteed by the *coeur*. We cannot prove rationally that we are not dreaming when we are awake, yet the *coeur* assures us that this is so. From this we conclude not that the reality of our existence is in doubt, but that our reason is weak and vacillating. But few truths are known to us in this way, and most have to be acquired by reason. The essence of our knowledge of reality is certain, supplied by the *coeur*, yet the greater area is exposed to the vacillations of reason. Reason can either confirm or doubt our knowledge which we have from the *coeur*, and therefore we are left with the paradox that we know in part, and at the same time we do not know.

This knowledge only serves to intensify not to palliate our misery, as it plunges us from the first term of the paradox of our nature into a still more paradoxical vortex in which the simultaneous perception of our misery and our greatness serves only to perpetuate the first term:[12]

> La grandeur de l'homme est grande en ce qu'il se connaît misérable; un arbre ne se connaît pas misérable.
> C'est donc être misérable que de [se] connaître misérable, mais c'est être grand que de connaître qu'on est misérable. (No. 114)

Grandeur is inseparable from *misère* as both are simultaneously seen at the centre and circumference of man's condition. Pascal makes each term of the paradox equally valid and adequate to describe man's nature, as he does in fragment 470 which equates 'la plus grande bassesse de l'homme' with 'la plus grande marque de son excellence'. At all times linguistically irreconcilable, both terms are in fact synonymous in the reality which they signify about man. For one term cannot be used without implying and evoking the other: *misère* implies the knowledge that man is miserable, and this in turn implies the *grandeur* of knowing one's misery, just as in Descartes' *cogito* doubt implies thought and thought the ability to doubt itself. Both terms must co-exist to give the only valid evaluation of man in Pascal's view, that is, as an existential paradox. Man can therefore have both self-respect for his capacity to seek truth and happiness and contempt for his inability to possess them; he is caught in the grip of his passions, yet his nature is capable of knowing what is morally good (No. 119). In the Pascalian dialectic one term of the paradox is constantly evoked by the other, so conscious is he of the fact that to omit either is tantamount to total misinterpretation of the reality of human nature. Hence his statement that it is dangerous to show that man is akin to the animals, without at the same time showing his *grandeur*, as did Montaigne when he wrote that 'Nous ne sommes ny au dessus, ny au dessoubs du reste';[13] and it is just as dangerous to show his *grandeur* without his *bassesse*. The greatest danger however consists in ignoring both his *grandeur* and his *bassesse*: 'Il ne faut pas que l'homme croie qu'il est égal aux bêtes, ni qu'il ignore l'un et l'autre, mais qu'il sache l'un et l'autre' (No. 121). So paradoxical is the subject of man, and the instrument which Pascal uses to explain his nature, reason, that either term of the paradox may be used with equally effective logic to prove the other, as Pascal points out by means of the contradictory views of the philosophers in fragment 122: 'La misère se concluant de la grandeur et la grandeur de la misère, les uns ont conclu la misère d'autant plus qu'ils en ont pris pour preuve la grandeur, et les autres concluant la grandeur avec d'autant plus de force qu'ils l'ont conclue de la misère même.'

To say that man is either miserable or great is to affirm the Pascalian paradox of *misère-grandeur* in his nature. Having made man's self-awareness the guarantor of each term of his existential paradox Pascal can now apply a self-validating test to it, just as Descartes confirmed his *cogito* by the act of doubting it, as he writes in the same fragment '. . . qu'à mesure que les hommes ont de lumière ils trouvent et grandeur et misère en l'homme'. The paradoxical circularity of *misère-grandeur* is the outcome of Pascal's use of the arguments of the Sceptics as well as his answer to them. By his use of the same sceptical arguments about man's inability to have real knowledge he establishes a picture of him which could not be more similar in detail and more divergent in implication. The *misère* which he establishes on Montaigne's criteria allows him to lift man out of the circle of perpetual doubt in which the Sceptics enclose him into the larger circle of his own making, in which *misère* perpetually implies *grandeur* and vice versa. The elaboration of the paradox *misère-grandeur* to a level at which one term logically implies the other both intensifies the mystery of man's nature and opens the way for a direct confrontation with the Pyrrhonists as well as with their philosophic counterparts, the dogmatists.

By casting doubt on the most commonly accepted criteria for receiving and evaluating knowledge, the Pyrrhonists reduce man to the position in which he cannot make any statement about the nature of reality which can claim to be more true than any other. All he can claim to possess by way of 'knowledge' are confused fragments of opinions, which by their relative nature cannot amount to knowledge in any real sense. The *Apologie* had already illustrated brilliantly the Pyrrhonist tactic; by exposing man to a series of arguments based on the tropes of Sextus Empiricus he is confronted with a range of incomprehensible and irreconcilable opinions about reality. The sceptical crisis thus engendered dissolves all previously held knowledge into doubt which is so embracing that it has no certainty of its own existence and must doubt itself.[14] Pascal attempts to break the Pyrrhonist hold over man's capacity to possess knowledge about himself not by arguing against the irreparable confusion of opinions which is found everywhere but by intensifying the Pyrrhonist tactic of mystification in his picture of man, who is infinitely more complex than even the Pyrrhonists have ever imagined him to be: 'Quelle chimère est-ce donc que l'homme? quelle nouveauté, quel monstre, quel chaos, quel sujet de contradictions, quel prodige? Juge de toutes choses, imbécile ver de terre, dépositaire du vrai, cloaque d'incertitude et d'erreur, gloire et rebut de l'univers' (No. 131).

Pascal develops an existential crisis of such proportions on the basis of paradox that it envelops even the sceptical crisis of total doubt which the Pyrrhonists engender. On the one hand, he has agreed with them that man does not possess truth, that it is beyond our capacity, whilst using our knowledge of first principles assured by the *coeur* to undermine their universal doubt. On the other hand, those philosophers who explicate man's nature in terms of his capacity to know truth through his reason are as simplistic, for they overlook the weakness of his speculative faculty which their opponents the Pyrrhonists illustrate so well. Once the range and depth of man's paradox are seen, the incompleteness and thus the partial truth of these arguments are manifest. But paradox by itself is not capable of explaining man's nature; it is merely an instrument in Pascal's hands to show that our nature cannot be understood in terms of reason alone, whether it be the reason of those who affirm that man can understand his nature and the world rationally or the self-doubting reasoning of the Pyrrhonists. Paradox is the means by which Pascal demonstrates the insufficiency of the philosophers' views on man, thus preparing our reason and will for the higher explanation of our condition which transcends paradox without demolishing it just as paradox itself has in its turn transcended all the fragmentary truths of the philosophers without demolishing them: 'Connaissez donc, superbe, quel paradoxe vous êtes à vous-même. Humiliez-vous, raison impuissante! Taisez-vous nature imbécile, apprenez que l'homme passe infiniment l'homme et entendez de votre maître votre condition véritable que vous ignorez. Ecoutez Dieu.'

The explanation of man's nature to which the paradox *misère-grandeur* leads is a far greater paradox of metaphysical proportions, involving the doctrine of the fall of man from a state of grace. Pascal takes us through various intermediary stages of this explanation in fragment 131, which in their structure and content remain true to man's paradoxical condition and to the ultimate paradox to which they point.

If man had never experienced corruption, he would still enjoy his former state of innocence, truth, and felicity; if, on the other hand, he had never been anything other than corrupt, he would have no present idea of that state of truth and felicity. On one hand we have an 'image de vérité' which corresponds to that former state of perfection; on the other, we have fallen from this state without having forfeited our awareness of it. The existential paradox of *misère-grandeur* ('nous avons une idée du bonheur et nous ne pouvons y arriver') can only be intensified by our perennial fluctuating between knowledge of and uncertainty about our condition, which renders us 'Incapables d'ignorer absolument et de savoir certainement....' It is not until we are brought to that ultimate paradox which underlies our existential paradox that we see the systematic way in which Pascal's ever-expanding argument of *misère-grandeur* prepares for and necessitates it to the point of being engulfed completely. For Pascal has deliberately made man incomprehensible to himself in order to present him with an explanation of his condition which must not only be incomprehensible if it is to account for the paradox of *misère-grandeur*, but which by its very incomprehensibility commends itself as the most rational way of understanding that paradox. Incomprehensibility is both the guarantee of the truth of the explanation for our condition and the ultimate logic behind our existential paradox. Pascal therefore stresses the incomprehensible nature of the Christian doctrine of original sin and its transmission to all the descendants of the first man, a doctrine which runs counter to all notions of reason and justice, in order to make way for the paradox behind the paradox, which is both source and explanation of our condition: 'Et cependant sans ce mystère, le plus incompréhensible de tous, nous sommes incompréhensibles à nous-mêmes.'[15] The doctrine of original sin presents itself as an overpowering theological and literary *tour de force,* for it is at once the mysterious objective to which all the argument of the *Pensées* leads, as well as the invisible principle which has conducted that argument. Within the economy of the apology it is the culminating point for Pascalian logic which lays bare our *misère-grandeur* only to reveal its own powerlessness in the process of achieving its supreme purpose: '... ce n'est pas par les superbes agitations de notre raison mais par la simple soumission de la raison que nous pouvons véritablement nous connaître'. (In parenthesis at the end of No. 131.)

Pascal moves abruptly away from the abstract mystery of original sin, with its explanation of man which is situated temporally and qualitatively both inside and outside his nature, to the practical consequences which it entails in Chapter VIII on *divertissement*. The existential paradox is stated here in a much lower register than in the previous chapter, but the compression of its form is no less startling and paradoxical than the formulae used to present the mystery of original sin. Considering men in their normal activities, Pascal writes, '... j'ai dit souvent que tout le malheur des hommes vient d'une seule chose, qui est de ne savoir pas demeurer en repos dans une chambre' (No. 136). The most conversational of styles is the vehicle for localizing man's moral and spiritual malaise within the spatial dimensions of a room. Pascal hastens to press home the force of the absolute proposition advanced: all classes of men are dependent on the same need for *divertissement*, and without it, the king is more miserable than the meanest of his subjects who has access to it. As is the case so often in the *Pensées*, the initial statement of paradox is used to overwhelm the reader, and only subsequently does Pascal furnish the reasons which underlie it. He begins with the universal need for *divertissement*, a need proved by the happiness which it induces as well as by the misery which its absence inflicts. After this generalization, however, the analysis of *divertissement* reveals underlying motivations as complex and as paradoxical as they are universal. If it is true that happiness is sought in and through *divertissement*, there is nevertheless a certain lucidity on the part of those who seek it in this way. We know that happiness does not reside in the acquisition of the ostensible aims of *divertissement*, yet this partial lucidity about our condition is both cause and symptom of our blindness as the attitude of the gambler to his game illustrates: 'Il faut qu'il s'y échauffe, et qu'il se pipe lui-même en s'imaginant qu'il serait heureux de gagner ce qu'il ne voudrait pas qu'on lui donnât à condition de ne point jouer....' Our awareness of the lack of intrinsic worth of the objects which we pursue and our paradoxical dependence on them are only to be explained in terms of the two opposing instincts in man's nature which are the consequence of his fall from perfection:

> Ils ont un instinct secret qui les porte à chercher le divertissement et l'occupation au-dehors, qui vient du ressentiment de leurs misères continuelles. Et ils ont un autre instinct secret qui reste de la grandeur de notre première nature, qui leur fait connaître que le bonheur n'est en effet que dans le repos et non pas dans le tumulte. Et de ces deux instincts contraires il se forme en eux un projet confus qui se cache à leur vue dans le fond de leur âme qui les porte à tendre au repos par l'agitation et à se figurer toujours que la satisfaction qu'ils n'ont point leur arrivera si en surmontant quelques difficultés qu'ils envisagent ils peuvent s'ouvrir par là la porte au repos.

We know by one of these instincts that happiness is to be found in *repos* only, and are led by the other to seek it in and through external activity; in seeking the end of the first instinct through the means of the second we compound our misery as we apply a temporary expedient to our permanent malaise. In no area of our activities is our search for happiness more demonstrably pathetic than in our attitude to death, as we attempt to escape from the reality of grief into the illusion which *divertissement* holds out to us. *Divertissement* is finally yet another product of our imagination, persuading us subtly that our happiness lies in illusion and our misery in reality: 'Sans divertissement il n'y a point de joie; avec le divertissement il n'y a point de tristesse.'

Chapter IX takes us back sharply to a consideration of the philosophers' ideas of God and our *summum bonum*, and is principally directed against Epictetus and the Stoics who believed that the chief end of man is to live according to nature and reason. It is by reason that man comes into harmony with the world and grows into the mind and will of God. The attempt by the Stoics to master natural limitations and come to knowledge of the truth through the exercise of reason counterbalances the intention of the Pyrrhonists who seek to divest man of his place at the centre of created being by integrating him into the rest of the animal kingdom. The doctrine of the Stoics is as true and as incomplete in its view of man as the doubt of the Pyrrhonists, for both are unaware of the paradox which unites their views by transcending and explaining them in and through the person of Jesus Christ.

Jesus Christ explains the paradox of man's *misère-grandeur*, of which the philosophers see but one term, by his incarnation, through which he is at once fully man and fully God, thus exemplifying to the highest degree possible both terms of the paradox. In the *Entretien avec M. de Saci* Pascal examines the ideas of Epictetus and Montaigne, which he regards as representative of the only two philosophical attitudes possible to man. Taken in isolation from each other, the emphasis of the first on the primacy of man's reason and of the second on man's inability to achieve knowledge are both deficient assessments of human nature. Taken together, they are incompatible from a rational viewpoint because they are mutually destructive in their nature. But by confronting and annulling each other, they open the way for the truth of the Gospels which reconciles the greatness of our nature which we have through grace with its infirmity which we have through original sin: 'Voilà l'union étonnante et nouvelle que Dieu seul pouvait enseigner, et que lui seul pouvait faire, et qui n'est qu'une image et qu'un effet de l'union ineffable de deux natures dans la seule personne d'un Homme-Dieu.'[16]

It is by faith in the revelation of God in the paradox of Jesus Christ that our own paradox is explained and our *Souverain Bien* assured (Ch. X). Faith is at once the bridge between this universal aspiration and the innumerable ways in which men seek to realize it, and the explanation for those ways (No. 148). We know that countless people have tried in vain to secure this by their own efforts. Knowledge and experience coexist with the illusion that we can succeed where all have failed, and our paradoxical pursuit of happiness once again underlines the depth of a particular need which can only be satisfied with the universal remedy:

'... ce gouffre infini ne peut être rempli que par un objet infini et immuable, c'est-à-dire que par Dieu même'.

The final chapter of the first part of the *Pensées*, Chapter XI, recapitulates the argument by following the ternary structure so basic to the paradox at its core.[17] (1) The visible *grandeur* in man implies that his true felicity is to be found only in God, and his visible *misère* implies that his real unhappiness comes from his separation from God. (2) The philosophers merely compound man's confusion by their contradictory fragments of the truth about his nature, which promote one side of that truth to the detriment of the balance of the total paradox of *misère-grandeur*. Man cannot know the truth about himself if this paradox is not kept intact, for it can only be explained by the greater paradox of Jesus Christ. (3) On the paradox *misère-grandeur* is superimposed the incomprehensible doctrine of the fall of man, which is 'explained' in this chapter in greater detail, not solely from the vantage point of man (as it was at the end of No. 131) but from the standpoint of 'la sagesse de Dieu' (No. 149). Man in the divine perspective which Pascal makes his own, was in a state of sanctity and perfection, but by ordering his life around himself usurped the rightful place of God. Abandoned by God, the god who failed was cast down to the level of the animals, but still retained an indistinct notion of his former status. The fall of man from grace is far from gratuitous, for in his double state of *misère-grandeur* which results there lies the hope of reconciliation with God through the incarnation in Jesus Christ. The Christian religion uses each of the terms of man's paradox to effect the reconciliation with God: it is through the humiliation of him in his *misère*, but not through his nature, that he is brought to seek penance, and it is through grace, but not through his nature, that he is finally reconciled to God. But the objection is raised by Pascal that the union of creaturely man with God is something that cannot be comprehended. This objection, legitimate if one restricts man's nature within the bounds of one term of the Pascalian paradox (*misère*) is answered by intensifying the objection to the point where man is reduced to a level at which he is incapable of understanding any of God's ways: from the point of view of reason, we are as incapable of comprehending union with God as we are of knowing the limits to his mercy: '... nous sommes en effet si bas que nous sommes par nous-mêmes incapables de connaître si sa miséricorde ne peut pas nous rendre capables de lui'. The gap between man and God, widened by the first term of the paradox in the depiction of man's *misère* and apparently narrowed by the superimposure of the second term (*grandeur*) is in reality infinite as Pascal stresses God's omnipotence, man's lack of knowledge of himself and of God, and the presumption of the creature questioning the designs of his creator. Skilfully Pascal reverts to the voice of 'la sagesse de Dieu' to counter the objection that an all-powerful God would not choose to reveal himself to man: God opens the way of salvation to all who truly seek him, but he can withhold it from those who harden their hearts against him and give unmerited grace to others.[18] But another objection is raised, this time not about the possibility of God revealing himself to man, rather about the lack of ambiguity which such a revelation ought to possess. Could such an omnipotent God not have made such an evident self-disclosure that no-one would have been left in doubt? Again Pascal's answer is paradoxical, as it incorporates the freedom of man's will to look for God and the omnipotence of God which enables him to withhold or reveal knowledge of himself as he pleases. Since it is man's corruption that makes him unworthy of God's mercy God can choose to disclose or conceal himself with perfect justice, yet his actions, although omnipotent, are not arbitrary, for he does not hide himself from those who seek him sincerely, just as he does not disclose himself in order to convince all. In fragment 427 Pascal adumbrates the principle of 'Deus absconditus' in answering the point that God does not reveal himself with sufficient clarity to us: sufficient light exists for those who wish to see him, and sufficient darkness for those who do not. In the face of objections that God cannot be known clearly, the Jansenist Pascal gives an answer which is deeply paradoxical in attributing this obscurity in part to God's omnipotence and in part to the degree of sincerity on the part of those who seek him. As he reaches that part of the apology where the will to believe of the unbeliever will be directly challenged (Ch. XII) Pascal subtly emphasizes the primacy of man's will in the search for God. It is the sincere wish of the unbeliever to know the omnipotent 'Deus Absconditus' which encourages the divine self-disclosure.

3

At the beginning of the second part of the *Pensées* Pascal addresses himself directly to man's faculty of will because he now deems this approach both possible and necessary. It is possible because the Christian religion has been shown to be 'vénérable', that is, capable of providing the explanation of the paradox *misère-grandeur* in man's nature which all other lines of thought are unable to resolve because of their human and unitary character. In its paradoxical diagnosis and explanation of human nature the Christian religion is both irrational and rational. It is irrational by virtue of the logically incompatible yet co-existent *misère* and *grandeur* which form man's existential paradox, and it is more rational than any other philosophy because it provides the unique explanation for that paradox. Its explanation is so wide in its scope, moving between the poles of man's sin and God's grace, that it allows Pascal to embrace rather than contradict all other views on man

The Paradox of Pascal's Pensées

as necessary fragments of that explanation. By its all-embracing explanation, the Christian religion has enabled him to refute automatically objections by integrating them into one of the terms of the paradox. The 'art de persuader' is therefore not just to be understood as a mere psychological tactic to make religion 'aimable' to the unbeliever: it originates from the paradox which he sees at the centre of the Christian explanation of man and its unique application to his nature:

> Quand on veut reprendre avec utilité et montrer à un autre qu'il se trompe il faut observer par quel côté il envisage la chose, car elle est vraie ordinairement de ce côté-là et lui avouer cette vérité, mais lui découvrir le côté par où elle est fausse. Il se contente de cela car il voit qu'il ne se trompait pas et qu'il y manquait seulement à voir tous les côtés. (No. 701)

The 'art de persuader' consists in appealing to man's reason by showing him the inadequacy of reason to comprehend the full truth about his nature as well as in appealing through that inadequacy to his will to believe. It is necessary for Pascal to stimulate the will to believe particularly at this point of his apology, for the Christian religion treats a matter of such import to all men that it cannot be considered with mere academic indifference: 'C'en serait assez pour une question de philosophie, mais ici où il va de tout....' (No. 150). The Christian religion not only provides the most complete explanation and therefore the unique answer to man's condition: its subject should compel a sense of existential urgency in all: 'Pour les partis vous devez vous mettre en peine de rechercher la vérité, car si vous mourez sans adorer le vrai principe vous êtes perdu' (No. 158). The objective in the search for truth is of such paramount importance that Pascal classifies people into three groups according to their respective attitudes towards it. There are those who serve God because they have found him, those who have not found the truth in him but who seek for it, and those who live without seeking or finding it (No. 160). It is clear that to Pascal's rigorously logical mind it was incomprehensible that people should know of the importance of the Christian religion to them and nevertheless remain indifferent to it. In fragment 427, which probably belongs by the nature of its argument to the beginning of the second part of the apology, Pascal describes his attitudes towards those people who search earnestly for the truth and those who live without apparent concern for it.[19] For those unbelievers 'qui gémissent sincèrement dans ce doute' (that is about the belief in the immortality of the soul) he experiences nothing but compassion. But it is a compassion compelled by their Pascalian reaction to their doubts which is manifest in the strenuous efforts on their part to come to know the truth. Their search exemplifies the paradoxical state of our natural knowledge which makes us

'Incapables d'ignorer absolument et de savoir certainement' (No. 131). His attitude towards the unbeliever who is indifferent to the question of what will happen to him after death is more complex, pointing up the way in which his logic and Christian instinct seem to contradict each other only to combine to reinforce powerfully his 'art de persuader'. It is by logic and not by spiritual zeal, he avers, that he is led to adopt the tactic of using what he himself terms invective against those unbelievers who flaunt their indifference to Christianity (No. 156) in order to awaken them to a matter which is of the utmost self-interest:

> Cette négligence en une affaire où il s'agit d'eux-mêmes, de leur éternité, de leur tout, m'irrite plus qu'elle ne m'attendrit; elle m'étonne et m'épouvante: c'est un monstre pour moi. Je ne dis pas ceci par le zèle pieux d'une dévotion spirituelle. J'entends au contraire qu'on doit avoir ce sentiment par un principe d'intérêt humain et par un intérêt d'amour-propre: il ne faut pour cela que voir ce que voient les personnes les moins éclairées. (No. 427)

'Invective' appears to be the last resort of Pascal's logic in his attempt to activate the will to believe in the person who remains bovinely indifferent to his situation in the universe, asking no questions about his origin, nature or destiny, but who allows himself to be borne along by circumstances to a death to which he has given no thought. Therefore Pascal strips him of every rational attribute, dehumanizing him after he himself has proved dead to the instinct which elevates him above the animal kingdom, and makes him into 'une si extravagante créature', redundant to himself and to all men. Indeed such an unbeliever is so bereft of reason that Pascal deems it an honour for the Christian religion to have such an antagonist, since he exemplifies most fully the first term of the Christian truth about man, that his nature is corrupt. Pascal has such a firm hold on reason that the sheer incomprehensibility of someone being sensitive to his temporal interest whilst remaining blind to his eternal one to which his nature points inexorably can only indicate a supernatural cause: 'C'est un enchantement incompréhensible, et un assoupissement surnaturel, qui marque une force toute-puissante qui le cause.' Yet he has at the same time an equally firm hold on the truth of religion; people who are indifferent to truth are not worthy of our concern, he writes, nevertheless it is necessary to have all the charity of the religion which they despise in order not to despise them. This attitude is imposed not by mere piety alone but springs from Pascal's vision of the humanly unpredictable and paradoxical effects of grace operating in human nature:

> Mais, parce que cette religion nous oblige de les regarder toujours, tant qu'ils seront en cette vie, comme capables de la grâce qui peut les éclairer, et de croire qu'ils peuvent être dans peu de temps plus

remplis de foi que nous ne sommes, et que nous pouvons au contraire tomber dans l'aveuglement où ils sont, il faut faire pour eux ce que nous voudrions qu'on fît pour nous si nous étions à leur place, et les appeler à avoir pitié d'eux-mêmes, et à faire au moins quelques pas pour tenter s'ils ne trouveront pas de lumières. (No. 427)

Grace begins at the point at which reason ends and operates without its necessary intermediation, but still compels the Christian to point the unbeliever towards the truth.

Such extreme cases of indifference to religion are ultimately inexplicable but not irredeemable. Most examples of professed scorn for religion are explicable by the fact that external attitude does not correspond to inward conviction: '... la plupart de ceux qui s'en mêlent se contrefont et ne sont pas tels en effet'. Pascal's sinuous logic imperceptibly brings this type of unbeliever within the orbit of his argument in two interrelated stages: if such people cannot be Christians, then let them at least be 'honnêtes gens' who abhor pretence, and they may then recognize that there are only two kinds of people who may be described as reasonable: 'ou ceux qui servent Dieu de tout leur coeur parce qu'ils le connaissent, ou ceux qui le cherchent de tout leur coeur parce qu'ils ne le connaissent pas'. The only rational attitude on the part of the unbeliever is that of the earnest seeker after truth.

The wager fragment (No. 418 in *Papiers non classés*) addresses itself to this second category of unbelievers who are not ill-disposed towards the Christian religion and are amenable to persuasion. It probably has its place at the beginning of the second part of the apology, where other related fragments of the *Copie* are placed by Pascal which sketch the argument for belief in God in similar terms of gain or loss (Nos. 153, 154, 158, 159). It constitutes as such not just a brilliant and more sustained set-piece but rather in the words of J. Mantoy 'l'entrée d'un ouvrage d'apologétique' in the overall design of the *Pensées*.[20] With its argument in favour of belief in God couched in mathematical terms of the ratios of gain to loss, the wager represents in a spectacular form the climax of the basic paradox underlying the *Pensées*, which consists in attempting to render faith in God as amenable as possible to logic whilst recognizing the impossibility of so doing. The progression of the argument to the unbeliever is conditioned explicitly by this paradox, as the four movements after the initial admissions of the difficulties in a finite creature having knowledge of God reveal. In the question of the existence of God, Pascal initially places reason out of court; then the argument for eternal life is couched in terms of the computation of the ratios between gain and loss in the wager and appeals simultaneously to the reason and the will; having overthrown the rational objections of the unbeliever to the idea of the wager by mathematical logic, Pascal transcends reason itself by asking him to imitate other Christians and in so doing stimulate his will to believe and prepare the way for faith in

God; finally, there is an appeal to the unbeliever's reason and will as Pascal compares the certainty of the infinite gain to be won in accepting the wager for God's existence with the smallness of the risk to be taken. By making the proposition of belief in the existence of God as rational and as attractive as possible to the unbeliever whilst admitting that reason itself can offer no absolute proof, the wager marks the climax of Pascal's attempt to combine the 'art d'agréer' and the 'art de convaincre', to make religion 'vénérable' and 'aimable' at the same time. The wager is then by its mode of argument and the proposition argued a wager within the larger wager of the *Pensées*, for in both it is God alone who converts, disposing the heart of the unbeliever to belief, with or without the intermediary of human argumentation. Yet Pascal is compelled to enter into the wager of the apology for Christianity by his understanding of and his reaction to man's situation in the universe, just as the unbeliever in the wager fragment is compelled to wager whether actively or passively by the very fact that he is 'embarqué', that is, finds himself in his particular existential situation.[21]

The main part of the dialogue with the unbeliever begins with the proposition that if there is a God, then we can know neither his nature nor his existence by reason alone. The objection to Christian belief on the grounds that its adherents are unable to prove it by reason is in any case invalid for they in fact claim that their religion is pure folly to those who do not believe in it. To ground it rationally would be to negate the basis for their belief since the strongest argument in its favour comes from its lack of proof. Since the question of God's existence can neither be proved nor disproved by reason alone, the unbeliever is brought to the point at which Pascal imposes a temporary suspension of reason by means of which he introduces the intrinsically irrational concept of the wager into the dialogue: 'Que gagerez-vous? par raison vous ne pouvez faire ni l'un ni l'autre; par raison vous ne pouvez défaire nul des deux.'

The unbeliever cannot consequently accuse those who choose to believe in the existence of God of being wrong since reason cannot determine the rightness or the wrongness of the choice. But can he not point out that they are wrong in having made a choice in the first place, since the reasons for and against their belief in God are equipollent? '... le juste est de ne point parier'. In the existential situation of man, however, Pascal finds the compelling reason overruling the attitude of neutrality towards the question which would appear to impose itself by the fact that Christian belief is not totally amenable to reason, just as he employed the knowledge of first principles to overrule the doubts of the Pyrrhonists regarding man's ability to attain objective knowledge in Chapter VIII.[22] Whichever choice the unbeliever may make, he cannot be more irrational in one than in the other. Pascal thus takes care to displace reason from the initial part of his proposition, overruling the rational objections of the unbeliever and concentrating his argument on the latter's willingness to accept it. 'If you wager in favour of God's

The Paradox of Pascal's Pensées

existence and win, you win everything, that is, eternal happiness: if you lose, you lose nothing.' The objection of the unbeliever, to the effect that he knows that he must wager but fears that he is placing too much at stake in doing so, forces Pascal to introduce the mathematical argument involving the ratios of gain to loss. Although reason cannot prove the existence of God in an absolute sense, there are reasons which may be advanced in favour of accepting the wager that he does exist. This argument begins by situating the ratios involved on a finite level. The wager in favour of God's existence is worthwhile even if the wagerer stands to gain only two lives and his stake involves equal chances of loss and gain; it is more advantageous if there is a chance of gaining three lives since he is in the position of having to wager in any event. On the lowest level of ratios, that of finite gain to finite chance of winning or losing, the wager presents itself as a rational proposition. Pascal seeks to make it more attractive to the will of the unbeliever by increasing the gain from finite to infinite proportions: 'Mais il y a une éternité de vie de bonheur.' In this case the unbeliever would be wrong to refuse to wager one life for two or three lives even though he may only have one of an infinite number of chances in his favour in a game in which he stands to win an infinite number of infinitely happy lives. The attractiveness of the proposition is still further enhanced by reducing the ratio of the chances of gain to loss to finite proportions, retaining the infinite amount to be gained and the finite stake, the unbeliever's earthly life. The proposition therefore attains its climax with the paradoxical wager which involves infinite gain and the finite ratio of the chance of gain to the chances of loss: 'Cela ôte tout parti partout où est l'infini et où il n'y a pas infinité de hasards de perte contre celui de gain.' In the existential situation of having to wager for or against God's existence, it is unreasonable to retain a finite form of life rather than risk it for the infinite gain which could be won by believing in his existence.

Rational objections still remain in spite of the apparent attractiveness of the proposition. Does the infinite distance between certain risk and uncertain gain not make the entire proposition infinitely irrational? Pascal's answer proceeds in three stages. All gamblers take a certain risk with the hope of uncertain gain, but the certainty of the finite stake in favour of uncertain finite gain does not mean that they are acting irrationally. The reason for this is that there is not infinite distance between the certainty of what one stakes and the uncertainty of the gain, but rather between the certainty of winning and the certainty of losing, since the uncertainty of gain stands in proportion to the chances of winning or losing. The certainty of the stake in the wager is equal to the uncertainty of the amount to be gained, but not infinitely distant from it. Since the chances of gain and of loss are equal and the stake is finite and infinite gain may be won, the proposition is at once infinitely rational and attractive.

Pascal has gone as far as he can in his attempt to make the wager for

God's existence and eternal life as rational and as attractive as possible; but with the admission of the unbeliever that although he recognizes the force of the existential and mathematical reasons in its favour he still cannot bring himself to the point at which he believes, a different approach must be adopted. His inability to believe proceeds now not from his reason but from the fact that his will is controlled by his passions. In this new situation, rational demonstration is of no avail, but Pascal elaborates a technique which may enable the unbeliever to minimize the influence of his passions over his will to believe. He proposes that the unbeliever should imitate the attitudes of those people who have found themselves in the same state of unbelief but who now believe: he will begin to believe in the way in which they began: 'C'est en faisant tout comme s'ils croyaient, en prenant de l'eau bénite, en faisant dire des messes, etc. Naturellement même cela vous fera croire et vous abêtira.' At first sight it seems that Pascal contradicts all his previous arguments in asking the unbeliever to submit his mind to the mechanical imitation of gestures and rituals which do not correspond to his actual state of belief. But it is not at all a question of denying the foregoing argument, rather of extending and complementing it to satisfy all the different facets in man's complex attitude towards belief. Fragment 821 contains remarks on the ways in which belief comes into being and may be fostered which are helpful in understanding the psychological undertones of the enigmatic term 'abêtira'.[23] It begins with the famous sentence: 'Car il ne faut pas se méconnaître, nous sommes automate autant qu'esprit' and in consequence argues that the methods of persuading the unbeliever to belief in religion are not to be simply equated with demonstrative proofs. Rational persuasion is not equivalent to conversion, but habit and custom bridge the gap imperceptibly and surely between reasoned argument and faith by building upon what reason has already achieved in the unbeliever's mind: 'Enfin il faut avoir recours à elle [la coutume] quand une fois l'esprit a vu où est la vérité afin de nous abreuver et nous teindre de cette créance qui nous échappe à toute heure, car d'en avoir toujours les preuves présentes c'est trop d'affaire.' If we are as much machine as mind, in the decisive act of belief we are nevertheless governed more by the first than by the second, for if that part of us which follows custom unthinkingly ('l'automate') is not disposed towards belief at the same time as our mind, we will not be converted to belief. The imitation of others is therefore both a technique and a necessary element in belief, for custom is nothing less than a second nature. The fragment which follows the wager points to the complementary roles played by both these aspects of custom, as they combine to lead us without thinking to the place where reason is already: 'La coutume est notre nature. Qui s'accoutume à la foid la croit....'[24]

Having transcended reason in order to dispose it towards belief, Pascal reverts to a summary of the wager and formulates a rational response for the unbeliever which anticipates his 'conversion' to the proposition advanced. He will now see such great certainty of gain where formerly he could only see uncertainty, since he will know that he has wagered for something infinite and certain and has risked nothing. The dialogue and the 'conversion' climax both Pascal's method of persuasion, consisting as it does in viewing the issues through the eyes of the interlocutor in order to lead him beyond his natural view of the truth to a more complete view of the truth, and his paradoxical attempt to render belief in religion at once logical to the mind and desirable to the will.

The apparently contradictory but in fact complementary roles of reason and custom in belief provide an excellent example of the subject of Chapter XIII, *Soumission et usage de la raison*. For Pascal, custom ('soumission') and the use of one's reason would only seem to oppose each other on a linguistic level. True Christianity, as No. 167 points out, consists in exercising both simultaneously. Submission and use of reason are not to be seen as representing mutually exclusive extremities in the operation of the mind but the harmonious functioning of reason which only Christianity is able to impart to it. The extremities which Christianity avoids are rather the wish to submit every truth of religion to the scrutiny of reason on the one hand (by which religion forfeits its mysterious and supernatural character and thus its unique ability to explain the otherwise inexplicable existential paradox of man) and the overriding of rational principles on the other, by which religion degenerates into something absurd and ridiculous (for it is by reason that man perceives his *misère* and can claim his *grandeur*) (No. 173). In other words, Christianity neither simply assimilates religion to reason nor dispenses with any of its operations. Few Christians however understand the proper exercise of reason in faith — many go to the extremity of credulous belief ('superstition') which is the opposite extremity of free-thought ('libertinage') (No. 179). Between these extremities, however, Christianity teaches reason how to operate properly by bringing it to the point at which it acknowledges its inadequacy: 'Il est donc juste qu'elle se soumette quand elle juge qu'elle se doit soumettre' (No. 174). The Christian view of reason allows proper scope to all the normal operations of the mind, such as doubting and rational demonstration, unlike the Pyrrhonist who applies doubt universally and the geometrician who does not proceed beyond demonstrative proof (No. 170). 'Soumission' climaxes the true exercise of doubt and of reason, for the abdication by reason of its claims to evaluate all areas of truth is both the outcome of properly exercised doubt and reason and the highest proof of its worth: 'La dernière démarche de la raison est de reconnaître qu'il y a une infinité de choses qui la surpassent. Elle n'est que faible si elle ne va jusqu'à connaître cela' (No. 188). Implicit in this highest exercise of reason is faith, faith on the part of reason in its own power to interpret phenomena with accuracy and faith in the evidence which that power provides of its inability to explain ultimate reality. Faith is the natural continuation of reason as it transcends itself and not its opposite. Similarly, faith is not the opposite of sight, but continues at the point where sight can see no further (No. 185). Put into the explicitly paradoxical terms of St Paul, religion is both 'sage' and 'folle' at the same time; although its proofs may be evaluated rationally, faith begins where reason ends — in the stumbling-block of the Cross of Christ (No. 842).[25]

In no question is the right use of our reason better illustrated than in that involving our knowledge of God (Ch. XIV). We can know God only in and through Jesus Christ. All the claims to prove God's existence without the knowledge of Christ rely on proofs which are relative and weak, for the validity of metaphysical proofs does not as a rule outlast the time it takes to demonstrate them (No. 190).[26] Yet if reason is powerless to prove God's existence beyond all doubt, it enables us to prove the existence of Jesus Christ by means of prophecies, miracles, and historical proofs. Because Christ is the mediator between God and man we are assured of knowledge of God, and without his intermediation, we know nothing about God: 'Mais par J.-C. et en J.-C. on prouve Dieu et on enseigne la morale et la doctrine. J.-C. est donc le véritable Dieu des hommes' (No. 189). Fragment 449 makes Jesus Christ the centre, focus and explanation of all things: 'Jésus-Christ est l'objet de tout, et le centre où tout tend. Qui le connaît connaît la raison de toutes choses.' Jesus Christ is the supreme reason for our knowledge of God and of ourselves, and all knowledge which bypasses him must therefore be partial and ultimately irrational. Knowledge of God without that of Jesus Christ leads to *orgueil*, whereas knowledge of our misery without the knowledge of God in Christ leads us to despair. Knowledge of Jesus Christ is the balancing *milieu* between *misère* and *orgueil*, enabling us to see him as the paradoxical point of reference and explanation for our own existential paradox: 'La connaissance de J.-C. fait le milieu parce que nous y trouvons, et Dieu et notre misère' (No. 192). In him we see the misery of our sinful nature and God's redemption through his death on the Cross. The paradox of *misère-grandeur* in man is but an aspect of Jesus Christ, the mediator between God and man, 'la raison de toutes choses' to whom our highest reason can but submit.

If knowledge of Jesus Christ — the divine *milieu* which situates all our fragments of knowledge and experience in the true perspective — provides the supreme explanation for reality, then there could be no greater contrast imaginable for Pascal than that between this *milieu* and the *milieu* which man occupies in the world. For apart from this knowledge of himself in Jesus Christ, his situation in a particular location in infinity ('ce milieu') is wholly contingent (No. 194). In the famous fragment entitled 'Disproportion de l'homme' (No. 199) the term *milieu* is used to locate man's point of reference between the infinite greatness and smallness of the universe, and as a means of defining his paradoxical relationship to the two infinities. Pascal progresses towards this definition by describing the two terms which make up the infinite paradox of the universe: the first term projects man and his environment into a series of ever-expanding conceptions of the universe and he is progressively diminished by comparison. Man is first of all placed within the majesty of nature, then the earth is seen as a mere speck in comparison to the sun's orbit, which in turn cannot be measured with the extent of the galaxies, and finally the visible world is merged into the immensity of which imagination alone can conceive and which is still incommensurate with the infinitely expanding universe: 'C'est une sphère infinie dont le centre est partout, la circonférence nulle part. Enfin c'est le plus grand caractère sensible de la toute-puissance de Dieu que notre imagination se perde dans cette pensée.'

The second term of the infinite paradox progressively enlarges man by contrast to the infinite smallness of the universe, which is illustrated by the microscopic sub-division *ad infinitum* of the anatomy of the tiniest insect. Spacially, man occupies the *milieu* between the infinity of the ever-expanding universe and the infinity of the ever-retracting universe and it is his relationship with the two infinities which allows Pascal to describe him as 'Un néant à l'égard de l'infini, un tout à l'égard du néant, un milieu entre rien et tout, infiniment éloigné de comprendre les extrêmes, la fin des choses et leurs principes sont pour lui invinciblement cachés dans un secret impénétrable'.[27]

Man is simultaneously at both extremities of the infinite universe, at once 'un néant', 'un tout', but also 'un milieu'. His position precludes him from ever piercing to the essence of phenomena, for he cannot hope to see into the working of either infinite greatness or smallness, but must be satisfied with fragmentary knowledge, a glimpse of 'quelque apparence du milieu des choses'. Thus in spite of his overweening presumption, his capacity remains strictly finite, and he occupies the *milieu* only in Pascal's conception of the universe. For the only *milieu* at which it is possible to know and mediate truth of the two infinities is an infinite *milieu* not situated merely by its quantitative aspect between the two infinities, as is the *milieu* of man, but rather one which is able to understand simultaneously the essential qualities of both: 'Ces extrémités se touchent et se réunissent à force de s'être éloignées et se retrouvent en Dieu, et en Dieu seulement.' Man's *milieu* on the other hand is situated between his desire to seek knowledge which elevates him above the animals and in which his true dignity resides and his inability to see into the life of things. We remain 'incapables de savoir certainement et d'ignorer absolument', pulled simultaneously between our desire for knowledge and our ignorance of final causes, and to suppress either term of our paradoxical *milieu* is to suppress man himself: 'C'est sortir de l'humanité que de sortir du milieu' (No. 518). As H. Friedrich has well pointed out, man's *milieu* in Pascal's view is far different from the *milieu* of Montaigne, which involves the renunciation of attitudes and beliefs counter to the relative nature of man and the consequent acquiescence in all the weakness and contradictions of our humanity: 'La grandeur de l'ame n'est pas tant tirer à mont et tirer avant comme sçavoir se ranger et circonscrire. Elle tient pour grand tout ce qui est assez, et montre sa hauteur à aimer mieux les choses moyennes que les eminentes.' The *milieu* of Montaigne rejoins the harmony and tranquillity of the natural order of things, which man's inordinate thirst for knowledge threatens to disrupt: 'O que c'est un doux et mol chevet, et sain, que l'ignorance et l'incuriosité, à reposer une teste bien faicte!'[28] To Pascal, this desire for knowledge situates man's paradoxical *milieu* above the beasts but below God, in which he vacillates until he finds the divine *milieu* in Jesus Christ without which the human one is inexplicable.

All the apparently different tiers of human intelligence are levelled in man's *milieu* of partial knowledge and partial ignorance of the universe and himself: 'Ce milieu qui nous est échu en partage étant toujours distant des extrêmes, qu'importe qu'un autre ait un peu plus d'intelligence des choses s'il en a, et s'il les prend un peu de plus haut, n'est-il pas toujours infiniment éloigné du bout. . . .' This *milieu* unites us all in our inability to know even basic principles of the universe which seem most familiar to us, such as the space which we occupy and the time in which we live. Because of the interrelated nature of all knowledge, to know man is to know the elements in which he lives, for one cannot know the part without knowing the whole. Pascal's *milieu* serves on the one hand to locate man spatially between the two infinities of greatness and smallness, revealing at once his external significance and insignificance in the universe, and on the other hand to demonstrate from an epistemological standpoint his inability to know the principles which govern the universe and himself. It is a concept which on a cosmic scale allows Pascal simultaneously to elevate and abase man, and so reinforces powerfully the central objective of the *Pensées* which is to point to the Christian faith as the only *milieu* able to harmonize the antinomies in his psychology and correct his sense of disorientation in the universe.

The criterion which determines the truth and error of the various religions is their ability or inability to provide man with the *milieu* where the greatness and the littleness of his nature may be fully explained: 'Qui l'a connue [notre nature] que la chrétienne?' (No. 215). The existential paradox of man underlies Pascal's validation of the claims of the Christian religion to be the true one, whether he looks at

The Paradox of Pascal's Pensées

the spectrum of religions from an abstract or a psychological viewpoint. If there is a unique principle governing the universe, then true religion must teach us how to adore it. But since we are unable to love a principle beyond ourselves, such a religion would have to show us how to overcome our limitations. Our inability to transcend self-love and the possibility of so doing are explained by the doctrine of the fall of man from grace impairing our relationship with God and by the restoration of that relationship through Jesus Christ (No. 205). The love of God is both the hallmark of the true religion and the only remedy for man's concupiscence (No. 214). Outside the divine *milieu*, other religions err by explaining man by one term of his paradox only — viewing him as either uncorrupted, or in despair, to the detriment of the other term and his paradoxical truth. The simple teaching of the Gospels brings us back to this true *milieu* in which the two terms meet and are explained but not abolished, for they are still resident even in redeemed human nature. Thus the believer still bears the seeds of corruption in his heart which render him liable to sin, error and death during his life, and the possibility of redemption is still open to the most impious unbeliever (No. 208). Christianity is further true for it not only explains human nature by the universal condition of *misère* and *grandeur* but it is also able to bring into balance the demands of reason and custom which vary from individual to individual. It satisfies simultaneously man's reasoning and his need for tradition by at once instructing the minds of those who follow ceremonial and using ceremonies to abase the pride of the intellectual (No. 219). By its ability to balance delicately the specific needs of the individual, Christianity reveals itself as the universal answer to man's need.

Pascal chooses the religion of Muhammad to point to the different values of human and divine religions. From the point of view of reason, he was a successful religious leader and Jesus Christ a failure. The former secured wealth and temporal power, the latter eschewed both, taking a course which led to his own death as well as that of his followers. Within the divine perspective, which transcends reason and seems paradoxical to us, human success is tantamount to failure and human failure to success (No. 209). The Scriptures are likewise superior to the Koran for paradoxical reasons: they are not less cryptic and obscure, for in places they are just as unintelligible to us, but what is clear is overwhelmingly more admirable in meaning and in the proofs which they give for their truth than the clearest parts of the Koran (No. 218).

In Chapter XVII the universality of the Christian religion is again invoked as one proof of its truth, but a fresh element is introduced into the comparison with other religions which inevitably is connected with the paradox of man's nature. Whereas the religion of Judaism is exclusively for its adherents, the redemption of Christ is available to all men by the very fact that it explains and embraces that paradox.

Considered within the state of human nature, therefore, Christians are on the same level as those people such as the Jews who are set apart by an esoteric belief as well as the pagans who have a rudimentary one: 'Les Juifs charnels et les païens ont des misères et les chrétiens aussi' (No. 222). Yet the two extremities of Judaism and paganism are united in that they have no present redeemer, and the Christian religion occupies the true *milieu* between them since its adherents have both *misères* and redemption.

From Chapter XVIII onwards (*Fondements*) Pascal deals with the ways in which God chooses to disclose himself to mankind through the Scriptural signs, prophecies and miracles. He is at once aware of the inadequacy of rational proofs in themselves to convince of the truth of the Christian religion, and of the necessity of submitting them, since the truth must be able to embrace the wholeness of man's nature of which reason is a part. Since the ways of reason are not those of God's truth however Pascal is driven towards the use of paradox as the only means of reconciling their divergencies in the same formula. He does not therefore see an unambiguously clear relationship between the Old Testament prophecies about the coming of Christ and his claims to fulfil them, for the hallmark of their interpretation is not clarity but paradox. The prophets did not prophesy that Jesus Christ would reveal himself manifestly to all men as God, but that he would be 'un Dieu véritablement caché' and that this deliberate obscurity would be a stumbling-block to many (No. 228). Thus it is by paradox that the rejection of Christ by the people from whom the prophets originated is reconciled with the Christian claim that Christ was the promised Messiah in Chapter XXIV, *Prophéties*. Fragment 324 sets down two apparently irreconcilable facts which appear to disqualify the Christian claim: the prophecies said that the Messiah would be king of the Jews and the Gentiles, yet both united to put Jesus Christ to death. These facts however are harmonized in and through the death of Christ by which the prophecy is fulfilled:

> Qu'il serait roi des Juifs et des gentils, et voilà ce roi des Juifs et des gentils opprimé par les uns et les autres qui conspirent à sa mort dominant des uns et des autres, et détruisant et le culte de Moïse dans Jérusalem, qui en était le centre, dont il fait sa première église et le culte des idoles dans Rome qui en était le centre et dont il fait sa principale église.

In the fulfilment of the prophecy, the Judaic tradition enshrining it is at once vindicated by the coming of Christ and overthrown by the foundation of the Christian Church which embraces Gentiles as well as Jews. The manner of Christ's coming as well as of his rejection by the Jews confirms the simultaneously clear and unclear character of prophecy in general: 'Pour faire qu'en voyant ils ne voient point et qu'en entendant ils n'entendent point rien ne pouvait être mieux fait' (No. 337). The same paradoxical intention in the teachings of Jesus Christ is seen as a mark of the continuity of the true prophetic spirit and the wisdom of God in him '... qui déclare son dessein et d'aveugler et d'éclaircir et qui mêle des obscurités parmi des choses claires qui arrivent' (No. 344). Rational objections to the prophecies on the ground of their lack of clarity are only valid on condition that the criterion for the distinction of true from false prophecy is a purely human one. When the design of God is rather to hide himself his obscure presence becomes the validating sign of true religion (No. 242). God wishes to dispose the will of man to belief rather than his reason, and the full clarity of his revealed purpose would merely hinder the operation of the will by enlightening the mind (No. 234). The Christian and the unbeliever are both subject to the same paradoxical revelation which God chooses to give of himself, for there is sufficient clarity to enlighten the former as there is obscurity to humble him, and sufficient obscurity to hide God from the latter as there is clarity to leave him without excuse for his unbelief (No. 236).[29]

The exegesis of Scripture must also have the same paradoxical character as prophecy. Since it emanates from God, it must be both beyond man's reason and amenable to rational interpretation if it is at all to account for our condition. On one hand, divine truth is conveyed by human means in the Testaments, and must appear contradictory to our reason. On the other, God's truth is by definition incapable of contradiction, therefore sound exegetical method must make apparent contradictions accord together (No. 257). The figurative method of interpreting the Old Testament is consequently proposed by Pascal as the only one capable of harmonizing what at first sight appear to be contradictions: 'Quand la parole de Dieu qui est véritable est fausse littéralement elle est vraie spirituellement. *Sede a dextris meis*: cela est faux littéralement, donc cela est vrai spirituellement' (No. 272). God's word, articulated by man's utterance, has of necessity the literal and limited expression attaching to all human speech: 'Car les choses de Dieu étant inexprimables elles ne peuvent être dites autrement....' (No. 272). Contradictions in Scripture are thus as necessary as the figurative exegesis which transcends them. Unspiritual Jews could only see one aspect of the multifaceted figure of divine truth, that which was immediately evident to them at a particular time and place. They were unable for example to reconcile the prophecy of the coming Messiah who would live for ever with the crucifixion of Jesus Christ, or understand his claim to pre-exist Abraham (No. 256). Similarly, they believed that their Law would last for ever and that God's approval could be earned only by adherence to all its demands. But the Law was not a self-sufficient end as it pointed to Christ as the one who would fulfil it perfectly by revealing its true meaning: 'Il a rompu le voile et a découvert l'esprit' (No. 260). Christ fulfils the Law, as St Paul showed, not by teaching the circumcision of the body, but of the heart, and by ushering in the kingdom of God not in flesh and blood, but as an inward and spiritual reality in the life of the believer (No. 270).[30] One word characterizes the fulfilment of the letter of the Law by the spirit of Christ — charity. This is at once the central objective towards which all the rest of Scripture tends and the principle which unifies in itself all apparently contradictory passages: 'Tout ce qui ne va point à l'unique bien en est la figure' (No. 270). But since we are human, God has chosen to mediate his central truth to us in diverse ways:

> Dieu diversifie ainsi cet unique précepte de charité pour satisfaire notre curiosité qui recherche la diversité par cette diversité qui nous mène toujours à notre unique nécessaire. Car une seule chose est nécessaire et nous aimons la diversité, et Dieu satisfait à l'un et à l'autre par ces diversités qui mènent au seul nécessaire. (No. 270)

In Chapter XX, *Rabbinage*, Pascal finds abundant evidence in rabbinical writings such as the Talmud, Mishna and Gemara for traditional beliefs similar to the biblical doctrine of the fall of man, as well as the anticipation that man's nature will be redeemed from its consequences. Historical evidence from the earliest times is thus given in favour of the dual nature of man, and the existential paradox of *misère-grandeur* corroborated by ancient documentation. Pascal also finds an argument in favour of the Christian religion in the fact of its continuing existence since time immemorial in defiance of all reason and probability (Ch. XXI, *Perpétuité*). It was anticipated before the biblical stories of creation by pagans who worshipped one true God through nature, and existed in inchoate form among the Patriarchs who believed in the fall of man from grace and dimly foresaw the coming of the promised Messiah. Although they and their successors lived in times of apostasy, they still clung to the belief that God would one day send his redeemer to deliver his faithful people. Amid all the schisms, mutations and perpetual opposition the Church still exists, now on the verge of destruction, yet always brought back as it were from the dead without its eternal message compromised by temporal interests (No. 281). Its existence is even more incomprehensible to reason when one remembers that it is the sole religion which seeks to curb the natural desires and passions of its members and runs directly counter to common sense (No. 284).

The relative importance which Pascal gives to his proofs for the Christian religion may be seen clearly in fragment 291 where he accumulates them only in order to demolish them at one fell swoop in favour of a more convincing and paradoxical proof. The proofs of the historicity of the Christian religion, together with its miracles and prophecies, are all extremely impressive when taken in themselves as well as corporately — but he is quite content to reject all of them in favour of

The Paradox of Pascal's Pensées

the folly of the Cross. He uses the paradoxical argument of St Paul in the first chapter of his first *Epistle to the Corinthians*, that the foolishness of God is wiser than the wisdom of men, to demolish rational proof and in so doing to demonstrate more effectively the irrational and overpowering divine reason which enables Christianity to dispense with human reason in its claims to be the true religion. He gives the Pauline paradox a practical extension which is not explicit in St Paul's use of it. Christians who reinforce their argument for their religion by rational proofs affirm that such proofs are totally ineffectual in changing man's moral nature so that he may know and love God. The 'folie' of the Cross alone is capable of effecting this change; in its origins the Christian religion is 'folle' and yet it is efficacious and wise in view of the wisdom which it imparts to those who believe and which cannot be procured by human wisdom.

In *Preuves de Jésus-Christ* (Ch. XXIII) Pascal is aware of the need to prove the authority of Jesus Christ from impartial secular sources in history and to deal with objections involving alleged contradictions in the accounts given by the Gospels of Christ's life and the charge that the story of the resurrection was fabricated by the disciples. But he devotes more space in his argument for the divinity of Christ to the latter's moral nature and to the relationship which it establishes with the human paradox. The humanity and divinity of Jesus Christ are evidenced by the fact that the Church has always had as much difficulty in establishing his humanity as his divinity (No. 307). Conversely, the Jews who sought to discover whether or not he was God demonstrated above all his humanity (No. 306). The Church and the Jews both approach the question of his nature with opposing preconceptions; yet the particular term of the paradox which they establish independently converges in favour of his divine and human duality.

Although Jesus Christ embodies the human paradox in order to explain it, the perfection of his moral nature places him beyond the orders of *corps* and *esprit*, which include the mass of humanity, into the order of the saints, that is the order of *charité*. Each order occupies its place in Pascal's moral hierarchy according to the degree to which its values are fashioned by materiality or immateriality. In the lowest of the orders, that of the *corps*, the values are based on the principle of crude materialism: to it belong all those people who strive for earthly dominion, power, ambition and wealth, and who seek no other self-fulfilment than that offered by the gratification of their senses. The honours distributed by this order have no value or attraction for those who belong to the higher order of *esprit*, in which the values of imagination, creativity and genius displace materialism. But the third and highest of the orders is that of wisdom and *charité*, transcending the natural orders of materialism and thought, for it alone derives its values from God. The values of the first order are formed predominantly by the sense of sight, as what is seen by the eye becomes the object coveted; the values of the second are fashioned by the mind's eye; but the saints are indifferent to the temporal values of these orders, for beyond the worlds of sight and thought they perceive values which can neither be diminished nor increased by those of time. It is to this supernatural order that Jesus Christ belongs, having no material acquisition or pretence to power or display of knowledge, but just humility, patience and holiness. But the apparent lowliness of his coming is only such to sight and reason. By his paradoxical values he overturns all human assumptions about life and man, for his appeal goes beyond the eye and the reason of man to the heart, the repository of our truest judgement: 'O qu'il est venu en grande pompe et en une prodigieuse magnificence aux yeux du coeur et qui voyent la sagesse' (No. 308).

Since so much of the *Pensées* deals with the bizarreness of man, the very strangeness of Christian moral teaching makes it entirely apposite for his nature (Ch. XXVI, *Morale Chrétienne*). It underlines his dual ability to become the recipient of divine grace even in his *misère* and to forfeit that grace even as a believer. Thus it both offers to the unbeliever the only way of bringing into balance the opposing elements of *misère* and *grandeur* in his nature and to the believer its doctrine and discipline which hold in check the antinomies in his life (Nos. 351—3). More specifically, it teaches the believer not to place his total trust in ceremonial on the one hand, yet on the other it makes him subject to the ritual of the Church as a corrective to his pride (No. 364). The teaching of the Christian religion emphasizes that the ultimate purpose of the Law is to be guided by the Holy Spirit (No. 367), that happiness is to be found in the renunciation of self-will and in the regulation of self-love (Nos. 362, 368). The believer does not rid himself of all trace of self-will and self-love: Pascal is aware that Christianity operates through humanity and not in spite of it. He rather disciplines his life by the awareness that he is not isolated in his belief, but is a member of a body of believers, the Church, whose head is Christ. Pascal takes over, *grosso modo*, the Pauline conception of the Church as the mystical body of Christ, but gives it a significantly Pascalian emphasis. In *I Corinthians* Ch. 12, vv. 12—30 St Paul uses the image of the physical body with its individual but interacting members to describe the functions of Christians within the Church. Just as each member of the body has a different but no less important function to fulfil in the functioning of the body as an harmonious entity, so too each Christian possesses a different charisma or gift of the Spirit which contributes to the edification of all members of the Church. In their mutual yet diverse service to the physical and mystical bodies, the members are mutually dependent. So the life of the body (the Church) is assured by the diverse functions of its members and its unity in and through diversity. If one member covets the function of another and neglects his own, the body does not function as it should do. Pascal points up the paradoxical and practical aspects of self-discipline for the believer within the body of the Church as the latter dies to himself and to his will in order to live through the corporate life of the Church: 'Etre membre est n'avoir de vie, d'être et de mouvement que par l'esprit du corps' (No. 372). Whenever the part tries to become its own centre and body without the principle of corporate life, it dies. Self-love is deeply and naturally ingrained in the member, but within the context of the body it may be transcended and sublimated into mutually edifying love: 'Mais en aimant le corps il s'aime soi-même parce qu'il n'a d'être qu'en lui, par lui et pour lui'. One loves oneself because one is a member of the body of Jesus Christ: 'Tout est un. L'un est en l'autre comme les trois personnes.' The self-love and life of the member are only possible and legitimate when expressed in and through the corporate love and life of the Church which embraces both member and the body of believers. The members love and live by the love and life of Christ, their head, to whom their love and life are in turn directed. No. 373 expresses the same paradox in the stark opposition of the love of God and hatred for oneself: 'Il faut n'aimer que Dieu et ne haïr que soi.' The member must hate himself sufficiently to die to self-love and his life in order to find true self-love and life in the love and life of the body of Christ. In this way the existential paradox of *misère-grandeur* attains the highest point of development possible at the end of the *Pensées* by the Pascalian extension of the doctrine of the Church as the body of Christ. It is not only explained by the death of Christ to unite the sinner to God but also transcended by grace as the believer shares the life of God in Christ and forfeits his formerly self-centred one.

The final chapter of the *Pensées* (*Conclusion*) places the stress on the wholly otherness of God and man, between whom no reconciliation is possible without a mediator (No. 378). In this work of reconciliation the initiative is entirely that of God in the incarnation: '... Dieu s'est fait homme pour s'unir à nous' (No. 381) as it is in the conversion of the unbeliever to belief in him: 'On ne croira jamais, d'une créance utile et de foi si Dieu n'incline le coeur et on croira dès qu'il l'inclinera' (No. 380). In the act of conversion Pascal emphasizes less the general connotation of the term in the New Testament where it denotes essentially the decisive turning to God of the sinner, than the change of mind and heart which conversion involves towards God and oneself (repentance). Hence the great gulf which he sees between an intellectual knowledge of God and love of him (No. 377). In conversion, God gives to the unbeliever both love for his creator and hatred for his own nature which place both in an entirely new relationship to each other (No. 380). For conversion involves the recognition on the part of the sinner that he has angered God so often that he could with perfect justice be annihilated at any moment and that he can do nothing without God (No. 378).

By affirming in his *Conclusion* that one should not be surprised to see many Christians who believe without need of proof, Pascal returns to the basic paradox with which the first chapter (*Ordre*) began, namely, that faith is a gift of God from first to last. In that case, all that the apologist for Christianity can do is to give reasons, which, however great their intrinsic cogency, may or may not convince or encourage the unbeliever to place himself in a ready state of mind and will in which God may inspire true faith in him. Whilst it is true to say that many of Pascal's proofs are inadequate and have been overtaken by modern biblical scholarship, this does not invalidate essentially the terms of reference of his argument of which he remains so consistently aware.[31] From the outset, the *Pensées* recognize the inability of reason to argue the unbeliever into faith (and this presumably would apply just as much to the twentieth century as to Pascal's own time) just as lucidly as they recognize that it is through reason that we perceive our misery and need of God. The *Pensées* seek to persuade of the necessity and attractiveness of Christianity not by lessening the distance between God and man, but by progressively widening it so that reason may comprehend the full extent of man's powerlessness and inexplicability without God. It is Pascal's supreme achievement to have placed this paradox both at the centre and circumference and at the beginning and end of his apology for the Christian religion and at the same time to have illustrated it so dramatically in and through the rational argument and structure of the *Pensées*.

6 Doubt and Certainty in Cartesianism

1

The *Discours* begins with the famous sentence which affirms, with ironic courtesy, the universal belief in the existence of 'le bon sens' and the fact that each person is fully satisfied with his allotted share of it: 'Le bon sens est la chose du monde la mieux partagée: car chacun pense en être si bien pourvu, que ceux même qui sont les plus difficiles à contenter en toute autre chose n'ont point coutume d'en désirer plus qu'ils en ont.'[1] Descartes here remembers both the tone and the content of one of Montaigne's remarks in the *Essais*: 'On dit communément que le plus juste partage que nature nous aye fait de ses graces, c'est celuy du sens: car il n'est aucun qui ne se contente de ce qu'elle luy en a distribué.'[2] If the first sentence of the *Discours* reminds us that Descartes was an attentive reader of the *Essais*, the second one defines the peculiarly Cartesian notion of 'le bon sens' and the need for a method by which it may be cultivated and brought to realize its potential. 'Le bon sens' or 'la raison' is for Descartes 'la puissance de bien juger et distinguer le vrai d'avec le faux' and is by nature equal in all men. The cause of the manifest diversity of opinion about what is and what is not 'le bon sens' is not that some people are more inherently reasonable than others, but that we direct our reason by different methods and so follow different objectives in our thinking.[3] The cornerstone of Descartes' thought in the *Discours* is not just that reason and truth are naturally within the reach of the universally existent 'bon sens' but that without the correct method to direct its operations the mind is bound to confound itself hopelessly in error: 'Car ce n'est pas assez d'avoir l'esprit bon, mais le principal est de l'appliquer bien.'[4] For Montaigne on the other hand the existence of 'le bon sens' and of a method for conducting it objectively in its search for truth is denied by the irreducible confusion and contradiction which reign in all branches of so-called knowledge. This confusion is adequate evidence for him of man's inability to probe to the underlying causes of phenomena and of the unreliability of the means by which he seeks to acquire knowledge, that is, of reason and the senses. He does, it is true, make an important distinction between the principle of reason which nature has implanted in all men, and what he terms 'l'humaine raison'. The first kind of reason is a firm and stable value, but whereas Descartes envisages the possibility of directing its operations by the application of the correct method, Montaigne views it as inaccessible to man: 'car la vraye raison est essentielle, de qui nous desrobons le nom à fauces enseignes, elle loge dans le sein de Dieu'. 'L'humaine raison' on the other hand is a relative and fluctuating norm which guides our thinking in the course of life, and is conditioned by custom, contingency, prejudice and error. It is constant only in its incapacity to arrive at truth:

> J'appelle tousjours raison cette apparence de discours que chacun forge en soy; cette raison, de la condition de laquelle il y en peut avoir cent contraires autour d'un mesme subject, c'est un instrument de plomb et de cire, alongeable et accommodable à tous biais et à toutes mesures.[5]

The diversity inherent in 'l'humaine raison' is used by Montaigne and the Sceptics to undermine man's claim to possess criteria for coming to objective knowledge about himself and the world, and thus they say that he neither knows the truth nor has adequate instruments to find it. Descartes agrees with them about the diversity which reigns in human opinions, but sees in it only the proof that an adequate method for conducting reason to the truth has not yet been found and applied. For him, reason, which is equal in all men, is 'la seule chose qui nous rend hommes et nous distingue des bêtes';[6] for Montaigne, 'l'humaine raison' is the precise cause of man's overweening desire to rise above his proper station in the animal kingdom by trying to know the unknowable and of his discontent and vanity: 'La peste de l'homme, c'est l'opinion de sçavoir.' He therefore endeavours to mitigate man's misery by inculcating in him a mistrust of reason in the affairs of life, thus bringing him closer to the natural state of ignorance which is for him the summit of wisdom: 'Il nous faut abestir pour nous assagir, et nous esblouir pour nous guider'.[7]

Just as Descartes' use of 'le bon sens' revalues that of Montaigne, so too his method for conducting it — doubt — revalues sceptical doubt for his own purposes. In view of the famous *tabula rasa* which Descartes makes of traditional disciplines in the first part of the *Discours* it is tempting to say that he begins at the point where Montaigne leaves off in the *Essais*, with the application of doubt to each branch of knowledge in turn.[8] But the *Discours* begins at a point anterior to this doubt with the belief in the mind's power to know the truth and apply a method to reason to this end. Point of departure and objective both remain unaffected by Montaigne's doubt, even though Descartes subjects reason to far more radical doubt in the fourth part of the *Discours* and in the second of the *Méditations Métaphysiques*. Doubt of the reality of his existence and the hypothesis that he is systematically deceived by a 'Dieu trompeur' are extreme dogmatic forms of doubt only possible within the Cartesian framework where reason all the while retains its ability to arrive at the truth. Doubt is the means of reaching truth, the necessary self-imposed obstacle and test which reason must surmount on its path to certainty. In the first of the

Méditations Métaphysiques Des choses que l'on peut révoquer en doute Descartes writes that he has accepted so many doubtful opinions as true in the past and that certainty is only possible on condition that he rid himself of all previously entertained opinions.[9] Even, or especially, when he is in possession of the indubitable knowledge from his method, doubt of it is simultaneously expressed. He tells us for example in the first part of the *Discours* of the confidence he has in his method which will enable him to make future discoveries, and then juxtaposes an image expressing doubt about it, doubt which at first sight may appear to be perfunctory modesty but which is the permanent concomitant of his method: 'Toutefois il se peut faire que je me trompe, et ce n'est peut-être qu'un peu de cuivre et de verre que je prends pour de l'or et des diamants.' Henri Gouhier has well noted that '*Le Discours de la Méthode* est l'oeuvre d'un philosophe content, content de sa philosophie et surtout de la méthode dont cette philosophie est la vérification continue'.[10] That philosophy is one of certainty and the method one of doubt, doubt which is always both more and less than sceptical doubt, as an examination of its functions throughout the *Discours* reveals.

2

Descartes' preponderantly negative review of contemporary education in the first part of the *Discours* is strongly reminiscent of Montaigne's strictures against the educational principles of his day, notably in his essay *De l'Institution des Enfans*. Although Descartes attended one of the most famous colleges of the time, that of La Flèche, the benefits derived by him were meagre and incommensurate with his expectations. Instead of acquiring the clear and assured knowledge to which he aspired, he discovered that he possessed only contradictions and doubts: 'Car je me trouvais embarrassé de tant de doutes et d'erreurs, qu'il me semblait n'avoir fait autre profit, en tâchant de m'instruire, sinon que j'avais découvert de plus en plus mon ignorance'.[11] He seems here to follow Montaigne's advice to the effect that the beginning of true wisdom or 'l'ignorance doctorale' as the latter terms it, consists in questioning the authority on which all received knowledge is founded, thus aiming to 'vuyder et desmunir la memoire'.[12] Descartes' apparently sceptical review of the various disciplines tends to support this similarity. In spite of the eminence of many philosophers, he sees that there is not a single principle in philosophy which is not subject to contestation. The same confused situation reigns in other branches of intellectual enquiry. In the *Apologie* Montaigne engages in a sceptical survey of the various disciplines and likewise concludes that each one is full of contradictions and none more so than the venerable profession of philosophy which is nothing less than 'une poësie sophistiquée'.[13] The similarity to Montaigne's doubt of traditional learning however is misleading in the extreme for the kind of doubt which forms Descartes' conclusion on the subject reveals that he is prepared to go farther than the former's sceptical questioning: '... je réputais presque pour faux tout ce qui n'était que vraisemblable' summarizes his attitude to the contradictions in philosophy.[14] In casting his first doubt about philosophy in this form, Descartes is prepared to be more negative and dogmatic than a true Sceptic would ever wish to be. As regards theology, on the other hand, his attitude duplicates that of Montaigne and is resolutely fideistic in its complete separation of the provinces of faith and reason as he acknowledges the sheer inability of the mind to pronounce on divine truth by itself. Montaigne had already preceded him in both the form and the content of his fideistic acceptance of religion:

> La participation que nous avons à la connoissance de la verité quelle qu'elle soit, ce n'est pas par nos propres forces que nous l'avons acquise. Dieu nous a assez apris cela par les tesmoins qu'il a choisi du vulgaire, simples et ignorans, pour nous instruire de ses admirables secrets: nostre foy ce n'est pas nostre acquest, c'est un pur present de la liberalité d'autruy.[15]

In his attack on rational disciplines, however, Descartes exempts one in particular from his criticism, the science of mathematics which attracts him on account of the certainty and evidence of its principles and reasoning.[16] In his exemption of mathematics from his strictures two characteristics of Descartes' doubt emerge clearly which serve to differentiate it from that of the Sceptics. He is prepared to exceed the doubt of the latter by his readiness to dismiss what is merely probable as almost wrong. The merely probable may, after all, prove to be true or false or doubtful, and the true Sceptic is not prepared to become a negative dogmatist since this would undermine his own philosophic position which is precisely that of the non-dogmatic doubter. Descartes' doubt does not bear on the certainty of mathematical reasoning, although he says that he did not at the time perceive the particular use which philosophy could make of it.[17] The deeply paradoxical character of his doubt, at once dogmatic and incomplete, underlines the paramount importance of certainty in Descartes' philosophical quest and makes assimilation to the perennial doubt of the Sceptics impossible.

Both aspects of Descartes' doubt are obscured by his decision to abandon the pursuit of the speculative type of knowledge in the traditional disciplines for the experience of the world at large: 'Et me résolvant de ne chercher plus d'autre science que celle qui se pourrait trouver en moi-même, ou bien dans le grand livre du monde. ...' In seeking thus to discover and cultivate his own judgement through experience rather than through bookish tradition he exemplifies Montaigne's scorn for 'une suffisance pure livresque' which stands in the path of empirical wisdom: '... tout ce qui se presente à nos yeux sert de livre suffisant ... le commerce des hommes y est merveilleusement propre, et la visite des pays estrangers'.[18] The travels of which Descartes tells us in the first part of the *Discours* confirm him in his view of the diversity of opinions and customs and detach him from adherence to fixed beliefs: '... j'apprenais à ne rien croire trop fermement de ce qui ne m'avait été persuadé que par l'exemple et par la coutume'. He is close here to Montaigne's attitude towards custom as the latter comments on its absence of rational foundation:

> Qui voudra se desfaire de ce violent prejudice de la coustume, il trouvera plusieurs choses receues d'une resolution indubitable qui n'ont appuy qu'en la barbe chenue et rides de l'usage qui les accompaigne; mais, ce masque arraché, rapportant les choses à la verité et à la raison, il sentira son jugement comme tout bouleversé, et remis pourtant en bien plus seur estat.

For both the first step towards wisdom is taken when one decides to discard the useless intellectual paraphernalia which clutters the mind and prevents it from seeing 'la Raison', the eternal principle to be followed and which is not hidebound by time and place. Wisdom is not, to use Montaigne's terms, 'un acquest' but rather 'une naturelle possession'.[19] Sceptical detachment seems then to characterize Descartes' attitude at the outset of his intellectual quest, but the will to think and act with certainty is not subject to that detachment as he makes clear at the end of the first part of the *Discours*: 'Et j'avais toujours un extrême désir d'apprendre à distinguer le vrai d'avec le faux, pour voir clair en mes actions, et marcher avec assurance en cette vie.' The will to attain such a method is responsible for his rejection of all the philosophical principles which he has acquired as well as for his decision not to allow his search for it to interfere in any way with the commonly held ideas in society. The motivation for his destruction of his previous opinions and knowledge is not therefore a sceptical one, but it issues in a sceptical attitude to society as he declares at the beginning of the second part that he will adhere nominally to the imperfect social structures of the day. The principle which he follows here is the sceptical one which argues that innovations are at best likely to be as deficient as the state which they purport to replace and at worst even more so. Descartes will not reconstruct a new social edifice but instead direct his thinking towards the construction of his own philosophic method, 'un fonds qui est tout à moi'.[20] His acknowledgement of the validity of the sceptical principle of diversity when applied to knowledge and custom does not discourage him from undertaking his own quest to establish whether or not anything may be known with certainty. His innate will towards certainty even as he doubts precludes him from rejecting all his previously held opinions without prior elaboration of a method by which he may continue to seek truth:

> ... je ne voulus point commencer à rejeter tout à fait aucune des opinions qui s'étaient pu glisser autrefois en ma créance sans y avoir été introduites par la raison, que je n'eusse auparavant employé assez de temps à faire le projet de l'ouvrage que j'entreprenais, et à chercher la vraie méthode pour parvenir à la connaissance de toutes les choses dont mon esprit serait capable.

Once again the two apparently incompatible aspects of Cartesian doubt are explicit as Descartes comes to the point at which he formulates the first rule of his method: his doubt is at once more dogmatic than that of the Sceptics in its rejection of all beliefs which cannot be justified by his reason, and less complete in that it allows him to incorporate into his method mathematical and geometrical reasoning which promises a firm foundation for it.[21]

These two aspects fuse to form the first rule of Descartes' method. He is not only prepared to submit every principle to doubt, as do the Sceptics, but also to reject every principle as false, deferring his assent until its truth imposes itself on his mind in irrefutable fashion: 'Le premier [précepte] était de ne recevoir jamais aucune chose pour vraie que je ne la connusse évidemment être telle; c'est-à-dire d'éviter soigneusement la précipitation et la prévention.' The first part of the first rule agrees with the sceptical attitude towards evidence, but the second goes far beyond it in implying that he is prepared to accept any proposition which presents itself so clearly and distinctly to his mind that he has no reason whatsoever to doubt it: 'et de ne comprendre rien de plus en mes jugements que ce qui se présenterait si clairement et si distinctement à mon esprit que je n'eusse aucune occasion de le mettre en doute'. The test for both Sceptic and Descartes in the examination of a proposition purporting to be true is to discover whether or not it is able to withstand doubt; the Sceptic doubts however that such indubitable knowledge is obtainable and suspends judgement, whereas Descartes is prepared to submit the proposition to persistent doubt and to accept it as true if it proves to be resistant. Evidence of knowledge becomes knowledge for Descartes, as Henri Gouhier has written, in the face of 'l'impossibilité de la mettre en doute expérimentée au cours d'une épreuve inventée à cet effet'.[22] The doubt of the Sceptic is not methodical in nature, that is, it has no other aim than that of establishing that there are reasons to doubt the proposition in question. If his doubt goes beyond this, it forfeits its claim to be non-dogmatic. Descartes' test for knowledge is that of finding a philosophic principle resistant to doubt by means of doubting and his doubt is therefore an integral part of his method. The character of indubitable knowledge is that it is at once 'clair' and 'distinct', not just intuitively, but because it remains so after having been subjected to doubt which is so severe that no further doubt is possible.[23] Between sceptical doubt and

Cartesian doubt there is a fixed gulf, created by the fact that the latter is inseparable from the will to seek and the method for seeking indubitable knowledge. In view of the intrinsic paradoxical nature of Descartes' doubt it is not surprising that at each stage of his philosophical journey it should point to the certainty obtainable even as he doubts (in the 'morale par provision' of Part III) and the certainty which may be obtained and confirmed through doubt (Part IV).

3

To describe the function of the 'morale par provision' in the intellectual itinerary of the *Discours* Descartes employs the image of a temporary construction erected to house the inhabitant who has destroyed his former dwelling, that is his previous opinions, but who has not yet completed the building of his new residence, that is, who has not acquired the clear and distinct knowledge on which to ground his thinking. The image is an appropriate one because it places the emphasis on the practical rather than on the philosophic aspects of the 'morale'. The relationship of the 'morale' to the method adumbrated in the preceding part of the *Discours* is somewhat ambiguous. Within the narrative framework of Part III the 'morale' is presented as having been formulated as a provisional way of directing Descartes' thought prior to his departure for Holland where he lived from 1619 until 1628 — it would accordingly precede the first elaboration of the method during the same period in the *Regulae ad Directionem Ingenii*. But Descartes adduces the 'morale' as the first necessary and practical consequence from his method of doubting: the title of Part III reads *Quelques Règles de la Morale tirée de la Méthode*.[24] The 'morale' is not drawn from the method as a particular truth deduced from a general one, but represents a logical stage in the process of the presentation of the method. The methodical doubt leads Descartes to define the requisite characteristics of knowledge (Part II), and the 'morale' acknowledges the absence of such knowledge and the necessity for the creation of the most rational conditions possible in which it may be pursued. In creating such conditions by elaborating the 'morale' the overriding consideration of Descartes is that the doubts to which his reason is exposed should in no way infect the way in which he acts: '. . . afin que je ne demeurasse point irrésolu en mes actions, pendant que la raison m'obligerait de l'être en mes jugements, et que je ne laissasse pas de vivre dès lors le plus heureusement que je pourrais. . . .'[25] The continuation of the methodical doubting of all presumed knowledge is vital to Descartes' objective of arriving at a proposition which may no longer be doubted and this may only be carried on within a framework of practical certainty in one's conduct. Whilst reason therefore still suspends its judgement about its beliefs the 'morale' is designed to foster the quest for philosophical certainty by preserving the will from the logical result of such suspension of judgement — the satisfaction with the merely probable or the possible as the ground for one's judgement. In this way Descartes hopes to avoid the pitfalls into which the Sceptics fall, the vacillation in decisions which betokens an inability and unwillingness to embrace any opinion with certainty. Montaigne describes the results of the Sceptics' doubt in the *Apologie* and its effect on reason and will as follows:

> Leur effect, c'est une pure, entiere et très-parfaicte surceance et suspension de jugement. Ils se servent de leur raison pour enquerir et pour debatre, mais non pas pour arrester et choisir. Quiconque imaginera une perpetuelle confession d'ignorance, un jugement sans pente et sans inclination, à quelque occasion que ce puisse estre, il conçoit le Pyrronisme.[26]

The first rule of the 'morale' consists in obedience to the laws and religion of one's country and adherence to the most moderate opinions available whilst retaining complete freedom of judgement. It has all the appearances of an impeccable sceptical maxim such as might be found in the pages of the *Apologie* or the treatises of Le Vayer. In fact it is but the first step towards overcoming the paralysing effect of scepticism in practice and in thought. Whilst Descartes places all his opinions in the doubt of his method, he scrutinizes the practice rather than the theoretical views of people of moderate opinion, hoping thus to minimize the scope for error in his judgement. The moderation of Descartes is not, as it is for the Sceptics, the end of doubt as they acquiesce formally in the commonly received opinions of the day, but a method adopted to place himself in the position in which he is most likely to perceive truth. The freedom of judgement which he insists on retaining is likewise similar in appearance to that of the Sceptics but different in purpose. Montaigne was careful to retain in all his actions that inner freedom of judgement unimpaired by prejudice and nominal adherence to custom which he terms his 'pensée de derrière': 'Quand ma volonté me donne à un party, ce n'est pas d'une si violente obligation que mon entendement s'en infecte.' If Descartes mistrusts *a priori* all excesses of opinion on the other hand, it is because they impair his freedom to choose his own opinions and prevent him from cultivating his reason to the point at which it is capable of recognizing truth:

> ... je me promettais de perfectionner de plus en plus mes jugements, et non point de les rendre pires, j'eusse pensé commettre une grande faute contre le bon sens, si, pour ce que j'approuvais alors quelque chose, je me fusse obligé de la prendre

pour bonne encore après, lorsqu'elle aurait peut-être, cessé de l'être, ou que j'aurais cessé de l'estimer telle.[27]

The doubt of the Sceptics leads to detachment of received opinion and goes no farther than the nominal acceptance of what it doubts. Descartes' doubt comes to the same stage of nominal acceptance of opinion, but this is seen only as a provisional halting-place for the mind and an opportunity to rid itself of some of the accretions which hinder its quest for indubitable knowledge.

The second maxim reveals the same dual character of Cartesian doubt as it shares the sceptical view of the relativity of all opinions whilst transcending it. In this maxim Descartes seeks to provide his actions with a firm basis even though the opinions which they follow are doubtful from a speculative point of view: 'Ma seconde maxime était d'être le plus ferme et le plus résolu en mes actions que je pourrais, et de ne suivre pas moins constamment les opinions les plus douteuses, lorsque je m'y serais une fois déterminé, que si elles eussent été très assurées.' The willingness to act on doubtful opinions in practice and follow them as though they were true is diametrically opposed to the methodical doubt by which Descartes must consider the doubtful as well as the probable false to the extent that both can never be indubitable. The necessity of action imposes the choice between alternative courses of conduct, but the choice, once taken, excludes comparison with those which have been rejected. This is illustrated by the example of the traveller lost in the forest who commits himself resolutely to one direction only, even though he may have chosen it arbitrarily. The principle followed is that it is better to do something rather than nothing at all. Doubtful or probable opinions once chosen become certain for the purposes of practical expediency, as they are considered henceforth 'non plus comme douteuses en tant qu'elles se rapportent à la pratique, mais comme très vraies et très certaines, à cause que la raison qui nous y a fait déterminer se trouve telle'. Descartes does not follow such opinions thinking all the while that they may be wrong and simply acting as though they were true, but rather in the conviction that on the evidence at the time of choice there were no better ones to be found (although others may be as valid) and that irresolution must be avoided. What is probable or doubtful does not suddenly become true or certain on account of situational expediency. But by regarding probable or doubtful opinions as the right opinions to follow at that particular time Descartes hopes to overcome irresolution in his conduct and eliminate futile future recrimination about the moral quality of the actions committed. The paradoxical 'provisional certainty' of the 'morale' emerges clearly in the letter which Descartes wrote in March 1638 to an anonymous correspondent in which he defends himself against the charge that he is in favour of persisting in following erroneous opinions in his maxim. On the one hand, he writes, doubtful opinions are to be followed as certain in practice precisely because there are no more certain opinions to be found. But on the other, this maxim in no way prevents him from changing these opinions followed if he discovers others which are better.[28]

The third maxim pursues the objective of the second one, to establish a basis for action which is unexposed to present hesitation and future remorse. Descartes seeks to stabilize this basis even more by accepting that his desires and thoughts are liable to be more easily modified than external circumstances and that in consequence true stability of judgement and happiness reside in the ability to accommodate the mind and will to reality. This signifies no mere contemplative retreat into the inner citadel of mind and will; the third maxim is rather designed as a philosophic supplement to the resolute conduct of the previous one and as a means of adapting the mind and will to possible failure or unforeseen consequences attendant upon one's actions: '... en sorte qu'après que nous avons fait notre mieux touchant les choses qui nous sont extérieures, tout ce qui manque de nous réussir est au regard de nous absolument impossible'. In the second maxim doubtful opinion became certain in the context of a practical situation; here unpredictable and possibly unpalatable reality is converted by reason and will into acceptable reality on the same principle, that is, '... faisant, comme on dit, de nécessité vertu'. In the emphasis of this maxim on the dependence of the will on reason in such a conversion ('... car notre volonté ne se portant naturellement à desirer que les choses que notre entendement lui représente en quelque façon comme possibles...') the 'morale' is strictly Aristotelian in appearance; but in fact it is more Augustinian in the extent to which it is inspired by the Cartesian will to act with certainty even in the midst of the mind's state of doubt. The 'morale' emphasizes at each stage Descartes' will to live as happily as possible by creating an interim basis for his actions free from indecision and remorse and by eliminating vain aspirations by the control of mind and will. In the 'morale par provision' reason proposes but will disposes in the end.[29]

At the end of the maxims, Descartes adds that he retained these principles of action together with his religious belief but did not hesitate to jettison all his remaining opinions. In 1638 he wrote that considerations of prudence as much as his need for peace of mind were responsible for the emphasis placed on the need for certainty in practical affairs and that he had thus hoped to forestall objections to the radical doubt applied to his opinions.[30] The 'morale' has without doubt the aim of mitigating the effect of his radical doubt, yet its primary function is to be understood within the framework of his thought in the *Discours*. It roots methodical doubt firmly to the will for certainty in practical matters as in speculation and anticipates the *Cogito* of Part IV.

4

Descartes' method incorporates the 'morale par provision' which provides certainty in action based on what is at the time at best true opinion, at worst error, as well as the freedom for doubt to function unhindered by prejudice. Following uncertain opinions in resolute conduct whilst pursuing methodic doubt to its ultimate conclusions makes the 'morale' an amalgam of logically incompatible elements held together by the will to act resolutely and to come to indubitable truth through the process of doubting. Having secured freedom for the will to doubt Descartes at the beginning of Part IV can continue the search for a secure foundation for knowledge in directions diametrically opposed to those taken by his conduct in its observation of commonly held opinions:

> ... mais pour ce qu'alors je désirais vaquer seulement à la recherche de la vérité, je pensai qu'il fallait que je fisse tout le contraire, et que je rejetasse comme absolument faux tout ce en quoi je pourrais imaginer le moindre doute, afin de voir s'il ne resterait point, après cela, quelque chose en ma créance qui fût entièrement indubitable.

In the first of the *Méditations Métaphysiques, Des choses que l'on peut révoquer en doute*, Descartes begins by setting out to destroy systematically all opinions which he has previously held. To this end, he states that it is not necessary to prove the falsity of each particular opinion. But since reason convinces him that he should be as vigilant in disbelieving what is not entirely true as in rejecting manifest error it follows that in his scrutiny of his various opinions the test for veracity must be strict: '... le moindre sujet de douter que j'y trouverai, suffira pour me les faire toutes rejeter'.[31] The objective of such far-reaching doubt, as the *Discours* affirms at the beginning of its fourth Part, is to discover whether or not there is any truth in a particular set of opinions which cannot be doubted. Whether or not there is any proposition which resists his doubts, Descartes writes in the second of his *Méditations*, he will persist in his doubting until he establishes one of the only two possible certainties, that is, either the certainty of indubitable knowledge or the certainty that nothing at all may be known with certainty.[32] Pierre Gassendi, in his *Disquisitio Metaphysica* (1642–4), containing his lengthy objections to Descartes' entire metaphysical system, begins by criticizing the nature and use of Cartesian doubt. Although there is disagreement about the extent to which Gassendi may properly be called a Sceptic, there is no doubt that his objections to the *Méditations* exemplify well the principles of sceptical as opposed to Cartesian doubt. In his *Doute Unique* relating to the method by which Descartes' doubt rejects all opinions, whether true or false, he is at a loss to understand the need to extend it to every branch of knowledge:

> La seule chose que je ne comprenne pas bien, c'est de savoir pourquoi vous n'avez pas cru qu'il suffisait, simplement et en peu de paroles, de tenir pour incertaines les choses que vous aviez jusque-là apprises pour mettre ensuite à part celles que vous reconnaîtriez pour vraies, au lieu qu'en les tenant toutes pour fausses, c'est moins un ancien préjugé dont vous vous dépouillez qu'un nouveau dont vous vous revêtez.

He cannot grasp why Descartes should wish to assimilate the true or the probable as well as the doubtful opinion to the same category, and is at pains to differentiate sceptical doubt from merely negative dogmatism. He thus makes the fundamental distinction between the sceptical attitude to phenomena perceived by the senses, and knowledge apprehended by the mind, noumena. The Sceptics are prepared to admit the first kind of knowledge non-dogmatically, that is, accepting the impressions received by their senses, but they say that everything in the second category is uncertain. The nature and range of their doubting of our knowledge is more restrictive than that of Descartes: '... les doutes des Sceptiques portaient seulement sur des choses réellement incertaines, et qui méritaient d'être soumises à la discussion; mais non pas sur les choses effectivement apparentes, et sur lesquelles il ne sert à rien de contester'. They admit the appearances of phenomena, but their doubts bear on what Gassendi calls '... la nature profonde de chacune de ces apparences, sur sa vérité', not on the appearances themselves. For Gassendi, if we cannot come to the point at which we are able to discern truth, we can arrive at probable knowledge, which at least is nearer to the truth than Descartes' unwarranted assumption that the merely probable is no different from what is false.[33]

Descartes uses doubt not in the manner advocated by Gassendi, to distinguish probable from false opinion, but simply to negate all his previous opinions as being wrong.[34] By intensifying his doubt into negation at the outset of the fourth Part of his *Discours* and by the stages through which he takes it as he systematically negates all possible ways of acquiring knowledge Descartes hopes to make the test for the evidence of true knowledge so severe that any proposition which resists it will by the same token automatically resist the less radical doubt of his philosophical opponents, the Sceptics. The first stage in what Henri Gouhier has called Descartes' methodical negation begins when the Cartesian will intensifies the sceptical principle for doubting knowledge: 'Ainsi, à cause que nos sens nous trompent quelquefois, je voulus supposer qu'il n'y avait aucune chose qui fût telle qu'ils nous la font imaginer.' This first stage of doubt is expanded in the first *Méditation* as Descartes states that he intends to apply doubt methodically to the principles underlying all knowledge, beginning with those which rely on the senses:

> Tout ce que j'ai reçu jusqu'à présent pour le plus vrai et assuré, je l'ai appris des sens, ou par les sens: or j'ai quelquefois éprouvé que ces sens étaient trompeurs, et il est de la prudence de ne se fier jamais entièrement à ceux qui nous ont une fois trompés.[35]

Gassendi jocularly likens Descartes with his total mistrust of his sense-impressions to a man who once or twice has found a particular food distasteful and has therefore decided that he is never going to eat it again. Prudence for Gassendi does not consist in considering every operation of the senses as necessarily deceptive, in spite of the fact that we have been deceived by previous sense-perceptions:

> ... elle ne conseille pas ... de considérer toute sensation comme douteuse ou fausse, parce que de temps à autre il y en a une qui nous trompe; mais bien de ne pas prendre pour certaine celle qui justement est douteuse, et de repousser justement celle qui est fausse, et d'autre part de considérer comme vraie celle qui a toujours été constatée comme vraie, et dont rien ne démontre qu'elle soit fausse.[36]

Nor does he accept the objection that the end of Descartes' doubt justifies its means, or that Descartes only considers sense-knowledge as false until he discovers the principle for separating truth from falsity, for the very reason that all our knowledge is not always or necessarily false but doubtful or probable. The Cartesian will cannot accept what is a basic philosophic principle to Gassendi, namely, that the senses may sometimes deceive and at other times mediate the truth, but instead seeks indubitable knowledge whilst Gassendi opts for the more modest way of discriminating between the deceptiveness and the veracity of the sense-impressions.

Descartes' second series of negations in the *Discours* bears on all knowledge which we claim to have by way of reason, and the form in which he negates these claims is identical to that employed in his first series. We know that our reasoning processes are capable of leading us astray regarding even the simplest subjects, and this leads him to the conclusion that '... jugeant que j'étais sujet à faillir autant qu'aucun autre, je rejetai comme fausses toutes les raisons que j'avais prises auparavant pour démonstrations'. The negation of all knowledge mediated by the senses and reason is now complete and so Descartes is ready to introduce the third and final stage of his negative argument as he deliberately induces the most extreme state of confusion which it is possible to produce in the mind, in which the activities of waking and sleeping merge into a continuum where reality may well be a form of dreaming and dreaming a form of reality, which we have no means of distinguishing from each other:

Et enfin, considérant que toutes les mêmes pensées que nous avons étant éveillés, nous peuvent aussi venir quand nous dormons, sans qu'il y en ait aucune pour lors qui soit vraie, je me résolus de feindre que toutes les choses qui m'étaient jamais entrées en l'esprit n'étaient non plus vraies que les illusions de mes songes.[37]

Montaigne in the *Apologie* saw so much error arising from the operations of the senses and the reason that he confessed himself unable to discriminate between the world of reality and the world of dreams, concluding that 'Nous veillons dormans, et veillans dormons'. He was however content to accept the blurred contours of his experience since they could not be placed in more exact focus: '... nostre veiller n'est jamais si esveillé qu'il purge et dissipe bien à point les resveries, qui sont les songes des veillants, et pires que songes'. Gassendi on the other hand takes this doubt of reality less far than Montaigne and the first of Descartes' *Méditations*, in which the difference between the states of waking and sleeping is completely dissolved, and rejects the procedure as an empty subtlety: 'Car encore qu'au milieu d'un songe nous ne puissions discerner si nous dormons ou veillons, il n'est cependant pas douteux, quand nous veillons, que nous sommes sûrs, que nous éprouvons la certitude d'être éveillés et de ne pas dormir.'[38] For Gassendi, to ask for evidence to distinguish between the two states is to resemble a man who in the full glare of the noon-tide sun asks for a torch in order to see his way. He rejects Descartes' means of doubting the difference between the states as in fact he rejects the possibility of so doing in practice. The confusion between what we normally take as reality and as dreams to the point at which the possibility is opened that life itself is a dream is the climax of the most extreme sceptical doubt to which the empirical Gassendi is not prepared to go. Descartes on the other hand accepts the sceptical confusion induced by this doubt but raises it to the highest possible level by making the criteria for the distinction between reality and dreaming not merely doubtful as did Montaigne but inexistent. The confusion of the Sceptics is induced by man's natural state of ignorance and his inability to perceive truth, whereas the higher Cartesian confusion is a necessary preliminary stage engendered artificially on the way towards the replacement of sceptical doubt by self-evident certainty. In the first two *Méditations Métaphysiques* Descartes raises the hyperbolic doubt of the fourth Part of the *Discours* to a still higher level in two stages. The first stage corresponds to the final stage of Cartesian doubt in the *Discours* prior to the *Cogito*, as Descartes imagines that all his thoughts are illusory by a process of studied intensification:

... j'emploie tous mes soins à me tromper moi-même, feignant que toutes ces pensées sont fausses et imaginaires; jusques à ce qu'ayant tellement balancé mes préjugés, qu'ils ne puissent faire pencher mon avis plus d'un côté que d'un autre, mon jugement ne soit plus désormais maîtrisé par de mauvais usages et détourné du droit chemin qui le peut conduire à la connaissance de la vérité.

The aim of this hyperbolic doubt in the *Discours* and the *Méditations* is to counter-balance the possible influence of his former opinions over his mind by eradicating them, since it could subsequently be objected that the affirmation 'Je pense, donc je suis' was present intact in Descartes' mind from the beginning of the entire demonstration of the *Cogito*.

The second stage of Cartesian doubt in the *Méditations* involves the hypothesis of a metaphysical source of doubt, by which Descartes is able to suppose not merely that all his opinions are erroneous but that they have been implanted in his mind expressly by a 'malus genius' for the purpose of deceiving him. The 'malus genius' is capable even of undermining the truth of mathematical logic: 'Je supposerai donc qu'il y a, non point un vrai Dieu, qui est la souveraine source de vérité, mais un certain mauvais génie, non moins rusé et trompeur que puissant, qui a employé toute son industrie à me tromper.' The hypothesis of the 'malus genius' seems to have been introduced to anticipate the basic objection to Descartes' doubt which Gassendi illustrates when he writes that is is impossible for someone to eradicate all his previous opinions from his mind since it is not in the power of the will to do so.[39] At the end of the first *Méditation* Descartes shows that he is aware of the difficulty in maintaining such a degree of total doubt or negation of all opinions in his mind which is all too inclined to lapse back into its acceptance of formerly discarded opinions as true through sheer force of habit, as well as of the danger which failure to maintain it presents to the demonstration of the *Cogito* as the truth which resists all doubt. The final stage of doubt in both *Discours* and *Méditation* therefore reveals his determination to overcome this difficulty and the potentially destructive objection to the *Cogito*. To this end, both stages of his doubt represent the culmination of a demonstrative technique invoked by the Cartesian will as it anticipates the foundation of certainty in his knowledge. This technique incorporates and utilizes two apparently antithetical forces which in fact are but complementary aspects of that will to certainty. The will to certainty incites the desire to reject all previous and present knowledge as false whilst using the force of its total negation to dispose the mind to certainty. The apparently negative desire to reject every opinion, which Descartes stresses in the fourth Part of his *Discours* ('... je voulus supposer, ... je me résolus de feindre ... pendant que je voulais ainsi penser que tout était faux ...') originates in the positive wish to affirm an indubitable truth.

The perspicacious Gassendi was not slow to see the full import for Descartes' philosophy of the hypothesis of the 'Dieu trompeur' which he demythologizes in ironic fashion: on the one hand he criticizes

Descartes' need to employ it in order to bolster his prejudice that all opinions are false, and on the other he objects that it is unnecessary since the enemy to the quest for indubitable knowledge is not at all the 'Dieu trompeur' but rather 'le peu de lumière de l'esprit humain et la seule faiblesse de notre nature'. Descartes' metaphysical fiction prevents us from seeking the causes for our deficient knowledge in naturally explicable ways. Even if it is true that the 'Dieu trompeur' exists to deceive us, says Gassendi, then it is *a fortiori* not in our power to neutralize his effect on our judgement.[40] To Gassendi, Descartes' hypothesis of the 'Dieu trompeur' is a sheer artifice, more necessary to the force of the argument than to the philosophic quest for truth. His fundamental grievance against his opponent is that the latter has falsified the evidence for our capacity to err by magnifying it for his own purpose of demonstration. Gassendi does not see indubitable certainty as falling within the compass of human powers, beyond the certainty of religion which he of course accepts fideistically, and hence does not understand Descartes' need for philosophic certainty, still less the elaborate superstructure of negations which he erects in order to achieve it.

Just as Descartes has orchestrated the negations at the beginning of the fourth Part of the *Discours* to their crescendo, the conclusion which has been implicit in the demonstration emerges: 'Mais, aussitôt après, je pris garde que, pendant que je voulais ainsi penser que tout était faux, il fallait nécessairement que moi, qui le pensais, fusse quelque chose.' The stress on the role of the will in intensifying the series of doubts in Descartes' mind that everything is false conceals the fact that the will is also the condition for producing the logical consequence from doubting — that of the certainty of thought. The certainty of the proposition, 'Je pense, donc je suis', is however neither necessary nor logical fact. As A. J. Ayer has well pointed out, if both parts of the proposition, 'Je pense' and 'je suis' seem to be necessary, it is only on account of the absurdity of denying them and not because the opposite proposition, 'Je ne pense pas', 'je ne suis pas', is self-contradictory.[41] The certainty of the *Cogito* is then only indubitable because it is doubted by the subject who expresses it. In the second *Méditation* the certainty of thought and of existence comes in and through the very act of Descartes supposing that he is being deceived by a metaphysical principle of doubt:

> Mais il y a un je ne sais quel trompeur très puissant et très rusé, qui emploie toute son industrie à me tromper toujours. Il n'y a donc point de doute que je suis, s'il me trompe; et qu'il me trompe tant qu'il voudra, il ne saurait jamais faire que je ne sois rien, tant que je penserai être quelque chose.

The fiction of the 'Dieu trompeur' opens the highest level at which doubt may be entertained in the mind and also the highest level at which it is possible to demonstrate that doubting implies thinking and thinking existence. Since doubt itself is a process of thought, it intuitively and permanently implies for Descartes the subject who thinks and exists. The actions of doubting and thinking therefore validate each other and the existence of their subject. In the second *Méditation* Descartes sets in motion this self-validating test of his own existence in the following terms: 'Mais qu'est-ce donc que je suis? Une chose qui pense. Qu'est-ce qu'une chose qui pense? C'est-à-dire une chose qui doute, qui conçoit, qui affirme, qui nie, qui veut, qui ne veut pas, qui imagine aussi, et qui sent.' The circular nature of the proof of his existence as a thinking subject (thinking is the condition of doubt which cannot do away with the certainty of thought, for to doubt even that one is thinking is to imply it) satisfies the criteria for indubitable knowledge laid down in the first rule of the method, namely that such knowledge should have the characters of clarity and distinctness after submission to the severest doubt. The certainty that the thought of the subject resists doubt is most clearly and distinctly revealed as thought attempts to negate itself completely by thinking that everything in the mind is illusory.[42]

Without Cartesian doubt, the certainty of Descartes' existence is open to doubt; without being doubted by the subject, the *Cogito* loses its logical axis and falls to pieces. Doubt leads him to ground his existence objectively in two further stages. His ability to doubt the existence of his body and environment but not his own existence enables him to place the first principle of his philosophy beyond the reach of material dependence such as physiological factors, which, say the Sceptics, play a role in the formation of our judgements. This first deduction from the *Cogito* places him at the point at which the third *Méditation* begins, seeing clearly and distinctly the truth of his proposition, which however is not guaranteed by anything other than itself. The certainty of his own existence as a thinking subject is objectively worthless if not validated by a metaphysical principle.[43]

The second deduction from the *Cogito* therefore centres on the presence in his mind of an idea of something more perfect than he thinks himself to be, that is, something whose existence cannot be doubted. As always, doubt is the test which clear and distinct knowledge must resist; the idea of perfection cannot be produced by an imperfect being who doubts, nor by his ideas of objects which are even less perfect, since their existence may be doubted whilst his own cannot.[44] In the third *Méditation* he examines various reasons in favour of the external origin of the ideas in his mind. By following the only reliable guide to truth, that is, knowledge which presents itself clearly and distinctly to the mind, he is able to objectify the idea of perfection in his mind:

.. car je ne saurais rien révoquer en doute de ce que la lumière naturelle me fait voir être vrai, ainsi qu'elle m'a tantôt fait voir que, de ce que je doutais, je pouvais conclure que j'étais. Et je n'ai en moi aucune autre faculté, ou puissance, pour distinguer le vrai du faux, qui me puisse enseigner que ce que cette lumière me montre comme vrai ne l'est pas, et à qui je me puisse tant fier qu'à elle.

This criterion enables him to see most objective reality in the idea in his mind of a sovereign, infinite and perfect God.[45] This idea exists not as a projection of his ability to doubt what is finite, but autonomously, pre-existing the idea he has of himself and enabling him to perceive his own imperfection. Its importance lies in the fact that it resists doubt more clearly than any other idea by its very presence in the mind as something perfect and infinite. It both validates and is validated by the criterion of clarity and distinctness required by indubitable knowledge, and guarantees his existence as the subject of the *Cogito*.

The circular relationship between his doubt and certainty may be seen in the postulate that this 'certitude métaphysique' is as indubitable as a geometrical demonstration. At the end of the fourth part of the *Discours*, as at the beginning, he elaborates the hypothesis that what we take as reality may in fact be a dream-like state, thus engendering another sceptical crisis about the criterion for distinguishing truth from falsehood. This has the effect of being less a proof of the metaphysical guarantee of the criterion than an illustration of its importance to the Cartesian method. How do we know, he asks, that the thoughts which we have when asleep are any more false than those which we have when awake, since the former may be just as clear and distinct as the latter? His answer is that it is not possible to do away with this objection to the criterion unless one presupposes the existence of God, for if we did not know that what we perceive clearly and distinctly is true because God exists, then there is no reason for thinking that such knowledge is true.[46] As Gassendi untiringly reiterates in his *Disquisitio*, Descartes is guilty of *petitio principii* regarding his criterion, since it states categorically that which needs to be proved. Yet Descartes is correct in assuming that the kind of doubt he has just raised will persist without a metaphysical guarantee for the accuracy of our knowledge. Framed by the sceptical crises which they need to provoke and by which they are themselves verified, the *Cogito* and its metaphysical guarantee are in necessary but precarious co-existence with Cartesian doubt — doubt which is less a philosophical doubt than the obverse of Descartes' wish to establish indubitable principles in philosophy.

7 The Paradoxes of Orasius Tubero

1

La Mothe Le Vayer is one of those writers who were well-known and widely read in learned circles of their time, but who are now numbered among the great background names in the history of thought of their century. The reasons for his relative obscurity are not difficult to find. Many of his writings are pedagogical in nature, prepared for the instruction of the young Louis XIV and his brother, the Duc d'Anjou. Others are pieces of political propaganda written to justify the political alliances of Richelieu. In particular, Le Vayer had a penchant for the archaic *genre* of the 'opuscule', or 'discours' or 'homilie académique', that is, formal disquisitions on themes as disparate as eloquence, travel, dress, friendship, wealth and poverty, life and death, philosophy, etc. An informal variation of the *genre* is seen in his one hundred and fifty *Petits Traités* dealing with subjects as diverse as agriculture, superstitions, dreams, the court, food, funerals, the law, literature etc., all of which are treated in his quizzical and digressive manner. His essays and dialogues are pedantic in style and ponderous in their wit, lacking the refined irony of Erasmus and the charming self-depreciation of Montaigne. Of the innumerable subjects treated, the principal one is that of his beloved scepticism or *epochē* as he prefers to term it, to which he remained attached from the first page of his voluminous work to the last. This provides the unifying principle of his work, but it is a unity in diversity since in his hands scepticism is capable of infinite nuances ranging from the tendentious scepticism of the early dialogues (1630—1) to the pure Pyrrhonic doubt of the essay on Pyrrhonism (1642) to that most conciliatory expression of Christian scepticism in the *Petit Discours Chrétien* (1637). In view of Le Vayer's temperamental need to cultivate paradox and practise mystification on the unwary reader, it is probably neither possible nor desirable to seek a coherent expression of his philosophy. He was known for his indifference to religious belief and practice, and it has generally been found convenient to classify him as an enigmatic successor to Montaigne and Charron, but more hostile to religion than either of them. With his acute sense of the diversity of opinions, Le Vayer would doubtless have been gratified to know that contemporary uncertainty about his orthodoxy in religion has been duplicated by posterity. For R. Pintard and Julien-Eymard d'Angers he is one of the most subtle of the *libertins érudits*, hostile to the very principles of religion;[1] for Sainte-Beuve and J. Grenier he is likewise 'un sceptique masqué';[2] for the abbé d'Olivet in the eighteenth century, R. Kerviler in the nineteenth and R. H. Popkin in the present one, he is a Christian Sceptic;[3] for E. Tisserand he is a precursor of eighteenth-century rationalism and probably not a Christian;[4] and for J. S. Spink 'while being obviously independent from Christian thought, he was not actually opposed to it'.[5] It is possible to adduce evidence in favour of each of these views from the innumerable expressions of scepticism which poured forth over a period of more than forty years. The earliest of his writings, however, his nine dialogues (1630—1) seem to me to be the most characteristic as well as the most revealing products of his thought, with the possible exceptions of the disabused *Prose Chagrine* (1661) and his last work, *Hexaméron rustique* (1670) which suffered the fate of being placed immediately on the Index.[6] The dialogues have the advantage of having been written before he came to act as propagandist for Richelieu's political and religious views as well as before his reception into the Académie Française and his long association with the court which was to last until his retirement in 1660. In the corpus of his works they occupy a place apart, for their spontaneity and frankness allow us to glimpse their author's mind more directly than most of his later writings in which the tactic of dissimulation is refined to the point at which it becomes a second nature.

2

The *Lettre de l'autheur* makes clear that the aim in writing the dialogues is purely personal, accounting for the outmoded dialogistic form. This illustrates Le Vayer's preference for unvarnished simplicity which he sees exemplified in the dialogues of Cicero, Lucian and Plato, as opposed to contemporary literary modes, deemed detrimental to spontaneity and feeling.[7] In addition, the dialogues, with real or fictional settings, are more capable of sustaining the illusion of real conversation than an essay or discourse, having arguments which develop simultaneously on two or more opposing fronts as the interlocutors take up or change their points of view according to the course of the conversation. It is easy to understand why such a form should have made a perennial appeal to Le Vayer, when one takes into consideration his brusque temperament, with its unpredictable sallies of wit, his inordinate penchant for contradiction and paradox which his scepticism gratifies so well.

Beneath the desultory erudition of the dialogues lies the unifying theme of scepticism which Le Vayer propounds relentlessly throughout his career. The first one, *De la Philosophie sceptique*, consists of an exposition of sceptical principles for the reader's benefit through the medium of a debate between the Aristotelian Eudoxus and the Sceptic Ephestion. It centres on the result of sceptical enquiry, suspension of judgement, the practice of which, the Aristotelian claims, leads to the absurd state of doubting the reality of universally agreed truths. Moreover, if nothing is certain, then opposing statements are as valid as those of the Sceptics. The sceptical rejoinder gives the classic statement about suspension of judgement from Le Vayer's master, Sextus Empiricus. The statement that 'nothing is true' is a non-affirmative and self-embracing axiom which, whilst undermining the claims to knowledge of its opponents, also undermines itself.[8] The marvellous suspension of judgement is brought about here by invoking the last of Sextus' ten modes or tropes which opposes opinion to opinion in such bewildering fashion that we see both the relativity and the tyranny of custom. What passes for folly in one country is wisdom in the next one: 'Il n'y a vertu qui ne soit prise pour un vice, ni vice qui ne tienne lieu de vertu ailleurs'.[9] Suspension of judgement (*epochē*) is achieved by the magical *ataraxia*, or intellectual detachment from all opinions, and by *metriopatheia*, or the moderation of the passions.

The first dialogue in its technique and 'conclusion' is a microcosm of so much of Le Vayer's opus. One cannot fail to discern the ludicrous disproportion between the effort expended on the demonstration that nothing is certain and the anti-climactic suspension of judgement, which, in spite of the grandiose claims on its behalf, merely replaces the vacuum created with the more finely worded sceptical one.

The second dialogue, *Le banquet sceptique*, also deals with objections to scepticism, and inadvertently lets us glimpse its main weakness as a practical philosophy. Since even the most perfect things are liable to corruption, declares the defender of scepticism, Orasius, it is not surprising that scepticism has its quota of eccentrics who doubt everything. The negation of reality, however, is not at all the Sceptic's ideal:

> Car se bander opiniâtrement contre tout ce que nous dictent les sens, ne recevoir aucuns phénomènes ... au lieu d'y acquiescer doucement, avec une raisonnable suspension, et sans épouser aucun parti ni opinion; ce n'est pas être légitime Philosophe sceptique ... mais être sans raison, ou sans sentiment quelconque ...[10]

This attack on the kind of hyper-scepticism shortly to be used by Descartes in the fourth part of his *Discours de la Méthode* raises the dilemma inherent in the sceptical attitude to phenomena. If the essence of reality is problematic and suspension of judgement the most rational attitude to adopt, is one not in bad faith if one acts and at the same time proclaims that one still suspends judgement? This is also the problem with which Descartes grapples in his 'morale par provision'. But by acting resolutely on the basis that there are no more certain reasons available at the time in question than those on which his action is grounded, his provisional certainty provides a more logical and ingenious solution of the problem than the imposed suspension of judgement of Orasius. The Sceptic attempts to forestall the problem by advancing that the suspension of judgement applies only to the nature of phenomena and allows for modest acquiescence in sense-impressions and reasoning. It is precisely at the point where he says that the mind 'neither affirms nor denies anything owing to the equipollence of the matters in question' and yet acts that he reduces himself to the kind of circular reasoning to which he drives his opponents. For we have no more guarantee that he neither affirms nor denies reality than those philosophers claiming to have true knowledge whose criteria are successively impugned by the Sceptics. He might after all be just a negative dogmatist masquerading under another name, that of Sceptic. In fact all he has done is to disclaim the title 'dogmatist' whilst refusing to follow the logic of his suspension of judgement to its ultimate conclusion, which is the cessation of all activity. If Le Vayer's character is unwilling to concede the title of Sceptic to those who suspend judgement about all phenomena, he seems to underline Pascal's point that 'On n'en peut venir là, et je mets en fait qu'il n'y a jamais eu de pyrrhonien effectif parfait'.[11]

The *Dialogue sur le sujet de la vie privée* treats a recurrent topic in Le Vayer's works as it debates whether or not it is better to live a life of philosophic seclusion or of social activity. In these strongly held antitheses we find the literary expression of Le Vayer's conflicting tendencies, to be seen later in his oscillation between avid search for formal recognition by court and Académie Française and subsequent disenchantment with both.[12] The debate between these two facets of his nature remains, like so many in his work, unresolved, principally because it is unresolvable in the mind of the author. In inconclusive debate he saw a kind of self-fulfilment, a means of maintaining his inner incompatibilities in harmonious co-existence, which life makes so difficult and scepticism satisfies so well.

The *Dialogue sur les rares et éminentes qualités des Anes de ce temps* illustrates, as the title suggests, the ponderous sceptical humour of Le Vayer. Even the most ridiculous objects, he intimates, have received their panegyric and he cites the example of Erasmus' *Encomium Moriae* (1511) which celebrates the wisdom of folly and the folly of wisdom. 'Cette petite ânerie' as Le Vayer calls his dialogue, is inspired by a sceptical attitude to reason and logic which have no objective meaning and may be used to buttress any opinion however intrinsically absurd or paradoxical. It is a burlesque illustration of Montaigne's description of reason in the *Apologie* as 'un instrument de plomb et de cire, alongeable, ployable et accommodable à tous biais et à toutes mesures'. The paradoxical argumentation demonstrates the malleable nature of reason and what Montaigne terms 'la suffisance de le sçavoir contourner'.[13] His praise of the intellectual prowess of the donkey is a *reductio ad absurdum* of the scholastic method of analysis, as he examines each attribute according to the time-honoured categories of prudence, justice, courage, etc. The donkey is pronounced exemplary in all categories and the asinine quality *par excellence* declared to be temperance in all things. His stolid immobile attitude under duress is compared to sceptical acatalepsy, although it is admitted that this could also be attributed to Stoicism. The burlesque subject thus gives Le Vayer the opportunity of investing something trivial with the trappings of scholarship and of providing a jocular illustration of his scepticism. What appears as mere asininity may after all be a comment on our relative and infirm speculative faculty, and a salutary reminder of the importance of suspending our judgement, of which the donkey is a symbol.

The last of the *Cinq dialogues*, the *Dialogue sur le sujet de la Divinité*, is without doubt the most important and complex on account of its theme and the way in which it is treated by Le Vayer. His treatment of religion has given rise to the vexed question of the relationship between his brand of scepticism and Christianity which has already been alluded to. Once again it is Orasius who undertakes to dispel doubts about scepticism, as he prides himself on having prepared his mind through it for belief in religion. Scepticism doubts the certainty of knowledge emanating from sciences and other branches of intellectual inquiry, but theology is exempt from its scrutiny since it is not 'une science qui demanderait des principes clairs et évidents à notre entendement, là où elle prend quasi tous les siens des mystères de notre foi, laquelle est un vrai don de Dieu, et qui surpasse entièrement la portée de l'esprit humain'.[14] His position at the outset is that of a thorough-going fideist in his radical separation of the provinces of reason and faith. Fideism does not of course imply in itself any doubting of religious truth, and many Christian fideists from Erasmus and Luther to Gassendi and Pascal have agreed with Orasius.[15] Once he has made the basic separation of faith and reason, he can proceed to show the concordance between scepticism and Christianity. Both are shown to stress the need for intellectual humility, and St Paul's strictures on human wisdom in the opening chapters of his first *Epistle to the Corinthians* are 'parfaitement Pyrrhoniens'.[16] The fideistic bond is deepened by Christ's reticence to reveal the time at which the world would end and to answer Pilate's query regarding truth. Up to this point it is perfectly possible and indeed necessary, in view of the difficulty inherent in any interpretation of fideism, to view Orasius within the tradition of orthodox Christian fideism. His exegesis of Christ's refusal to explain what truth is however is something of a watershed in the dialogue, since to Orasius it places him on the same level as other human beings who share our lack of knowledge of final things. The exegesis as such is plausible, but disturbing from the pen of one who professes himself to be a Christian. He has laboured hard to erect a sceptical foundation for the Christian faith, and this has been possible because scepticism stresses the uncertainty of human knowledge and the Christian faith the fallible state of man. But he finally overstretches himself here, for the foundation is not equal to the weight placed upon it by the incorporation of Christ as the prime example of sceptical uncertainty. By subtly making the founder of the Christian religion into an albeit unacknowledged exponent of scepticism, his unique claim to be the revelation of God's truth to men is in effect nullified.

The end of the conciliation of scepticism and Christianity has been reached and the former is extolled as 'une heureuse préparation Evangélique'. The conclusion is the same as that of Montaigne and Charron. The former saw in scepticism 'une carte blanche préparée à prendre du doigt de Dieu telles formes qu'il luy plaira y graver' and the latter wrote that it induced in the mind the 'vacuité de résolution' thus presenting man as 'blanc, nud et prest' for the reception of God's truth.[17] But both restricted sceptical uncertainty to the operation of preparing the mind for the revelation of truth; their claims remain more modest and preparatory in character than those of Orasius, who sets out with much ado to effect a spectacular conciliation between scepticism and Christianity. In fact the much heralded conciliation does not take place at all, because scepticism has been extended to embrace the Christian faith, the founder of which has been shown to be no more exempt from error than the founder of any other philosophical sect. Nowhere has that faith been seen to command the assent of the will, which in Montaigne and Charron had remained ostensibly unaffected by their use of scepticism. Montaigne's scepticism enabled him to see Christianity as providing a traditional religious channel through which man's spiritual aspirations could seek fulfilment, and in the confusion of opinions which it revealed, encouraged him in practice to rely solely on the established authority of the Church. For Charron, scepticism stripped man of his pride by revealing the weakness of his judgement, and in so doing disposed his will to accept true piety.[18] With Orasius, however, the sceptical will to doubt is everywhere revealed, and no limit, certainly not that of his will to believe, has been set against it.

With the divorce of faith and reason, the sceptical bent of Orasius need be hemmed in no longer by the necessity of appearing orthodox, and the way is opened for the demolition of the idea that God's existence is proved by universal consent. Audacity and gratuitous defence of the Christian faith alternate, as he advances St Thomas' argument for the existence of God, based unfortunately on universal consent which has just been demolished! The double-edged argument concedes that the atheistic viewpoint does not lack cogency; immediately, the cosmological proof is invoked only to be discredited. The way is also opened for the secularization of Christianity, as Christ is no longer the divine Logos but the principle of natural reason in which all men share. All who follow this natural reason, be they reputed atheists, may be accepted as Christian.

The climax of Orasius' argument has been reached and the general purpose is clear. By the initial separation of faith and reason, successive sceptical crises have been engendered: the sceptical comparative approach to religions deprives Christianity of the unique status of revealed religion which it claims; all the rational arguments accumulate insidiously on the side of the unbelievers, but after each accumulation we are told that this imbalance is unimportant since faith does not rest on reason. Indirectly the will to believe has been undermined all the while by innumerable examples of credulous belief in the face of rational evidence.

Descartes was not slow to see the dangerous implications for religion in this dialogue, for he almost certainly alluded to it in his correspondence of 6 May 1630 with Père Mersenne as 'le meschant livre' and even thought of publishing his own edition containing a refutation of each of its arguments. In the event he did not carry out his intention but this dialogue in particular doubtless acted as an additional stimulus in his later elaboration of the proof of God's existence in the *Discours de la Méthode* and the *Méditations Métaphysiques*. On 25 November of the same year he wrote to Mersenne in this connexion: 'Le plus court moyen que je sçache pour répondre aux raisons qu'il apporte contre la Divinité, et ensemble à toutes celles des autres Athées, c'est de trouver une démonstration évidente, qui fasse croire à tout le monde que Dieu est.'[19] One can understand such a reaction, for the mode of argument creates a highly unfavourable impression of Le Vayer's attitude to the faith he professes to uphold, an impression which had not been created by the frequently similar sceptical arguments of Montaigne and Charron. In spite of the latters' philosophical doubts, both are in the last analysis prepared to accept the final authority of the Church in faith and practice and a presumption in favour of their religious belief, if not of their orthodoxy, is created. Descartes' conclusion is encouraged by the sustained ironic tone of the dialogue, by the absorption of Christianity into scepticism, and by the barely concealed intention to jolt the reader from traditional orthodoxy. However, the overall impression from the dialogue is that it is less a work of studied miscreance than a boisterous, irreverent and often facetious revolt against the stability of traditional Christian belief, less a manifesto of *libertinage érudit* than a highly unconvincing and unsubtle attempt to show the religious gain to be derived from scepticism. In short, the dialogue seems to be nothing more than a belated 'péché de jeunesse' in which Le Vayer's rhapsodical espousal of scepticism impels him to indulge, and which, once gratified, loses much of its attractiveness for his iconoclastic mind, as evidenced by the numerous subsequent modulations of his professed Christian scepticism in his work.

3

The first of the *Quatre autres dialogues, De l'ignorance louable*, is directed against Aristotle's definition of knowledge as a divine science and its extension in the Stoic maxim that 'sapientia est rerum humanarum divinarumque scientia'. The sceptical ideal opposed to this by Orasius is 'une ignorance honorable, et vraiment philosophique, laquelle s'accommodant à l'obscurité de la nature, et se mesurant à la portée de l'esprit humain, ne promet rien au-delà de ses forces'. Entrance to this happy state of philosophic ignorance is only possible by coming to that stage beyond knowledge which Montaigne termed 'l'ignorance doctorale', that is, the paradoxical degree of knowledge which makes us aware that the essence of things cannot be known. The Aristotelian Télamon asserts that knowledge is the natural prerogative of man. Following Montaigne, Orasius maintains that if this were so, we would acquire it effortlessly and with pleasure. But this is manifestly not the case with the philosophers who convert it into pedantry and dogmatism. Great learning does not go hand in hand with sound judgement.[20] This dialogue represents the most incisive and sustained criticism of established philosophy in the dialogues as the ubiquitous Orasius, in page after page of devastating sceptical doubt, demonstrates that all systems of ethics and philosophy are arbitrary in the extreme, and that true reason may be closer to the state of the animals than to those 'Poètes de la Mythologie', the philosophers.[21]

The *Dialogue sur l'opiniâtreté* between Ephestion and Cassander provides a discussion of the psychological and philosophic reasons underlying our intransigent defence of those opinions which we cherish most. Scepticism is seen as a bulwark against all kinds of inflexibility: Ephestion reminds us that our past mistakes should render us cautious about promulgating our opinions as truth for all to receive as such. But this is not always the case, since 'la philautie' or self-love is such a potent factor in shaping our judgement and making us cling obdurately to an opinion once we have advanced it. Cassander adds that our judgement is so often beclouded by prejudice that the object of our discussions is not to establish the truth but rather the triumph of a partisan point of view.[22] Ephestion offers an interesting insight into the psychology of people who never retract an opinion. Just as there are physical illnesses which are incurable, so too there are maladies of the mind of which what he terms quaintly 'cette jalousie des opinions' is one against which reason is powerless. Self-love is the underlying cause of our self-delusions, accounting for the natural contradictoriness in our behaviour: 'Pour le moins en voyons-nous beaucoup qui n'ont pas moins d'inclination à se roidir contre tout ce que les autres approuvent que de certains poissons à nager toujours contre le fil de l'eau'. With the view of the incurable and perverse obduracy with which men cling to their vision of things, so that they are impervious to reason, these remarks anticipate in a striking way the psychology of Molière's greatest comic heroes who are sustained in their aberrations by the opposition of all who do not conform to their particular fixation. In *L'Avare* Valère describes Harpagon as one of those people who have 'des tempéraments ennemis de toute résistance, des naturels rétifs, que la vérité fait cabrer, qui toujours se roidissent contre le droit chemin de la raison' (Act I, Sc. 5).[23] Perhaps the best example of such monolithic comic rigidity is seen in the comedy of Alceste, of whom Célimène says penetratingly

> Et ne faut-il pas bien que Monsieur contredise?
> A la commune voix veut-on qu'il se réduise,
> Et qu'il ne fasse pas éclater en tous lieux
> L'esprit contrariant qu'il a reçu des cieux?
> (*Le Misanthrope*, Act II, Sc.4, lines 669–72).

The *imaginaire* in Molière's theatre cannot conceive of an opinion other than his own as having a right to exist. It is as impossible for Orgon to realize that his idolatry of Tartuffe is not universally shared as it is for Alceste to understand why the rest of the world is not outraged by the adverse result of his lawsuit or for Argan to comprehend why his daughter need not marry a doctor. As this dialogue makes clear, our differences of view stem from the different constitutions of our minds, from the different ways in which they incline us to look at reality and from our inability to pierce to the truth of things since we see only what we wish to see. Some thirty-five years before *Le Misanthrope* Le Vayer anticipates the lines which Molière will give to Éliante about the subjective criteria governing our judgement and of which the character of Alceste is the supreme comic illustration. Ephestion's conclusion is similar to the judgement deeply embedded in the dramatic structure of the play and illustrated in the character of Philinte, as he advises us to cultivate 'cette belle indifférence et cette souplesse d'esprit, laquelle nous rendant commodes et sociables partout, nous donne encore une assiette reposée'.[24]

In the *Dialogue traitant de la politique sceptiquement* the traditional forms of government are progressively stripped of all substance as they fall under the sceptical purview of Orontes. Each begins with high principles but inevitably degenerates into the common absurdity and vanity. Whilst the manoeuvres of politics and politicians are stigmatized as products of 'l'imbécillité de notre nature', no positive alternative is suggested as a means of ordering human affairs. Instead, the purely personal ideal of 'ce doux repos et cette agréable tranquillité' is extolled and provides the pretext for Orontes to rhapsodize about the natural innocence of men which politics corrupt. True independence of thought and action is seen as incompatible with politics, from which the wise man can only withdraw to laugh at the folly of human enterprises, exemplifying the sceptical principle of the dialogues enunciated in the *Lettre de l'autheur*, to the effect that 'notre vie n'est, à le bien prendre, qu'une fable, notre connaissance qu'une ânerie, nos certitudes que des contes: bref, tout ce monde qu'une farce et perpétuelle comédie'. The difficulty even for Le Vayer in achieving this supremely negative ideal is borne out by the constant tension in his later writings between his desire for independence and public recognition. Orontes will always be a part of Le Vayer, but Le Vayer is always more than his dialogist.[25]

The last dialogue, *Sur le mariage*, is without doubt the most burlesque of Le Vayer's early writings. Eleus, the bachelor seeking advice as to whether or not he should marry, sums up the conclusion at the beginning by saying that marriage is like all other conditions of life 'qui nous réussissent faciles ou importunes, selon que la fortune, ou notre adresse et bonne conduite nous permet d'en bien ou mal user'.[26] Cassander and Philocles give their advice sceptically, that is, both are sufficiently detached from their own state to proffer an opinion which directly contradicts it. Thus the bachelor Cassander advises marriage and the married Philocles inveighs against it.

Cassander celebrates the industry, intelligence and superiority of women, dismissing as 'calomnies forgées à plaisir' the traditional criticism by men. It is jealousy on the part of a husband which he sees as the greatest obstacle to marriage, and he develops a line of thought entirely in keeping with the speeches of Ariste and Chrysalde in Molière's *Ecoles*.[27] According to his liberal attitude, jealousy only serves to make the husband miserable and often attracts the attention of rivals who otherwise would have remained indifferent to the wife.[28] Exercise of good judgement in the choice and treatment of a wife will not of itself ensure a marriage free of trouble. In the final analysis one can only hope that fortune will be kind by not providing real grounds for jealousy. Following the well-known arguments of tradition and anticipating Chrysalde, Cassander undertakes the apology for cuckoldry, 'la plaisante imagination des cornes'.[29] Sacred and secular sources both make favourable mention of horns, and the tangible benefits are evidenced in the affluence of many homes. But the greatest advantage lies in the fact that the cuckold is assured of the reality of his dreams — 'fortis imaginatio generat casum'.

Like Arnolphe, Philocles has long been a student of feminine wiles which result in neglect of household duties and preference of the *galant* to the onerous ties of marriage. Liberalism is a misnomer where honour is at stake, for fear of cuckoldry is both natural and rational. Its dread reality cannot be trivialized or mitigated by arguing that it may bring social advantages in its wake.[30] Several types of women are anathema to this traditionalist as to the retrograde cast of mind of Arnolphe and Sganarelle. Women brought up on the romantic doctrines of *L'Astrée*, like their successors Cathos and Magdelon, are viewed as threatening the fabric of marriage and society, as are viragos who rule husband and family with a rod of iron and bluestockings 'qui ignorent tout ce qu'elles pensent savoir, et ne savent que ce qu'elles feignent ignorer'.[31] A submissive and obedient wife is the ideal, but in view of the concomitant troubles of a wife and family 'il fait fort bon se garder d'une mauvaise, et ne se guère fier en la meilleure'.[32]

The opposing arguments annul each other, underlining Eleus' conclusion spoken at the outset, that everything depends on the way one adapts to contingency. The argumentation proves superfluous, serving only as a sceptical *reductio ad absurdum* of reason, which is, as Montaigne wrote, 'un pot à deux ances, qu'on peut saisir à gauche et à dextre'.[33] The dialogue is a game, a paradox in form and content, into which the speakers enter with alacrity, arguing for and against positions which they do not hold. The last dialogue is in fact a microcosm of the others and allows us to glimpse the spirit of paradox which animates them. The dialogues as a whole can only take place on condition that the intellect is at variance with the will, for suspension of mind begins with detachment from one's opinions, evidenced here in the ability to make them into a playful spectacle.

The dialogues represent the enthusiastic discovery of scepticism by Le Vayer and are an early experiment in the process of self-detachment which was to continue unabated over the next forty years or so. Thanks to his opposing characters, Le Vayer is in them and beyond them simultaneously as he uses them to provoke and sustain the most diverse arguments. As such, the dialogues are more often than not self-conscious and prolix, more an overstatement of scepticism than a studied philosophic outlook, too replete with gratuitous adolescent-like mystification to pose a serious challenge to established authority and religious orthodoxy. To take them more seriously and literally is to fall victim to the author's manifest wish to disconcert us at all costs. Bayle glimpsed something fundamental to the inspiration and enigmatic mind behind them when discussing Le Vayer's alleged lack of religious belief:

> Il est sûr qu'il y a beaucoup de libertinage dans les Dialogues d'Orasius Tubero: mais qui en voudroit conclure, que l'Auteur

n'avoit point de Religion se rendroit coupable d'un jugement téméraire; car il y a une grande différence entre écrire librement ce qui se peut dire contre la foi, et le croire très véritable.[34]

Notes

Abbreviations of periodicals correspond to the conventions used in the bibliography of *The Year's Work in Modern Language Studies*.

INTRODUCTION

1. A. Gide, *Préface* to *L'Immoraliste* in *Romans, récits et soties* (Paris, 1958), p. 367.
2. Quoted by W. G. Moore, in his *French Classical Literature, An Essay* (Oxford, 1961), p. 18.
3. See W. G. Moore's *Molière, A New Criticism* (Oxford, 1949); *Racine: Britannicus* (London, 1960); and *French Classical Literature* quoted above.
4. P. Larthomas, *Le langage dramatique, sa nature, ses procédés* (Paris, 1972).
5. His third *Discours* on dramatic poetry in Pierre Corneille, *Writings on the Theatre*, ed. H. T. Barnwell (Oxford, 1965), p. 63.
6. See P. Bénichou, *Morales du grand siècle* (Paris, 1948).
7. *Maxime* 43.
8. *Essais*, éd. M. Rat (Paris, 1962), III, Ch. 2, p. 227.
9. See the suggestive remarks of E. R. O. Borgerhoff in this connexion in *The Freedom of French Classicism* (New York, 1950).

CHAPTER 1

1. G. Lanson, 'Le héros cornélien et le 'généreux' selon Descartes', *RHLF*, I (1894) pp. 397–411; see also A. J. Krailsheimer, *Studies in Self-Interest from Descartes to La Bruyère* (Oxford, 1962), pp. 47–60.
2. P. Bénichou, *Morales du grand siècle* (Paris, 1948); O. Nadal, *Le sentiment de l'amour dans l'oeuvre de Pierre Corneille* (Paris, 1948).
3. O. Nadal, op. cit., pp. 305ff.
4. Ibid., p. 127; cf. G. Poulet, *Etudes sur le temps humain* (Edinburgh, 1949), p. 127.
5. P. Bénichou, op. cit., p. 20.
6. La Bruyère, *Les caractères, ou les moeurs de ce siècle* (Paris, 1962), p. 88.
7. The phrase is from P. Bénichou, op. cit., p. 25; see also the chapter on the topic in O. Nadal, op. cit., pp. 126–36.
8. Quotations are from *Théâtre complet de Corneille* (Paris, 1962), 3 vols.
9. Cf. Pauline's similar role in front of Sévère, *Polyeucte*, Act II, Sc. 2.
10. L. Herland, *Horace ou la naissance de l'homme* (Paris, 1952), pp. 71ff.
11. L. Herland sees Horace here as a hero who intoxicates himself with martial rhetoric to protect his feelings (ibid., p. 105).
12. Ibid., pp. 111ff.

13. Camille curses Rome in a passionate outburst (lines 1301–18), an entity which symbolizes to her the malefic force delighting to rob her of Curiace (see also Act IV, Sc. 4).
14. Corneille, *Writings on the Theatre*, ed. H. T. Barnwell (Oxford, 1965), p. 111.
15. Ibid., p. 111.
16. Ibid., p. 9; see the illuminating study by R. C. Knight, 'A minimal definition of seventeenth-century tragedy', *FS*, 10 (1956), pp. 297–308.
17. J. Morel sees a belief in his heroism underlying the passive attitude of Horace in the scene of judgement, 'A propos du plaidoyer d'Horace', *RR*, LI (1960), p. 32.
18. The conclusion has been advanced that Horace comes to the end of the play without recognizing the tragedy of his position, notably by R. J. Nelson, *Corneille, his Heroes and their Worlds* (Philadelphia, 1963), p. 93; for the contrary view, see M-O. Sweetser, *La dramaturgie de Corneille* (Geneva–Paris, 1977), pp. 118–19.
19. See M-O. Sweetser, 'Importance du personnage d'Auguste dans la dramaturgie cornélienne', *RR*, LII (1961), p. 262, and op. cit., pp. 122–3; A. D. Sellstrom, 'The structure of Corneille's masterpieces', *RR*, XLIX (1958), p. 275.
20. S. Doubrovsky, *Corneille et la dialectique du héros* (Paris, 1963), p. 193; G. Lanson, art. cit., p. 401.
21. L. Herland, 'Le pardon d'Auguste dans *Cinna*', *TR*, 158 (février 1961), pp. 113–26.
22. See the perceptive remarks on Auguste's pardon by O. Nadal, op. cit., p. 135.
23. *Maximes* 15 and 16 by La Rochefoucauld are apposite in this connexion.
24. *Maxime* 24; for the view of the *Maximes* as the antithesis of the heroic ethic, see P. Bénichou, op. cit., pp. 13–51, 97–111.
25. Corneille, *Writings on the Theatre*, pp. 117, 28–36.
26. R. Lebègue, 'Remarques sur *Polyeucte*', *FS*, III (1949), p. 218; cf. A. Adam, *Histoire de la littérature française au XVIIe siècle* (Paris, 1962), I, pp. 538–9.
27. R. Chauviré, 'Doutes à l'égard de *Polyeucte*', *FS*, II (1948), p. 6; J. Schlumberger more perceptively sees this apparent difference in Polyeucte's attitude as the result of Corneille's observation of the rule of the unity of time, *Tableau de la littérature française* (Paris, 1939), p. 22.
28. On the importance of emulation in *Polyeucte*, see L. E. Harvey, 'The role of emulation in Corneille's *Polyeucte*', *PMLA*, LXXXII, 5 (October 1967), pp. 314–24.
29. See B. Dort, *Corneille* (Paris, 1957), and S. Doubrovsky, op. cit.
30. Lytton Strachey, *Landmarks in French Literature* (Oxford, 1964), p. 39 (1st ed. 1912); also E. Faguet, *En lisant Corneille* (Paris, 1913); J. Calvet, *Polyeucte de Corneille* (Paris, 1932); P. Bénichou, op. cit.; O. Nadal, op. cit.
31. J. Pineau, 'La seconde conversion de Polyeucte', *RHLF* (1975), p. 548.
32. This is, in varying degrees, the thesis of S. Doubrovsky (op. cit., p. 251), P. Bénichou (op. cit., p. 33) and A. J. Krailsheimer (op. cit., p. 54). For a refutation of this viewpoint, see J. d'Angers, '*Polyeucte*, tragédie chrétienne', *XVII S*, 75 (1967), pp. 49–69.

Notes

33. See R. Tobin, 'Le sacrifice et '*Polyeucte*', *RSH* (1973), p. 595, n. 18.
34. *John*, Ch. 15, v. 13 (*La Bible de Jérusalem*).
35. Cf. the comment of A. Stegmann that Polyeucte in his offer to Sévère 'est sublime jusqu'au ridicule', *L'Héroïsme cornélien—genèse et signification* (Paris, 1968), I, p. 590.
36. The Greek term is formed from the verb 'heauton ekenōsen', 'he emptied himself', and the divine 'kenosis' is the subject of St Paul's christological hymn in his *Epistle to the Philippians*, Ch. 2, vv. 6–11.

CHAPTER 2

1. B. Weinberg, *The Art of Jean Racine* (Chicago, 1963), p. 106.
2. L. Goldmann, *Le dieu caché. Etude sur la vision tragique dans les Pensées de Pascal et dans le théâtre de Racine* (Paris, 1955), p. 355.
3. A. Adam, *Histoire de la littérature française au XVIIe siècle* (Paris, 1962), IV, p. 318.
4. Quotations are from *Oeuvres de J. Racine* (Paris, 1923), II.
5. Cf. her admiration for his heroic deeds on learning of his return to her from Andromaque, lines 851–4.
6. Cf. her earlier evocation of the fall of Troy to Pyrrhus, lines 928–30.
7. A. Ubersfeld sees Andromaque as an unselfish heroine in her edition of the play (Paris, 1961), p. 50; A. Adam on the other hand speaks of the cruelty in her role (op. cit., p. 318).
8. It is this ingenuousness which makes the materialistic interpretation of her decision by L. Goldmann incompatible with her character (op. cit., p. 361).
9. On the development of the word 'autel' as a symbol, see J. C. Lapp, *Aspects of Racinian Tragedy* (Toronto and Oxford, 1955), Ch. 4.
10. On the ways in which Racine renovates certain *précieux* words so that they assume symbolic force, see ibid., Ch. 4.
11. As the action moves towards her decision in Act IV, Sc. 1, references to her tears become less frequent: see Act I, Sc. 4, lines 263, 266, 278, 281, 304, 338, 362, 374; Act III, Sc. 4, lines 861, 880; Act III, Sc. 6, line 897; Act III, Sc. 7, line 949; Act III, Sc. 8, line 1021; Act IV, Sc. 1, line 1126 is a reference by Andromaque to the tears of Céphise.
12. Cf. lines 645–7, where he explains to Phoenix his intentions behind his blackmail.
13. Cf. *Britannicus*, Act II, Sc. 2, line 402.
14. On the power of the 'regard' see J. Pommier, *Aspects de Racine* (Paris, 1954), pp. 195–6, 268ff; J. Starobinski, 'Racine et la poétique du regard', *L'oeil vivant* (Paris, 1961); C. Amat, 'Le thème de la vision dans l'*Andromaque* de Racine', *RSH* (1973), pp. 45–54.
15. See the remarks of J. D. Hubert on the way Andromaque's glance achieves revenge over Pyrrhus, *Essai d'exégèse racinienne, les secrets témoins* (Paris, 1956), pp. 84ff.
16. Unwilling to witness the ultimate triumph of Andromaque's glance in her marriage to Pyrrhus, Hermione nevertheless is anxious that he should know who is responsible for his murder; see lines 1269–70.
17. Cf. *Phèdre*, Act IV, Sc. 4 and 5, where Phèdre learns of Hyppolyte's love for Aricie.

18. Cf. lines 1060-2, 1217-19.
19. See the perceptive remarks on the opening of the play by L. Goldmann (op. cit., p. 364).
20. This is one of the key-words in her role, reflecting her obsession with power and her dread of removal from its source; see line 143, line 1276.
21. The play has well been called 'a drama of watcher and watched' by J. C. Lapp (op. cit., p. 8).
22. After the murder of Britannicus she sees the extent to which Narcisse has betrayed her (line 1696).
23. J. Brody, '"Les yeux de César", The language of vision in *Britannicus*', *Studies in Seventeenth Century French Literature* (Ithaca, 1962), p. 190.
24. O. de Mourgues speaks of 'The genuine passion born in the heart of Néron', but sees 'a strain of sadism in him'; *Racine or, the Triumph of Relevance* (London, 1967), p. 19.
25. On the power of Agrippine's look, see J. Brody, art. cit., pp. 196-7.
26. B. Weinberg, op. cit., p. 110.
27. See Act II, Sc. 2, lines 371-419.
28. Cf. lines 105ff., 171ff., 211ff., 301ff., 691ff.
29. Rome is considered as a backcloth to the drama in the edition of the play by C. L. Walton (Oxford, 1965), pp. 23-4; in *Andromaque*, however, there is the suggestion in the *dénouement* that Troy is a destructive as well as a noble influence; in *Britannicus* Rome is pictured as the unwitting accomplice of Néron in the speeches of Burrhus, Act I, Sc. 2. On the difference between Rome in *Britannicus* and in *Bérénice*, see H. T. Barnwell, 'La gloire dans le théâtre de Racine', *Jeunesse de Racine* (1962), pp. 10ff.
30. L. Goldmann, op. cit., p. 374.
31. P. F. Butler, 'The tragedy of *Bérénice*', in *Racine*, ed. R. C. Knight (London, 1969), p. 212.
32. P. F. Butler, *Classicisme et Baroque dans l'oeuvre de Racine* (Paris, 1959), p. 239.
33. On the refusal of the tragic character to recognize the truth of his situation, see H. T. Barnwell, 'Le tragique dans la tragédie française', *Jeunesse de Racine* (1967), pp. 67-9.

CHAPTER 3

1. F. Brunetière, 'La philosophie de Molière', *RDM*, C (1890), pp. 657, 676-7; see also his *Etudes sur le XVIIe siècle* (Paris, 1907), pp. 179-242.
2. E. Faguet, *En lisant Molière* (Paris, 1914), pp. 95-6.
3. G. Michaut, *Les luttes de Molière* (Paris, 1925), pp. 108, 227.
4. R. Fernandez, *La vie de Molière* (Paris, 1929), pp. 108-9.
5. W. G. Moore, *Molière, A New Criticism* (Oxford, 1949), p. 74; R. Bray, *Molière homme de théâtre* (Paris, 1954), p. 32.
6. See J. D. Hubert, *Molière and the Comedy of Intellect* (Berkeley, 1962), pp. 48-9; J. Guicharnaud, *Molière, une aventure théâtrale* (Paris, 1963), pp. 358-9.
7. L. Gossman, *Men and Masks, a Study of Molière* (Baltimore, 1963), pp. 242-4; F. L. Lawrence, 'The "Raisonneur" in Molière', *EsC*, VI (1966), pp. 156-66.

8. R. W. Herzel, 'The Function of the Raisonneur in Molière's Comedy', *MLN*, 90 (1975), pp. 564–75; H. C. Knutson also sees ambiguity in the character, who uses rhetoric to impress the audience and *imaginaire* rather than to put forward a point of view; *Molière: An Archetypal Approach* (Toronto and Buffalo, 1976), p. 177.
9. R. Fargher, 'Molière and his reasoners', *Studies in French Literature Presented to H. W. Lawton* (Manchester, 1968), pp. 105–20; A. Eustis, *Molière as Ironic Contemplator* (The Hague, 1973), pp. 182–92.
10. On the evolution of the character, see R. McBride, *The Sceptical Vision of Molière, a Study in Paradox* (London, 1977).
11. Quotations are from Molière, *Oeuvres complètes*, éd. G. Couton (Paris, 1971), I.
12. *Essais*, éd. M. Rat (Paris, 1962), I, Ch. 23, pp. 123, 125.
13. See, for example, the opening scenes of *L'Ecole des Femmes, Dom Juan, Le Misanthrope, L'Avare, M. De Pourceaugnac, Les Femmes Savantes*.
14. The title of *récits* and dances performed in 1655 at Montpellier in which Molière took part.
15. A. Eustis views Chrysalde as both foil and protatic character (op. cit., pp. 185ff.); for the latter view, see F. L. Lawrence, art. cit.
16. Sc. 3.
17. Ibid., Sc. 3.
18. Bossuet overlooked entirely this context in his attack on Molière's supposed advice to husbands, *Maximes et Réflexions sur la comédie*, Ch. 5.
19. See A. Adam, *Histoire de la littérature française au XVIIe siècle* (Paris, 1962), III, p. 381.
20. F. L. Lawrence, art. cit., p. 158.
21. A. Eustis maintains that Ariste and Chrysalde 'take themselves seriously most of the time', op. cit., p. 185; for L. Jouvet, on the other hand, the advice of the character was not to be taken at all literally, 'Molière', *Conferencia* (1 September 1937), pp. 292–3.

CHAPTER 4

1. *Maximes*, éd. J. Truchet (Paris, 1967), p. 578.
2. *Pensées* (No. 211, Lafuma), in *Oeuvres complètes* (Paris, 1963).
3. Ed. cit., pp. XXIII–V.
4. Sainte-Beuve, *Portraits de Femmes* (Paris, 1854), p. 296.
5. The *Discours de la Chapelle-Bessé* is at pains to present La Rochefoucauld as an amateur writer, éd. cit., p. 270.
6. P. E. Lewis in *La Rochefoucauld: the Art of Abstraction* (Ithaca and London, 1977) revives the view of the predominance of self-love in the *Maximes* whilst conceding that their author was not intent on constructing a system.
7. 'De la gloire', *Essais*, éd. M. Rat (Paris, 1962), II, Ch. 16, p. 15; see the suggestive remarks on *amour-propre* by W. G. Moore in *La Rochefoucauld, His Mind and Art* (Oxford, 1969), Ch. 9; also E. D. James, 'Scepticism and positive values in La Rochefoucauld', *FS*, XXIII, 4 (1969), pp. 349–61.

8. This remark is well illustrated in the *salon* scene, Act II, Sc. 4.
9. Cf. the images of 'branle' and flux which Montaigne uses at the end of his *Apologie de Raimond Sebond* to suggest the ever-changing nature of personality and judgement, op. cit., pp. 678ff.
10. 'De la Retraite', éd. cit., p. 224.
11. Cf. No. 412.
12. Cf. the co-ordination of *amour-propre* and *intérêt* in *Maximes Supprimées*, No. 1.
13. Pascal sees *intérêt* as producing only blindness in us, *Pensées*, No. 44.
14. On the variations in judgement brought about by physical causes, see Montaigne, *Essais*, II, Ch. 12, pp. 633-9.
15. One of the best accounts of the theory is to be found in F. Bernier's *Abrégé de la philosophie de Gassendi* (Lyon, 1678), VII, 7, Ch. 1; Molière makes great play with this fixed view of the human organism, see *L'Amour Médecin*, Act II, Sc. 4.
16. Montaigne had made the same point in the *Apologie*, op. cit., p. 633; see also Pascal, *Pensées*, No. 44.
17. Ed. cit., pp. 257-8; for a similar view, see Molière's *Préface* to *Tartuffe* (1669).
18. Erasmus, *Eloge de la Folie*, tr. P. de Nolhac (Paris, 1953), p. 56.
19. *Essais*, II, Ch. 2, pp. 380-1.
20. Cf. Montaigne's similar remark in ibid., II, Ch. 12, p. 636.
21. See the two scenes of seduction, Act III, Sc. 3, Act IV, Sc. 5.
22. For a discussion of *folie* in this play and in the work of Molière's friend, La Mothe Le Vayer, see R. McBride, *The Sceptical Vision of Molière* (London, 1977), pp. 143—50.
23. See *Essais*, I, Ch. 50, p. 337; in the *Maximes*, weakness is presented as the only irremediable fault (No. 130), the enemy of sincerity (No. 316) and more opposed to virtue than vice (No. 445).
24. See the passage in the *Lettre* on the manifestation and perception of the ridiculous in human nature, in Molière, *Oeuvres complètes*, éd. cit., I, p. 1174.
25. *Essais*, II, Ch. 20, p. 78, Ch. 1, p. 370.
26. Cf. the same sentence in ibid, II, Ch. 1, p. 372.
27. *Pensées*, No. 131.
28. P. Bénichou, *Morales du grand siècle* (Paris, 1948), pp. 97-111.
29. Mme de Rohan did not conceal her surprise in finding it in this context, see éd. cit. p. 588; but some of the *Maximes Posthumes* written at the same time allow for genuine humility (Nos. 37, 38).
30. Cf. *Pensées*, No. 21, on the importance of the correct perspective in judgement.
31. For the same idea, see No. 287, 'Du faux', éd. cit., p. 208, 'Des goûts', pp. 202-3.
32. 'De la différence des esprits', éd. cit., p. 219.
33. See Nos. 258, 451.
34. On the date of composition of the *Réflexions* see M. Leconte, 'Recherches sur les dates de composition des 'Réflexions diverses' de La Rochefoucauld', *RSH* (avril-juin 1965).
35. 'Des goûts', éd. cit., p. 202.

36. Ed. cit., pp. 185–6.
37. 'De la différence des esprits', éd. cit., p. 218.
38. This basic idea of *honnêteté* is more fully developed in R. McBride, op. cit., pp. 150ff., 188ff.
39. Ed. cit., p. 189.
40. Faret, *L'honneste homme, ou l'art de plaire à la cour* (Paris, 1630), p. 35; Méré, *Oeuvres complètes* (Paris, 1930), II, pp. 36–7.
41. The same maxim is repeated in 'Du faux', éd. cit., p. 208; the amateur spirit of the *honnête homme* is underlined in similar terms by Méré, op. cit., II, p. 45.

CHAPTER 5

1. In a fragment attributed to Pascal by Marguerite Périer Descartes' use of the idea of God in his philosophy is criticized (No. 1001) in *Oeuvres complètes*, éd. L. Lafuma (Paris, 1963). The history of the editions of the *Pensées* as well as the extremely cogent reasons in favour of following the order of the *Copie* as does L. Lafuma are given in full by J. Mesnard in *Les Pensées de Pascal* (Paris, 1976), pp. 13–50; cf. also his remarks on this edition, pp. 7–8.
2. Cf. St Paul's *Epistle to the Ephesians*, Ch. 2, v. 8.
3. Ed. cit., p. 355.
4. H. Friedrich, 'Pascals Paradox. Das Sprachbild einer Denkform'. *ZFRP*, 56 (1936), pp. 322–70.
5. Ed. cit., p. 356.
6. Montaigne, *Essais*, II, Ch. 12, pp. 632–3, 676; on Pascal's use of Montaigne's scepticism, see L. Brunschvicg, *Descartes et Pascal, lecteurs de Montaigne* (New York, 1944), Ch. 3; the borrowings from the *Essais* are analysed systematically by B. Croquette, *Pascal et Montaigne, étude des réminiscences des Essais dans l'oeuvre de Pascal* (Geneva, 1974).
7. Pascal here adapts a remark of Montaigne, structuring it to underline sharply the misery of man without God (*Essais*, I, Ch. 3, p. 11); cf. the similar remark in III, Ch. 13, pp. 573–4.
8. Cf. *Essais*, II, Ch. 12, p. 651.
9. Cf. *Essais*, III, Ch. 1, p. 212, and Ch. 13, p. 524.
10. Cf. the former's sentence in *Essais*, I, Ch. 54, p. 346; for Le Vayer's refinement of Montaigne's ideal, see Ch. 7 (3) below.
11. *Essais*, III, Ch. 10, p. 447; see also I, Ch. 23, p. 125.
12. H. Friedrich defines paradox as used in the *Pensées* as '. . . die Formel, mit welcher die Vereinigung zweier Unvereinbarkeiten an einem einzigen Subjekt oder Objekt als in der Gleichzeitigkeit verwirklicht gedacht und ausgedrückt wird', art. cit., p. 334.
13. *Essais*, II, Ch. 12, p. 504; the theme of 'cette equalité et correspondance de nous aux bestes' is developed at great length in the *Apologie*, pp. 496–540.
14. On the ways in which Montaigne uses the sceptical principles of Sextus Empiricus, see R. H. Popkin, *The History of Scepticism from Erasmus to Descartes* (Assen, 1960), Ch. 3.
15. On the divine folly of original sin, see No. 695.

16. Ed. cit., p. 296; cf. St Paul's expression of the same paradox in *II Corinthians*, Ch. 5, v. 21, *Ephesians*, Ch. 2, vv. 14-16.
17. On the basis of the position of the title of this chapter, *A.P.R.*, at the head of the second column in the table of contents in the *Copie*, J. Mesnard concludes that it marks the beginning of the second part of the apology, *Les Pensées de Pascal*, pp. 178, 226, 240. This revises his earlier conclusion that the first part ended with Chapter XI and the second began with the following chapter, *Commencement*; see *Pascal* (Paris, 1962), pp. 138, 144. The nature of the argument in Chapter XI appears to me to support the earlier view, held notably by L. Lafuma. The first sentence, 'A.P.R. commencement, après avoir expliqué l'incompréhensibilité', indicates that a new part of the apology (XII, *Commencement*) begins after the Christian explanation for man's paradoxical nature, which the philosophers only explain partially. This explanation, given in Chapter XI, involves the fall of man from a state of perfection and his retention of an awareness of his former nature which makes him dissatisfied with all human answers to his dilemma. It thus transcends the partial explanations of Chapters VII and IX and prepares the way for Pascal's direct challenge to the unbeliever in Chapter XII. The conclusive and transitional aspects of XI may account for its position in the table of contents of the *Copie*.
18. Cf. *Romans*, Ch. 9, vv. 14-18.
19. As No. 11 on *Ordre* makes clear, this fragment was intended to precede 'le discours de la machine' ('Le Pari').
20. J. Mantoy, *Des Pensées de Pascal à l'Apologie* (Paris, 1955), p. 75; the wager fragment is classified in Chapter 12 of the edition of the *Pensées* by L. Lafuma (Paris, 1960), pp. 201-5; see also the remarks in this connexion of J. Mesnard in *Pascal*, pp. 144-5, *Les Pensées de Pascal*, pp. 314-7; on the various positions suggested for the wager fragment in the apology see H. Gouhier, *Blaise Pascal, Commentaires* (Paris, 1966), pp. 297-306.
21. H. Gouhier has well underlined the fact that the wager is not a demonstration of the existence of God, but an argument for an existential choice (op. cit., p. 288); G. Brunet however has pointed out that Pascal does not justify the necessity for the wager, but rather states the necessity of making a choice, and that this ambiguity is deliberate, *Le Pari de Pascal* (Paris, 1956), pp. 122-4.
22. In No. 577 Pascal argues that if our actions are to be calculated on the sole basis that we shall be certain about their result, nothing will be done for nothing is certain. But by the rule of probabilities there is more certainty in religion than that we shall see tomorrow.
23. Cf. Montaigne's injunction in the *Apologie*, op. cit., p. 545: 'Il nous faut abestir pour nous assagir, et nous esblouir pour nous guider.' On the difference between Pascal's usage of the term and that of Montaigne, see E. Moles, 'Pascal's Use of *Abêtir*', *FS*, 19 (1965), pp. 379-84.
24. On the force of custom in regulating our daily affairs, see No. 634; in the words of G. Brunet, custom for Pascal is 'une racine commune à la raison et à la foi', op. cit., p. 99.
25. Cf. *I Corinthians*, Ch. 1, v. 18.
26. No. 449 states that rational proofs for the articles of Christian belief are useless without the knowledge that God has manifested himself in Jesus Christ.

Notes 185

27. Pascal here goes farther than Le Vayer and Gassendi in affirming man's inability to understand basic principles: the former restricts himself to a non-dogmatic view of man's capacity to penetrate the workings of nature in *Doute sceptique* (Paris, 1667); Gassendi's scepticism is more creative in character, as may be seen from this sentence written in 1634: '... je ne dirai pas que la vérité des choses soit impossible à comprendre, mais du moins il me semble pouvoir dire qu'elle n'a jusqu'ici jamais été comprise', quoted by H. Berr, *Du scepticisme de Gassendi* (Paris, 1960), p. 66.
28. H. Friedrich, art. cit., pp. 343–4; *Essais*, III, Ch. 13, pp. 571, 526.
29. Cf. *Romans*, Ch. 1, vv. 18–23.
30. See *Romans*, Ch. 2, vv. 28–9, and *Galatians*, Ch. 3, vv. 19–26.
31. See the remarks in this connexion by A. J. Krailsheimer in the introduction to his translation of the *Pensées* (London, 1966), p. 21.

CHAPTER 6

1. *Descartes oeuvres et lettres*, éd. A. Bridoux (Paris, 1953), p. 126.
2. Montaigne, *Essais*, II, Ch. 17, p. 61.
3. Ed. cit., p. 126; H. Gouhier notes that this sentence marks the beginning of the Cartesian method, *La Pensée Métaphysique de Descartes* (Paris, 1962), p. 16.
4. Ed. cit., p. 126.
5. *Essais*, II, Ch. 12, pp. 605, 634; on Montaigne's concept of reason, see A. Levi, *French Moralists, the Theory of the Passions 1585 to 1649* (Oxford, 1964), pp. 58ff.
6. Ed. cit., p. 126.
7. *Essais*, II, Ch. 12, pp. 540, 545.
8. See A. J. Krailsheimer, *Studies in Self-Interest from Descartes to La Bruyère* (Oxford, 1962), p. 31; L. Brunschvicg places the question in perspective in *Descartes et Pascal, Lecteurs de Montaigne* (New York, 1944), p. 115.
9. Ed. cit., p. 267.
10. Ed. cit., p. 127; cf. similar expressions of contentment in Part II, p. 139, Part III, p. 144; H. Gouhier, *Essais sur Descartes* (Paris, 1949), p. 56.
11. Ed. cit., p. 128.
12. *Essais*, I, Ch. 54, p. 346, II, Ch. 12, p. 548.
13. Ibid., II, Ch. 12, p. 599; cf. I, Ch. 26, p. 172.
14. Ed. cit., p. 130.
15. Ibid., p. 130; *Essais*, II, Ch. 12, p. 554.
16. Ed. cit., p. 130.
17. In the first *Méditation Métaphysique* Descartes says that the propositions of arithmetic and geometry are indubitable whether one is awake or asleep. This does not however prevent him from extending the hypothesis of his 'Dieu trompeur' to such propositions in the hope of coming to an indubitable truth (éd. cit., p. 270).
18. Ibid., p. 131; *Essais*, I, Ch. 26, p. 163.
19. Ed. cit., p. 132, *Essais*, I, Ch. 23, p. 123, I, Ch. 25, p. 153.
20. Ed. cit., pp. 131, 134, 135; cf. *Essais*, I, Ch. 23, p. 125.
21. Ed. cit., pp. 136, 138.

22. Ibid., p. 137; H. Gouhier, *La Pensée Métaphysique* . . . p. 21.
23. See *Les Principes de la Philosophie*, 43, 45, éd. cit., pp. 590-1.
24. See G. Rodis-Lewis, *La Morale de Descartes* (Paris, 1957), p. 14.
25. Ed. cit., p. 140.
26. Op. cit., p. 560.
27. Ibid., III, Ch. 10, p. 457; éd. cit., pp. 141-2.
28. Ed. cit., pp. 142, 1000-1.
29. Ibid., pp. 142-3.
30. Ibid., pp. 144, 1001.
31. Ibid., pp. 147, 268.
32. Ibid., p. 274.
33. Gassendi, *Disquisitio Metaphysica Seu Dubitationes et Instantiae Adversus Renati Cartesii Metaphysicam et Responsa*, texte établi, traduit et annoté par B. Rochot (Paris, 1962), pp. 30, 70, 54.
34. See 'Doute méthodique ou négation méthodique?' in H. Gouhier, *La Pensée Métaphysique* . . . , pp. 15-40.
35. Ed. cit., pp. 147, 268.
36. Gassendi, op. cit., p. 46.
37. Ed. cit., p. 147.
38. Op. cit., p. 672; Gassendi, op. cit., pp. 48-50; on the theme of the interchangeable nature of reality and fantasy in contemporary drama, see J. Rousset, *La littérature de l'âge baroque en France, Circé et le Paon* (Paris, 1954).
39. Ed. cit., p. 272; Gassendi, op. cit., pp. 36, 44.
40. Gassendi, op. cit., pp. 31, 56, 50; cf. the similar comment by A. J. Ayer, *The Problem of Knowledge* (London, 1956), pp. 44-5; Gassendi does not distinguish between the 'Dieu trompeur' and the 'malin génie' of the first *Méditation*. But the first idea appears to be a metaphysical hypothesis and the second a methodological tactic, as H. Gouhier has pointed out in *La Pensée Métaphysique* . . . , pp. 119-21.
41. A. J. Ayer, op. cit., pp. 45-6.
42. Ed. cit., pp. 275, 278; B. Russell, however, raises the point that Descartes nowhere proves that thoughts need a thinker, although the pronoun 'I' is grammatically convenient, *History of Western Philosophy* (London, 1961), p. 550.
43. Ed. cit., pp. 148, 286.
44. Ibid., pp. 148, 149.
45. Ibid., pp. 288-9.
46. Ibid., pp. 150-3.

CHAPTER 7

1. R. Pintard, *Le libertinage érudit dans la première moitié du XVIIe siècle* (Paris, 1943), I, pp. 131-7; J.-E. d'Angers, 'Stoïcisme et libertinage dans l'oeuvre de François La Mothe Le Vayer', *RSH*, 75 (1954), pp. 259-84.
2. Sainte-Beuve, *Nouveaux Lundis* (Paris, 1866), VI, p. 382; J. Grenier, 'Le sceptique masqué, La Mothe Le Vayer', *TR*, XXII (1949), pp. 1504-13.
3. P. Bayle, *Dictionnaire Historique* (Rotterdam, 1722), IV, Art. Le Vayer; R. Kerviler, *François de La Mothe Le Vayer, Etude sur sa vie et sur ses écrits*

Notes

(Paris, 1879), p. 110; R. H. Popkin, *The History of Scepticism from Erasmus to Descartes* (Assen, 1960), p. 98.
4. E. Tisserand (ed.), *Deux dialogues sur la divinité et l'opiniâtreté* (Paris, 1922), pp. 56–8.
5. J. S. Spink, *French Free-Thought from Gassendi to Voltaire* (London, 1966), pp. 18–19.
6. *Cinq dialogues faits à l'imitation des anciens par Oratius Tubero, Quatre autres dialogues du mesme auteur, faits comme les précédens à l'imitation des anciens par Oratius Tubero*, both published in Paris. Quotations are from the edition published in Frankfurt, 1716.
7. See the article by B. Beugnot, 'La fonction du dialogue chez La Mothe Le Vayer', *CAIEF*, 24 (mai 1972), pp. 31–41.
8. Ed. cit., pp. 19–20; cf. Sextus Empiricus, *Outlines of Pyrrhonism*, in *Works*, tr. Rev. R. G. Bury (Cambridge, Mass., 1935), I, Ch. VII.
9. Ed. cit., pp. 29, 42–7.
10. Ibid., pp. 162–3.
11. *Pensées*, éd. cit., No. 131; see the similar objections to scepticism by Hume in R. H. Popkin's excellent survey of the subject, *Encyclopaedia Britannica*, 16 (1974), p. 833.
12. See *De la conversation et de la solitude*, in *Oeuvres de François de La Mothe Le Vayer* (Dresde, 1756–9), II, 2e partie, 4e vol.; *De la retraite de la cour*, in VII, 1re partie, 13e vol.; *Prose Chagrin* (1661); *Promenades en Neuf dialogues* (1662–4); *Soliloques sceptiques* (1670).
13. *Essais*, II, Ch. 12, p. 634.
14. Ed. cit., p. 333.
15. On the debate between Erasmus and Luther about the criterion for religious truth, see R. H. Popkin, op. cit., pp. 1–7; on Luther's attitude to reason, see E. F. Rice, *The Renaissance Idea of Wisdom* (Harvard, 1958), pp. 131–43; B. Rochot remarks that fideism is the 'caractéristique dominante de l'esprit gassendien', *Pierre Gassendi, sa vie et son oeuvre* (Paris, 1955), p. 103.
16. Ed. cit., pp. 336–7.
17. Ibid., pp. 336–42; Montaigne, *Essais*, II, Ch. 12, p. 562; Charron, *De la Sagesse* (Paris, 1820–4), II, Ch. 2.
18. Montaigne, *Essais*, I, Ch. 27, Ch. 12, pp. 487ff; Charron, op. cit., II, Ch. 2; on Montaigne's attitude to Christianity, see H. Friedrich, *Montaigne* (Berne, 1949), pp. 138–49.
19. *Correspondance du P. Marin Mersenne*, éd. C. de Waard (Paris, 1945), 2, pp. 479, 563.
20. Ed. cit., pp. 26–7; the hiatus between knowledge and judgement is one of the major themes of Montaigne's essays 'Du Pédantisme', and 'De l'Institution des Enfans', *Essais*, I, Chs. 25 and 26.
21. Ed. cit., pp. 118–71, 168; cf. Montaigne's description of philosophy as 'une poësie sophistiquée', *Essais*, II, Ch. 12, p. 599.
22. Ed. cit., pp. 186–98; cf. Montaigne, 'De l'art de conférer': 'Nous entrons en inimité, premièrement contre les raisons, et puis contre les hommes. Nous n'aprenons à disputer que pour contredire, et chascun contredisant et estant contredit, il en advient que le fruit du disputer c'est perdre et aneantir la verité', *Essais*, III, Ch. 8, p. 360.
23. Ed. cit., pp. 200–1.

24. Act II, Sc. 4, lines 711–30; for analogies between Le Vayer's scepticism and the dramatic vision of Molière's play, see R. McBride, *The Sceptical Vision of Molière* (London, 1977), Ch. 5.
25. Ed. cit., pp. 357, 341, 349ff.; see in this respect *De la Liberté et de la Servitude* (1643), and *Prose Chagrine*.
26. Ed. cit., p. 361.
27. Ibid., pp. 375–8; this similarity in argument is developed by R. McBride in 'The Sceptical View of Marriage and the Comic Vision in Molière', *FMLS*, V, 1 (January 1969), pp. 26–46.
28. Ed. cit., pp. 392, 393–4; for similar liberal ideas on marriage, see Rabelais, *Le Tiers Livre*, Chs. 30, 33, 34, and the abbé de Pure, *La Prétieuse, ou le Mystère des Ruelles*, éd. E. Magne (Paris, 1938), I, IIe partie, p. 216.
29. Ed. cit., p. 396; cf. Erasmus, *Encomium Moriae*, XX; Montaigne, *Essais*, III, Ch. 5, pp. 294–7.
30. Ed. cit., pp. 428ff; cf. Molière's *Amphitryon*, lines 1898–9, and *George Dandin*, Act II, Sc. 2, for arguments similar to that of Cassander.
31. Ed. cit., p. 455; cf. *L'Ecole des Femmes*, lines 84–94, *Les Femmes Savantes*, lines 671–4.
32. Ed. cit., p. 456; cf. the closing lines of *L'Ecole des Maris*.
33. *Essais*, II, Ch. 12, p. 654.
34. P. Bayle, op. cit.

Index

Abraham, 141
Académie Française, 166, 168
Adam, A., 37
Amour-propre, 91–6, 97, 98, 99, 103, 108, 109, 116
Angers, J.-E. d', 165
Anjou, Duc d', 165
Aristotle, 172
Art de persuader, 113, 115, 129
Ataraxia, 167
Ayer, A. J., 162

Bayle, P., 175
Bénichou, P., 7–8
Bray, R., 74
Brody, J., 53
Brunetière, F., 1, 74
Butler, P. F., 67, 69

Charité, 143–4
Charron, P., 165, 170, 171
Christ, *see* Jesus Christ
Christianity, 27, 90, 112, 130, 132, 135, 139, 143, 144, 146, 169–72
Cicero, 166
Coeur, 104, 121, 123
Conversion, 135, 145
Corneille, P., 3, 4, 5, 7–36
    Cinna, 22–6
    Horace, 5, 11–21
    Le Cid, 5, 8–11
    Polyeucte, 27–36
Corps, 143–4
Custom, 78, 118, 134, 151, 154, 167

Descartes, R., 1, 3, 5, 112, 121, 122, 147–63, 167–8, 171
Devoir, 15–18, 66, 69
Divertissement, 124–6

Ennui, 119
Epictetus, 126
Epochē, 165, 167
Erasmus, D., 102, 165, 168, 169
Esprit, 143–4
Esprit, Père Thomas, 90

Faguet, E., 1, 74
Faret, N., 111

Fernandez, R., 74
Fideism, 150, 169
Folie, 104–8, 143
Fortune, 100–1
Friedrich, H., 113, 138

Galen, 100
Gassendi, P., 157–62, 164, 169
Gemara, 142
Générosité, 22–3, 25
Gide, A., 2
Gloire, 7, 9–11, 14–15, 17, 18–19, 20–1, 22, 25–6, 30–2, 35, 65, 69, 72
Goldmann, L., 37, 64
Gouhier, H., 149, 152, 158
Grenier, J., 166

Herland, L., 14, 16
Hippocrates, 100
Honnête homme, 91, 109–11
Humanism, 102
Humeur, 100–1, 104, 109

Inconstance, 118
Intérêt, 98–9, 103

Jansenists, 90, 102, 128
Jansenius, 90
Jesus Christ, 34, 114, 126–7, 135–6, 138, 139, 140, 141, 142–3, 144–5, 169–70
Judaism, 139–40

Kenosis, 36
Kerviler, R., 166

La Bruyère, J. de, 8
La Mothe Le Vayer, F. de, 1, 5, 9, 90, 120, 154, 165–76
La Rochefoucauld, F. Duc de, 3, 4, 5, 25, 26, 90–111, 116
Lanson, G., 1, 7, 10
Larthomas, P., 3
Lebègue, R., 28
Lefebvre, H., 2
Louis XIV, 165
Lucian, 166
Luther, M., 169

189

Mantoy, J., 131
Méré, Chevalier de, 111
Mersenne, Père Marin, 171
Metriopatheia, 167
Michaut, G., 74, 76
Milieu, 136-9
Misère-grandeur, 114-15, 120-2, 126-8, 135, 136, 139, 142, 144
Mishna, 142
Molière, J.-B. P., 2, 3, 4, 49, 74-89, 92, 100, 103, 104, 105, 110, 173, 174
  L'Ecole des Maris, 74, 75-82
  L'Ecole des Femmes, 74, 75, 82-8
Montaigne, M. E. de, 1, 5, 78, 92, 99, 102, 104, 106, 115, 116, 118, 119, 120, 122, 126, 138, 147-8, 149-54, 160, 165, 168-9, 170, 171, 172, 175
Moore, W. G., 3, 74
Muhammad, 139

Nadal, O., 7-8

Olivet, Abbé d', 166
Orgueil, 96-7, 98, 99, 119, 136
Original sin, 123-4

Pascal, B., 1, 3, 5, 90, 112-45, 168, 169
Passions, 101-3
Pilate, 169
Pintard, R., 165
Popkin, R. H., 166
Plato, 166
Puissances trompeuses, 104, 115-17
Pyrrhonism, 165
Pyrrhonists, 120, 122, 123, 126, 132, 135

Racine, J., 2, 3, 4, 8, 37—73
  Andromaque, 37—51
  Bérénice, 63-73
  Britannicus, 51-63
Reason, 135-6, 147-8, 151
Repos, 125
Richelieu, Cardinal de, 165, 166

Sablé, Mme de, 91
Saci, M. de, 126
Sainte-Beuve, C.-A., 90, 166
St Paul, 136, 142, 143, 144-5, 169
St Thomas, 170-1
Sceptics, 148, 150, 152, 154-5, 158, 160, 163
Scripture, 141-2
Seneca, 90
Sextus Empiricus, 116, 122, 167
Sirmond, Père, 90
Spink, J. S., 166
Stoicism, 102-4, 126, 169
Strachey, L., 30

Talmud, 142
Tisserand, E., 166
Tobin, R., 34

Vanité, 26, 115, 118
Visé, D. de, 85

Wager, 131-5
Weinberg, B., 37, 58